THE
SPHINX
IN THE CITY

Urban Life, the Control of Disorder, and Women

ELIZABETH WILSON

UNIVERSITY OF CALIFORNIA PRESS

BERKELEY · LOS ANGELES · OXFORD

University of California Press
Berkeley and Los Angeles, California

University of California Press, Ltd.
Oxford, England

© 1991 by Elizabeth Wilson

First published by Virago Press Limited, 1991
First University of California Press edition published 1992

Library of Congress Cataloging-in-Publication Data

Wilson, Elizabeth, 1936–

The sphinx in the city: urban life, the control of disorder, and
women / Elizabeth Wilson.
p.   cm.
Includes bibliographical references and index.
ISBN 0-520-07850-0 (cloth). — ISBN 0-520-07864-0 (paper)
1. City and town life.   2. Urban women.   3. City planning.
4. Cities and towns.   I. Title.
HT361.W55 1992
305.4′09173′2—dc20   91-31209

Printed in the United States of America

9 8 7 6 5 4 3 2

The paper used in this publication meets the minimum requirements of
American National Standard for Information Sciences—Permanence of Paper
for Printed Library Materials, ANSI Z39.48-1984. ∞

Contents

For Helen Thornton and Robert Tuck

SPHINX: 'the strangling one', a she-monster . . . She is said to have proposed a riddle to the Thebans, and to have murdered all who were unable to guess it . . . The . . . Greek Sphinx . . . [had] a winged body of a lion, the breast and upper part being the figure of a woman.

Smith's Smaller Classical Dictionary

1

Into the Labyrinth

Autobiography has to do with time, with sequence and with what makes up the continuous flow of life. Here, I am talking of a space, of moments and discontinuities.

Walter Benjamin, *One Way Street* (1932)

'Now let me call back those who introduced me to the city', wrote Walter Benjamin in the 1930s, remembering his childhood in old Berlin. In his case, it was nursemaids; in mine, my mother. She planted within me, never to be eradicated, a conviction of the fateful pleasures to be enjoyed and the enormous anxieties to be overcome in discovering the city.

Every excursion we made together was an immense labour, a strenuous and fraught journey to a treacherous destination: we waited for buses that never came, were marshalled into queues that never grew shorter, walked down endless streets in the hot sun. Our destinations also were terrible. The Tower of London, Hampton Court and Madame Tussaud's were theatres of cruelty: *here* was the exact spot upon which Anne Boleyn was beheaded; *this* was the gallery along which Catherine Howard ran desperately to beg Henry the Eighth for mercy; here was the Chamber of Horrors with its electric chair.

There were also the crowds of that first, weary, hot, London summer. I had never seen crowds like those. The insolence, the promiscuity of the crowd, jostling my mother and myself, seemed like a vast yawn of indifference. The stale suits and rayon dresses brushed against us, bodies against bodies. The air seemed yellow with a kind of blasé fatigue. My mother tried to keep her hat tipped forward, her little veil in place, her corsage of soft suede anemones – blue, rose-red and purple – crisply pinned against the navy crêpe of her dress, but I felt the vulnerability of her pretensions exposed, and together we seemed so insignificant and lost.

I saw and snatched a pound note from beneath the feet that tramped across a mosaic floor in the food hall of our local department store. I was offered the forbidden chewing gum by departing American soldiers. We took boat trips down the Thames. And on one occasion there were fireworks: the crowd swarmed darkly, softly, beneath the trees; there was a hiss, and gold, white and magenta stars burst silently towards us, to melt away just out of reach.

Our visits to the Zoo and to Kensington Gardens expressed some longing for what was so absent from the stony streets in which we lived and wandered: a memory of the rural life we had left behind. Walter Benjamin recalled the park as a scene of bourgeois domestic harmony:

> There were serpentine paths near the lake and . . . benches . . . at the edge of the sand pit with its ditches, where toddlers dig or stand sunk in thought until bumped by a playmate or roused by the voice of a nursemaid from the bench of command; there she sits stern and studious, reading her novel and keeping the child in check while hardly raising an eyelid until, her labour done, she changes places with the nurse at the other end of the bench, who is holding the baby between her knees and knitting. Old, solitary men found their way here, paying due honour, amid these scatterbrained womenfolk, among the shrieking children, to the serious side of life: the newspaper.[1]

and perhaps my mother hoped to find a lost tranquillity in the green vista with its lines of trees in faultless perspective. The flowers and especially the spring blossoms, like all flowers in cities, appeared as a luxury item set against the urban fabric, rather than as an invasion of nature or a rural enclave; they symbolised some other, idealised world.

The Zoo was a very different experience, for there again were the crowds, jostling to stare at the infant gorilla and the apes. This was an old-time crowd, more of an eighteenth-century 'mob' come to stare at whatever exotic spectacle was on offer – a hanging, lunatics at Bedlam. Screams of laughter greeted the antics of the chimpanzees, those caricatures of humanity. Family groups approached the tiger's cage with a frisson of fear. Always for me the great question was whether to brave the reptile house, where huge snakes lay so creepily still. Their malevolent, horrible inertia gave me nightmares, yet I could never resist. 'I won't look' – but I always did.

The reptile house was for me that Minotaur's chamber cited by so many writers who liken the city to a labyrinth. Benjamin's Minotaur was 'three-headed', being the three prostitutes in a small Parisian brothel. In either case, fear mixed with an obscure or suspect pleasure lay at the heart of the city's secret courtyards and alleyways.

In Benjamin's adolescence the Berlin cafés played their part in introducing him to the world of pleasure that is one layer in the geology of the social city, and years later he remembered the names of those cafés like an incantation: the Romanisches Café, the Viktoria, the West End Café. Those salons were neither exactly public nor private space, and yet partook of both, and in them bohemia and the bourgeoisie mingled as part of the quintessential urban spectacle:

> For one of the most elementary and indispensable diversions of the citizen of a great metropolis, wedged, day in, day out, in the structure of his office and family amid an infinitely variegated social environment, is to plunge into another world, the more exotic the better. Hence the bars haunted by artists and criminals. The distinction between the two, from this point of view, is slight. The history of the Berlin coffeehouses is largely that of different strata of the public, those who first conquered the floor being obliged to make way for others gradually pressing forward, and thus to ascend the stage.[2]

There were, of course, no comparable cafés in London in the mid 1950s, when I was myself of an age to explore the city alone, coffee bars and jazz clubs offering a poor substitute. Soho drinking clubs were barred to me, in any case unknown. I nevertheless roamed London, solitary, engaged in that urban search for mysteries, extremes and revelations, a quest quite other than that of the wanderer through the natural landscape: a search less hallowed, yet no less spiritual.

Christine Mallet Joris's *Into the Labyrinth* was the title of the second lesbian novel I ever read (the first being, of course, Radclyffe Hall's *The Well of Loneliness*). *Into the Labyrinth* was French, and, unlike Radclyffe Hall's Edwardian romance, fitted precisely into my aimless, desperate walks and rides round London's streets, squares and inner suburbs. The heroine, a schoolgirl, discovered love in a house on a street called, romantically – and inappropriately – the *Rempart des Béguines* (the Rampart of Nuns). The adventures and sufferings attendant upon her sexual initiation took place in the bedrooms, hotels, the theatres and cafés of a great city – a city like a magic set of boxes, with, inside each box, a yet smaller and more secret one.

This recurring image, of the city as a maze, as having a secret centre, contradicts that other and equally common metaphor for the city as labyrinthine and centreless. Even if the labyrinth does have a centre, one image of the discovery of the city, or of exploring the city, is not so much finally reaching this centre, as of an endlessly circular journey, and of the retracing of the same pathways over time.

Yet one never retraces the same pathway twice, for the city is in a constant process of change, and thus becomes dreamlike and magical, yet also terrifying in the way a dream can be. Life and its certainties slither away from underfoot. This continual flux and change is one of the most disquieting aspects of the modern city. We expect permanence and stability from the city. Its monuments are solid stone and embody a history that goes back many generations. Rome was known as the 'Eternal City'. Yet, far from being eternal, in the sense of being outside time, Rome, like all cities, is deeply time-bound.[3] Although its history gives it its character, and a patina of durability, in modernity especially the city becomes ever more changing. That which we thought was most permanent dissolves as rapidly as the kaleidoscopic spectacle of the crowds and vehicles that pass through its streets. As Siegfried Kracauer wrote of Berlin in the 1920s:

> If some street blocks seem to be created for eternity, then the present day Kurfurstendam is the embodiment of empty, flowing time in which nothing is allowed to last . . . Many buildings have been shorn of the ornaments which formed a kind of bridge to yesterday . . . Only the marble staircases that glimmer through the doorways preserve memories: those of the pre-war world.[4]

Walter Benjamin noted this constant destruction and replacement in his inventory of the cafés he had once frequented. The Viktoria Café 'no longer exists. Its place – on the corner of Friedrichstrasse and Unter den Linden – has been taken by one of the noisiest luxury cafés of new Berlin, against which the earlier one, however luxurious it may have been in its day, stands out with all the magic of the age of chandeliers, mirrored walls and plush comfort.'[5]

Even if the building itself – a café, hotel or department store – survives, its life may have long departed. It is still possible to visit some of the original Vienna cafés, famous at the turn of the century for their astonishing intellectual and bohemian life. Today they are almost empty, and dust floats down the bars of sunshine that reveal worn velvet and threadbare carpet, while a bad-tempered waitress surveys her deserted realm.

The London of the 1990s, for all the destruction that has occurred, is a livelier place than gloomy 1950s London. Today I am nevertheless sometimes conscious of a nostalgia for that vanished city: for the hushed interior spaces of long-defunct department stores with their carpeted trying-on rooms; for the French provision stores of Soho, replaced first by stripshows, later by fashion boutiques; but most of all for the very gloom and shabbiness now banished by gentrification, redevelopment and the commercialisation of leisure. It felt safe, and as you wandered through the streets you sensed always that pervasive English privacy, of lives veiled by lace curtains, of a prim respectability hiding strange secrets behind those inexpressive Earls Court porticoes.

In my mid teens I was unfamiliar with the writings of Benjamin, but I intuitively identified with an urban consciousness of which his reminiscences are one of the most beautiful examples. This consciousness had been developed by the dandies and '*flâneurs*' (strollers, loiterers) of mid-nineteenth-century Paris. They had relished the kaleidoscope of urban public life and had created from it a new aesthetic, perceiving a novel kind of beauty in streets, factories and urban blight. In the 1930s the anthropologist Claude Lévi-Strauss discovered this beauty in an even more intense form in the Latin American cities he visited. He wrote that although 'São Paulo was said at the time to be an ugly town . . . I never thought São Paulo was ugly; it was a "wild" town, as are all American towns.' This quality of 'wildness' was, Lévi-Strauss felt, due to exaggerated and surreal contrasts. Extremes of wealth and poverty, of enjoyment and misery, made an essential contribution to this perception of the city. It was just those things that were shoddy and awful about city life that constituted its seduction, its peculiar beauty. What Lévi-Strauss found strange and evocative about the cities of the New World was their premature decrepitude, the incongruity of concrete skyscrapers alongside shanty towns, of Victorian Gothic churches jumbled up with bleak warehouses, creating a stone landscape as melancholy as it was striking.[6]

His perception, like that of the dandies, 'makes strange' the familiar and disregarded aspects of city life. It inverts our values: what was once seen as marginal becomes the essence of city life and that which makes it truly beautiful, even if its beauty is a beauty of ugliness. This new definition of beauty and meaning places the underside or 'Other' of city existence at the centre of consciousness. The nineteenth-century Parisian *flâneur* did not care about the pomp of the 'official', public city being created by Napoleon III and Baron Haussmann; it was the trivial, fragmented aspects of street life that appealed to him.

Lévi-Strauss was a latterday *flâneur* who discovered in the streets of São Paulo and Chicago a heartrending nostalgia not for the past but for the future. Their street canyons and windswept vistas suggested a lost future that was never to be, and ached with the yearning of human aspirations destined ever to fall short of the grandiose hopes that inspired them.

This sophisticated urban consciousness, which, as we shall see, reached a high point in central Europe in the early twentieth century, was an essentially male consciousness. Sexual unease and the pursuit of sexuality outside the constraints of the family were one of its major preoccupations.

This in itself made women's very presence in cities a problem. The

city offers untrammelled sexual experience; in the city the forbidden
– what is most feared and desired – becomes possible. Woman is
present in cities as temptress, as whore, as fallen woman, as lesbian,
but also as virtuous womanhood in danger, as heroic womanhood
who triumphs over temptation and tribulation. Writers such as
Benjamin concentrated upon their own experience of strangeness in
the city, on their own longings and desires, but many writers more
definitely and clearly posed the presence of women as a problem of
order, partly *because* their presence symbolised the promise of sexual
adventure. This promise was converted into a general moral and
political threat.

Nineteenth-century planning reports, government papers and
journalism created an interpretation of urban experience as a new
version of Hell, and it would even be possible to describe the
emergent town-planning movement – a movement that has changed
our cities almost beyond recognition – as an organised campaign to
exclude women and children, along with other disruptive elements –
the working class, the poor, and minorities – from this infernal urban
space altogether.

Sexuality, was only one source of threatening ambiguity and
disorder in the city. The industrial city became a crucible of
intense and unnerving contrasts. The hero, or less often the heroine, of urban literature was lured by the astonishing wealth and
opportunity, threatened by the crushing poverty and despair of
city life. Escape and entrapment, success and disaster offered
heightened, exaggerated scenarios of personal triumph or loss of
identity.

There was another contradictory aspect of city life. The sociologist
Max Weber argued that the western city developed a typical form of
political organisation: democracy. Feudal lords found that they were
unable to retain their hold over their vassals, bondsmen and serfs
once these had settled in cities. It was in the western late medieval
city that men and women for the first time came together as
individuals rather than as members of a kin group, clan or feudal
entourage. The western city evolved political organisations which
displaced existing paternalistic and patriarchal forms, and so the way
was opened both to individualism and to democracy during the
transition from feudalism to capitalism.

By the nineteenth century this had become contradictory because
commentators and reformers of that period claimed to value individualism and democracy, but as cities grew, the mob became a
revolutionary threat. The dangers seemed especially clear in American cities, already becoming for Europeans a paradigm of all that was
new, and Alexis de Tocqueville was one of the first to voice this

heightened, paranoid fear of the crowd in the nineteenth-century city, reporting that:

> the lowest classes in these vast cities are a rabble more danger-ous even than that of European towns. The very lowest are the freed Negroes, condemned by law and opinion to a hereditary state of degradation and wretchedness. Then, there is a crowd of Europeans driven by misfortune or misbehaviour to the shores of the New World; such men carry our worst vices to the United States.

As he saw it, it was 'the size of some American cities and especially the nature of their inhabitants' that constituted a danger, even 'threatening the future of the democratic republics of the New World'. He predicted that the new urban crowd would destroy those infant republics 'unless their government succeeds in creating an armed force . . . capable of suppressing their excesses'.[7]

There were women as well as men in the urban crowd. Indeed the crowd was increasingly invested with female characteristics, while retaining its association with criminals and minorities. The threatening masses were described in feminine terms: as hysterical, or, in images of feminine instability and sexuality, as a flood or swamp. Like women, crowds were liable to rush to extremes of emotion. As the rightwing theorist of the crowd, Le Bon, put it, 'Crowds are like the sphinx of ancient fable; it is necessary to arrive at a solution of the problems offered by their psychology or to resign ourselves to being devoured by them.' At the heart of the urban labyrinth lurked not the Minotaur, a bull-like male monster, but the female Sphinx, the 'strangling one', who was so called because she strangled all those who could not answer her riddle: female sexuality, womanhood out of control, lost nature, loss of identity.[8]

Yet the city, a place of growing threat and paranoia to men, might be a place of liberation for women. The city offers women freedom. After all, the city normalises the carnivalesque aspects of life. True, on the one hand it makes necessary routinised rituals of trans-portation and clock watching, factory discipline and timetables, but despite its crowds and the mass nature of its life, and despite its bureaucratic conformity, at every turn the city dweller is also offered the opposite – pleasure, deviation, disruption. In this sense it would be possible to say that the male and female 'principles' war with each other at the very heart of city life. The city is 'masculine' in its triumphal scale, its towers and vistas and arid industrial regions; it is 'feminine' in its enclosing embrace, in its indeterminacy and labyrin-thine uncentredness. We might even go so far as to claim that urban life is actually based on this perpetual struggle between rigid,

routinised order and pleasurable anarchy, the male–female dichotomy.

Perhaps the 'disorder' of urban life does not so much disturb
women. If this is so, it may be because they have not internalised as
rigidly as men a need for over-rationalistic control and authoritarian
order. The socialisation of women renders them less dependent on
duality and opposition; instead of setting nature against the city, they
find nature *in* the city. For them, that invisible city, the 'second city',
the underworld or secret labyrinth, instead of being sinister or
diseased as in the works of Charles Dickens and many of the writers
we will encounter later on, is an Aladdin's cave of riches. Yet at the
same time, it is a place of danger for women. Prostitutes and
prostitution recur continually in the discussion of urban life, until it
almost seems as though to be a woman – an individual, not part of a
family or kin group – in the city, is to become a prostitute – a public
woman.

The city – as experience, environment, concept – is constructed by
means of multiple contrasts: natural, unnatural; monolithic, fragmented; secret, public; pitiless, enveloping; rich, poor; sublime,
beautiful. Behind all these lies the ultimate and major contrast: male,
female; culture, nature; city, country. In saying this I am not arguing
(as do some feminists) that male–female difference creates the deepest
and most fundamental of all political divisions. Nor am I arguing
that the male/female stereotypes to which I refer accurately reflect
the nature of actual, individual men and women. In the industrial
period, nonetheless, that particular division became inscribed on
urban life and determined the development and planning of cities to a
surprising degree and in an extraordinarily unremarked way. It will
be one purpose of this book to explore how underlying assumptions,
based both on this unconscious division and on consciously spelt-out
ideas about women's rightful place, have determined the shape of
contemporary cities.

We shall also explore how women have lived out their lives on
sufferance in the metropolis. For although women, along with
minorities, children, the poor, are still not full citizens in the sense
that they have never been granted full and free access to the streets,
industrial life still drew them into public life, and they have survived
and flourished in the interstices of the city, negotiating the contradictions of the city in their own particular way.

The contradictions and intensity of urban life have produced
strong responses, one of which has been a corrosive anti-urbanism.
For many years I took for granted the assumption that a great city
was the best place to live, and Paris and New York seemed the only
possible – and even more magical – alternatives to the shabbier but

comfortable and accommodating ambience of sub-bohemian London. It was only my involvement in 'alternative' radical politics in the 1970s which alerted me to the hatred many 'progressive' people feel for cities, and to an alien point of view, which self-righteously attacked the ugliness and vulgarity of urban life while setting out some rural or small-town idyll as the desired alternative. I had known that many rightwing writers feared the modern city as destructive of the traditional patriarchal order; but to me the anti-urbanism of the left seemed like a betrayal, and made me permanently disillusioned with utopianism. William Morris in particular – a writer who seems exempt from any criticism by socialists to this day – demonstrated in his utopian *News from Nowhere* a retreat from modernity and a nostalgia for patriarchalism that I found suffocating.

Anti-urbanism has a long history, partly related to industrialisation; developments in the 1980s and early 1990s have served to make such ideas even more threatening and more plausible. One development is our growing ecological consciousness; another the redevelopment of inner cities as uninhabited office or business districts; a third the parallel growth of inner-city ghettoes inhabited by a so-called 'underclass'; fourthly, the simultaneous suburbanisation of more and more of the countryside. The result is that today in many cities we have the worst of all worlds: danger without pleasure, safety without stimulation, consumerism without choice, monumentality without diversity. At the same time, larger and larger numbers of people inhabit zones that are no longer really either town or countryside.

We need a radically new approach to the city. We will never solve the problems of living in cities until we welcome and maximise the freedom and autonomy they offer and make these available to all classes and groups. We must cease to perceive the city as a dangerous and disorderly zone from which women – and others – must be largely excluded for their own protection. There are other issues, of course, equally important. Leisure and consumption must cease to be treated purely as commodities controlled by market forces, nor can adequate housing ever be provided so long as it is regarded as a mere byproduct of urban development and property speculation.

Yet at the 'commonsense' level of our deepest philosophical and emotional assumptions, the unconscious bedrock of western culture, it is the male–female dichotomy that has so damagingly translated itself into a conception of city culture as pertaining to men. Consequently, women have become an irruption in the city, a symptom of disorder, and a problem: the Sphinx in the city.

Women are placed at the centre of my argument for this reason.

For a woman to make an argument in favour of urban life may come as a surprise. Many women and much feminist writing have been hostile to the city, and recent feminist contributions to the discussion of urban problems have tended to restrict themselves narrowly to issues of safety, welfare and protection.[9] This is a mistake, since it re-creates the traditional paternalism of most town planning. Women's experience of urban life is even more ambiguous than that of men, and safety is a crucial issue. Yet it is necessary also to emphasise the other side of city life and to insist on women's right to the carnival, intensity and even the risks of the city. Surely it is possible to be both pro-cities and pro-women, to hold in balance an awareness of both the pleasures and the dangers that the city offers women, and to judge that in the end, urban life, however fraught with difficulty, has emancipated women more than rural life or suburban domesticity.

With so vast a subject as life in cities, much has inevitably been left out. Many omissions have been regretted but deliberate. Necessarily, the result is something of a collage, as fragmentary and partial as the experience of city life itself.

In assembling this 'collage' I have used a variety of texts – fiction, journalism, government reports – assuming that all contribute on equal terms to a 'discourse' about the city. In using the term discourse, I wish to alert the reader to the idea, often expressed in the urban literature, that the city itself is a 'text' – that is to say, that it is something to be read and interpreted. It is an artefact, a work of art, created by the human mind and imagination, and contains many layers of meaning. Yet paradoxically (because the city is always contrasted with 'nature') it also appears as a *natural* phenomenon. Marcel Proust described Venice as 'a network of little alleys' and these, 'packed tightly together', dissected 'in all directions with their furrows a chunk of Venice carved out between a canal and the lagoon, as if it had crystallised in accordance with these innumerable, tenuous and minute patterns':

> Suddenly, at the end of one of these alleys, it seemed as though a distension had occurred in the crystallised matter. A vast and splendid *campo* of which, in this network of little streets, I should never have guessed the scale, or even found room for it, spread out before me surrounded by charming palaces silvery in the moonlight. It seemed to be deliberately concealed in a labyrinth of alleys, like those palaces in oriental tales whither mysterious agents convey by night a person who, brought back home before daybreak, can never find his way back to the magic dwelling which he ends by believing that he only visited in a dream.[10]

Here, the texture of the city is both natural – crystalline matter – and the substance of dreams, which are the involuntary workings of the mind.

Perhaps we should be happier in our cities were we to respond to them as to nature or dreams: as objects of exploration, investigation and interpretation, settings for voyages of discovery. The 'discourse' that has shaped our cities – the utilitarian plans of experts whose goal was social engineering – has limited our vision and almost destroyed our cities. It is time for a new vision, a new ideal of life in the city – and a new, 'feminine' voice in praise of cities.

2

From Kitsch City to the City Sublime

> With cities it is as with dreams: everything imaginable can be dreamed, but even the most unexpected dream . . . conceals a desire or, its reverse, a fear. Cities, like dreams, are made of desires and fears, even if the thread of their discourse is secret, their rules are absurd, their perspective deceitful, and everything conceals something else.
>
> Italo Calvino, *Invisible Cities* (1972)

On a wet afternoon we sheltered in the arcades beneath the front, separated from the beach by a litter-blown promenade. The sea churned and sucked at the pebbles a few yards below, but here we entered a zone of images, divorced from nature.

Each boy gambler – some were alone, some in little clusters – faced his machine as if it were a destiny, pulled knobs and twisted wheels to bring an ideal world on to his screen: but this life desired was a place of death, and each game re-enacted an ultimate struggle between Good and Evil. Armed police gunned down robots with laser rays and the cavern echoed with imitation machine-gun fire.

I too sat mesmerised. In front of me unreeled the straight road to infinity, and on the horizon a skyscraper city rose beyond a lake. We raced towards it. Suddenly the expressway passed between the clifflike blocks and we were in the city. Skyscrapers pressed in on us, casting their shadow along the street. The automobiles ricocheted through in silence, swerving from side to side. And then we'd left the city behind, we were back where we'd started, once more we were hurtling towards the city of the future, which was as far away on the horizon as it had been at the beginning of the journey, once more a mirage beyond the stretch of water.

This empty city was familiar. I recognise it now. It's a memory, an illusion now reborn as a computer game, debased but authentic, of Le Corbusier's Radiant City, in which magnificent motorways converge towards the towers, monumental, empty, and white, the mirage of a perfect city. Here, in the half-life of the amusement arcade, where human existence is at its most inconsequential, where thwarted holidaymakers loiter and loaf away an afternoon spoilt by the rain, failing to ward off boredom, Le Corbusier's grand design fleetingly revives in the form of a computerised memory flicker. The difference is that his city, born as a dream of the future, now suggests some hideous hallucination of the present.

Popular culture, in this case children's culture, brings into circulation all sorts of ideas about cities. A future without cities is projected,
for example, by the children's video *He Man and Shera*. The
characters inhabit a landscape which combines nursery-picture
graphics with memories of moon landings. The Rebels live in a land
of Robin Hood; the Evil Horde inhabit futuristic interiors hewn out
of rock. This world is both pre-industrial and post-holocaust. Cities
no longer exist.

An alternative image of the city is found in the Babar books. Jean
de Brunhoff wrote *Babar the Elephant* and *Babar the King* in the 1930s,
when the architect Le Corbusier was designing his Radiant City; and
Babar the elephant, unlike the creatures of *He Man and Shera*, still had
confidence in the city: a city, that is, of a certain kind. He set up the
city he founded, Celesteville (named after his wife), as an enlightened
Cité Industrielle or garden city: 'our houses will be by the water in the
midst of flowers and birds'.

Although Babar's first sight of 'civilisation' when he left the jungle
was a French colonial (African) town, his own Celesteville, 'most
beautiful of towns', is based on the principles of French reforming
socialism that were influential in early-twentieth-century France.
'Each elephant has a house of his own.' Life is wisely zoned and
regulated in Celesteville – the 'Palace of Work' (with a library) is next
to the 'Palace of Pleasure'; and all the elephants are issued with 'good
working clothes and lovely holiday costumes'. The infant school is a
progressive one; the children do not sit in regimented rows to learn
by rote, but in small groups at round tables.

The adult elephants work in the mornings, and 'in the afternoon
they do whatever they like. They play, go for walks, read and
dream.' Some play tennis, others bowls, yet others swim or sail. In
the evenings they watch French classical theatre. The high point of
the year is the *Grand Fête* when the armed forces and the arts and
crafts guilds march together in procession. The fact that it is guilds
rather than trades unions is another reminiscence of the French
non-revolutionary socialism of the period between the wars.

Babar's paternalistic city, with its colonial undertones, is a
reformist utopia. In this perfect city, 'health', 'happiness', 'work',
'learning', 'perseverance' and other virtues have driven out 'despair',
'indolence', 'ignorance', 'cowardice' and 'laziness'.[1]

Celesteville is one example of the close links between the planning
of cities and utopian ideals, of the belief that a perfect city can be
built, a city that will solve all social and human problems. This belief
is not new. In the late twentieth century, however, it has been recast.
Utopia for the year 2000 is Disneyland: a 'degenerate utopia'.

In Disney World, Florida, Walt Disney planned the creation of a whole city of the future – although the plan was not carried out. Where the classic utopia offered an alternative vision of society and often a critique of existing ones, Disneyland oppressively confirms the inevitable triumph of world capitalism on American lines. In Disneyland, historical events and geographical locations are reworked in such a way that they seem to lead inevitably to 'Tomorrowland' – the triumph of science and technology and a consumer paradise. There is an illusion of freedom and choice, but Disneyland actually pre-empts choice, both physically, in the layout and organisation of its space (not to mention the long queues for all exhibits, often described as hellish), and in its presentation of ideas. The single future offered by Disneyland excludes from consciousness all memory of the underside of capitalism. Instead of an acknowledgment of colonialism there is simply a journey through exotic, primitive places; instead of genocide there is the triumphal conquest of the American West; instead of poverty and unemployment there is Main Street, USA, the small-town paradise of American popular culture: the answer to Metropolis.[2]

In each of these utopian scenarios women play their appropriate role. In Celesteville women participate in social life but not in paid employment: companionate marriage and 'equality in difference' are the rule – the middle-class ideal of the mid twentieth century. Shera, the feminine equivalent of He Man, has Barbie Doll looks but plays an active role in the narrative, especially because she is equipped with a sword, which transforms her into the Princess of Power: a phallic woman for today.

In the amusement arcade we have reached a further stage. Instead of a coherent space, however oppressive, there is fragmentation and lack of meaning. The vision of the ideal city is reduced to a mere memory trace, no longer either dream or nightmare. About this depopulated city we feel nothing. It is a contemporary city seen and experienced as though it were in the future and *simultaneously* a ruin. The post-catastrophic urban landscape is simply *there*, and police and rebels, warriors and fugitives wrest an existence from it by killing. This city through which rival gangs hunt and slaughter is a city that has finally become wholly masculine. The domestic sphere, a high point of the industrial city, has disappeared. So have nature and women.

Almost from the beginning, the presence of women in cities, and particularly in city streets, has been questioned, and the controlling and surveillance aspects of city life have always been directed particularly at women. Urban life potentially challenged patriarchal systems. 'Civilisation', which meant luxury and consumerism (although only for a minority), threatened the virtuous authority of the family. This theme has been a potent and enduring source of ambivalence towards city life.

In early Babylonian times, women enjoyed great freedom. Semiramis and Nicrotis were two famous and powerful queens of Babylon, and women are mentioned in documents as engaged in a wide variety of professions and callings. The temple priestesses and woman functionaries enjoyed high esteem and a respected position in their society. Sacred marriage and fertility cults centred on the temple. Female sexuality appears to have been reverenced as a civilising force. Very gradually, however, the status of women declined, a decline probably associated with military conquest, slavery and the impoverishment of the farmers, on whose agriculture the wealth of Babylon was based. Commercial prostitution developed and respectable women were gradually segregated from non-respectable or 'public' women. This segregation was symbolised in the veil, and in public laws and edicts regulating its use. Women were eventually controlled by a patriarchal form of family.[3]

In a famous satire the Roman poet Juvenal, writing in the early days of the Roman Empire (around AD 100), attacked Roman womanhood with unbridled hatred. Usually, this satire is explained as an expression of 'misogyny', which does no more than state the obvious. While the poem must, of course, be understood in its social and historical context, its theme is actually a perennial one: it links female immorality with the many opportunities provided by urban life for women to escape the authority of family and husband.

While Juvenal attacked the immorality of all aspects of Roman life, he regarded the women of Rome, or at least the women of the Roman upper classes, as the most vicious of all. Married or not, they made love with low-class gladiators and actors; Messalina, the wife of the Emperor Claudius, even went to the brothels to satisfy her lust. Juvenal implied that the corruption of Rome was founded upon the decline in female morality: the city gives free rein to women's sexual lusts, which escape control and become unbridled, defiled and even murderous.

In the mid fifteenth century Leon Battista Alberti wrote an architectural treatise that revolutionised Renaissance concepts of city planning. He also wrote a book on the family, undeterred by the fact that as a priest he never married. The form of the family in Alberti's rational and scientifically planned city was to be patriarchal. Women would be under the authority of their husbands, and their place was the private sphere. The family of which Alberti wrote was an early form of the bourgeois family, with its much vaunted virtues of thrift and hard work, and modesty and domesticity in women.[4]

Both western and non-western societies have regulated women's movement in cities, although to varying degrees. The protection and control of women have everywhere gone hand in hand, but cities have posed a challenge to men's ability to retain their hold. The city is the zone of individual freedom. There, the ties of family and kinship may be loosened and avenues of escape may open up.

Even in nineteenth-century Korea, a culture in which upper-class women were rigidly confined, a strange nocturnal licence operated. The lives of Korean women of the upper class were spent largely in seclusion, but sometimes the Korean lady left her house to visit family friends. During the journey it was imperative that she remain invisible, so she travelled in a sedan chair. Its bearers retired when she entered and left it in the enclosed courtyard for her to emerge from unseen. (The imperative of invisibility did not apply to working women, and the Korean lady's sedan chair was always accompanied by a slave girl or servant, who ran alongside the vehicle.)

At night, these restrictions were reversed. After the city gates were closed, it was men (save for officials and the blind) who were forbidden to appear on the streets, and the city was turned over to women, who were then free to walk abroad. They strolled and chatted in groups with their friends, carrying paper lanterns. Even in this dim light, however, they used unfurled fans to protect themselves from being seen, or held their silk jackets over their faces.[5]

So often, this has been women's experience of the city: to live in it, but hidden; to emerge on sufferance, veiled.

With the coming of 'modernity' the cities of veiled women have ceded to cities of spectacle and voyeurism, in which women, while seeking and sometimes finding the freedom of anonymity, are often all too visible. They are in fact a part of the spectacle, and the kaleidoscope of city life becomes intensely contradictory for women. Commerce, consumerism and pleasure seduce them into its thoroughfares, yet men and the state continue their attempts to confine them to the private sphere or to the safety of certain zones. Since the Industrial Revolution a deadly struggle has been waged over women's presence in cities.

This struggle has often been carried on in a covert way, and in order to appreciate its persistence it is necessary to investigate many of the more general ideas about the development of cities and the conduct of urban life: controversies which often act to conceal an underlying disquiet that women are roaming the streets.

There is another and perhaps more profound way in which the male–female dichotomy has structured western thought about the city. The very possibility of the idea of the city implies its contrast to nature, rural life or the wilderness. The city cannot exist without its opposite. And mapped on to the opposition of city and country, culture and nature, is male and female: man is culture and woman is the earth.

Central to Greek and Roman thought was a concept of 'civilisation', and since ancient times the idea of the city has been central to the idea of civilisation in western culture. Peoples were defined as 'civilised' or 'barbarous' and the civilised were the city dwellers: citizens. As early as 2000 BC the nomadic way of life was an alternative to the urban, suited to areas that could not easily have been cultivated by settled communities. In practice the two ways of life were complementary and even necessary to each other, yet they were seen as contrasting and antagonistic; there was conflict between the nomadic herdsmen and the settled farmers who began to build cities.[6]

Above all, ancient cities were sacred. The Babylonian cities had archetypes in the constellations, their form copied from an ideal celestial form. For the ancients, the building of a new city represented symbolically the act of creation; the city represented a microcosm of the universe; and thus the map of Babylon showed the city just as the Sumerians imagined Paradise. The Romans would dig a trench round the site where a city was to be founded, and this marked the point at which the nether regions met the celestial. It is in this sense that cities are perceived as 'eternal' – and they are in this way to be contrasted with deserts, the wilderness and uncultivated regions, which represent the chaos of the world before Creation.[7]

If the contrast between the city and nature stands also for the contrast between the male and female principles, then the building of a new city as an act of creation implies the merging of these two principles. One of the most influential twentieth-century writers on the city, Lewis Mumford, described the inevitable rise and decline of 'the city' through history. He traced the emergence of the first real cities to the merging of two earlier periods: the 'male' paleolithic period with its phallic tools; and the neolithic womb-like 'feminine':

> Under woman's dominance, the neolithic period is pre-eminently one of containers: it is an age of stone and pottery utensils – of vases, jars, vats, cisterns, bins, barns, granaries, houses, not least great collective containers, like irrigation ditches and villages . . .
>
> The order and stability of the village, along with its maternal enclosure and intimacy and its oneness with the forces of nature, were carried over into the city.[8]

Mumford believed that these qualities were perpetuated in the contemporary urban neighbourhood or community. For him, even in the city woman represented the local, particular and domestic.

Mumford was one of the most ferocious opponents of the vast metropolis of the twentieth century. He believed that the city run out of control became 'megalopolis', and finally 'necropolis' (city of death). Socialists have been as uncritical of Mumford's views as they have of William Morris's. The dislike both men expressed for the huge metropolitan city, and their favoured solutions, have seldom been challenged or questioned, and it has hardly been noticed that one of the underlying reasons for their dislike was that the metropolis provided women with an escape from patriarchal relations. As we shall see later, Mumford's support for the 'garden city' was based in part on his belief that it would restore women to their primary maternal role.

Although sacred, Babylon and Rome were also worldly cities: urbane, civilised. The city represented freedom and an expansion of experience. Babylon lives on as the supreme – almost mythical – example of cosmopolitan wealth, beauty and refinement. Babylon is also a – feminine – cultural metaphor for wickedness. Modern culture inherits this association from Judaism. The Jews were a nomadic people, and for them Babylon represented not splendour and the civilised life, but exile. Nebuchadnezzar took the Hebrews captive and brought them to Babylon (commemorated in Psalm 137 with its lines: 'By the rivers of Babylon we sat down, yea we wept. We hanged our harps upon the willows'). They therefore associated Babylon's eventual destruction with just revenge. The Old Testament story of the destruction of Babylon implied that this was God's retribution and a punishment for its wickedness. The Protestant Church reworked this idea as the wickedness of Roman Catholicism and the Pope, whose Rome became the 'whore of Babylon'.[9]

In the Renaissance and Baroque periods the discourse on the city underwent a profound change. The city was detached from its religious origins, from the tradition that cities were always organised in accordance with sacred and religious imperatives. The city became secular; it became a spectacle, and an expression of the grandeur and power of the state.

The Renaissance rediscovered the classical Greek debate about the ideal political state. What should government be like? How should it take place? At the same time, Renaissance architects and artists tried in their work to express the ideal 'polis' or seat of political power in the form of their own city states.[10]

At this time two new kinds of writing about cities were invented: the architectural treatise (giving guidance on how to plan, design and build actual cities); and utopian literature (books about imagined ideal cities and societies). These genres, which might seem very different, and which are usually discussed quite separately, not only arose at the same period, but both directed thinking about urban life and urban planning into certain channels which have endured until the present day.

Leon Battista Alberti's treatise on architecture and planning inaugurated an entirely new field of knowledge. His book was the model for many others – and even for the whole concept of planning, urbanism as an academic subject, and ultimately the town-planning movement.[11] Alberti wished for a rational, scientific approach to planning. His work aimed to elucidate the underlying universal and timeless principles which determine how a city – all cities – ought to be built.[12]

As the city's sacred function was eclipsed, it began to appear as the crucible for human perfectibility and order. Once its form was no longer determined by divine forces, it became the mission of men to create the perfect city, and the imagining of utopias was the result.

The utopia as a distinct literary form goes back to Sir Thomas More's *Utopia*, published in 1516. The classic utopian work is a description of an ideal city and society, an entity in which the town plan and the architecture – the totality of the organised, planned space – embody the political and social ideals of the society which has created this city. It is the embodiment in stone of a political order: the 'solid geometry' of a perfect way of life.

Utopia was Thomas More's response to the gradual breaking up of feudal society, the beginnings of early capitalist forms of agriculture, the rise of a merchant class, which was beginning to challenge the power of the aristocracy, and the growing centralised power of the state under the monarchy. It was also inspired by the recent discovery of the 'New World' – the Americas.

More's utopia was an anti-consumerist one, in which the main object was to give its citizens as much time as possible for leisure pursuits and study. There was to be little differentiation in the way in which the populace was clothed or housed. Their society was patriarchal, yet women played a full role in it. One function of the perfect city – a microcosm of the perfect society – was that it wiped out all social antagonisms, including that between the sexes; yet this problem was not to be solved by introducing equality between men and women. Rather, utopia rendered the patriarchal order benign, and above all rational.

Alberti claimed that architecture was the greatest of the arts. The architect, who reorganises the human world in accordance with his own vision, was the Renaissance 'complete man', the hero or superman. This idea, too, has lasted into the twentieth century,

when architects such as Le Corbusier have still claimed the right to
design a perfect world.

There is a sense in which all town planning contains both a utopian
and a heroic, yet authoritarian, element. Although its purposes may
seem purely practical, it does claim to offer, like the utopian work, a
permanent solution to the flux and flow of the ever-changing city.
The plan is always intended to fix the usage of space; the aim, the
state regulation of urban populations. This includes the fixing of
women in their 'rightful' place.

The utopia, on the other hand, claims to be a vision of an ideal,
and therefore offers, at least implicitly, a liberating vision. Yet it
equally legislates against the possibility or need for change and
spontaneity. Both the utopia and the architectural treatise proceed
from the assumption that human deviance and unreason can be
wiped out by the perfect plan. The utopia aims to stop history.

In the eighteenth century, or 'Enlightenment', the city signified
both public hierarchy and grandeur and an essentially moderate and
'civilised' approach to urban living. The squares and terraces of
Bloomsbury in London were built for city dwellers of varying
classes and 'demonstrated an ideal of harmony and decorum over and
above display and vulgar individualism'. Some of the Georgian 'new
towns' (in Edinburgh, for example) were built in accordance with a
growing desire to segregate the different classes of society, but the
ideal remained social integration.[13] The moderate-sized pre-
industrial city formed the basis for the philosophy of the new liberal
economy of the late eighteenth century: in Adam Smith's *The Wealth
of Nations* (1776), such a city represented the ideal form of social
organisation within which political economy could proceed
smoothly.

The intellectual leaders of the Enlightenment emphasised the
harmony that linked human endeavour, God and nature. Harmony
did not, however, rule out hierarchy; on the contrary, authority and
hierarchy were essential to harmony, an important dimension of
which was the contrast between men and women. Each sex had an
appropriate role to play, but women's was essentially subordinate.

In spite of the Enlightenment emphasis on reason and harmony,
new and more disturbing ways of perceiving the city also had their
origins in eighteenth-century thought. A concept of the 'Sublime'
took shape. At first, in the eighteenth century, the concept appeared
as an extension of the Enlightenment ideal of civilisation. Gradually,
however, it came to suggest certain much more extreme aspects of
urban experience that emerged with the Industrial Revolution.

To begin with, the sublime or vast in nature served to reveal the
omnipresence of the divine. The sublime was on a more than human

scale, but its grandeur would be destroyed by too great a sensation of dread. In 1757, however, Edmund Burke published a famous and influential essay, *A Philosophical Enquiry into the Origin of Our Ideas of the Sublime and Beautiful*. This brought dread closer to the central meaning of the sublime. The sublime, wrote Burke, 'operates in a manner analogous to terror', and was 'productive of the strongest emotion which the mind is capable of feeling'. For Burke, the vast, the rugged, magnitude and infinity were sources of the sublime: dark and gloomy colours, night rather than day, silence and solitude.

In early-nineteenth-century German philosophy the concept of the sublime underwent further development, and became the attempt – necessarily doomed to failure – to express the infinite. External existence can never be adequate to the representation of the infinite, and thereby becomes degraded in comparison. The sublime becomes a tragic absence (the absence of God). Its meaning today has shifted again, for now it is used to describe the representation of the unrepresentable – that which cannot be spoken.

Burke and many of his contemporaries felt that the greatest and best architecture should be capable of 'fitting the mind with great and sublime ideas'. Massive, uniform buildings were thought to suggest infinity – and the sublime was an expression of infinity. For Burke, furthermore:

> All edifices calculated to produce an idea of the sublime ought rather to be dark and gloomy . . . darkness itself on other occasions is known by experience to have a greater effect on the passions than light . . . To make anything very terrible, obscurity seems in general to be necessary.[14]

These precepts were consistent with Neo-classical theory. Neo-classicism developed in the late eighteenth century, a revolutionary style which expressed the spirit both of the Enlightenment, and of the French Revolution. Architecturally and artistically it came as a reaction to the ornamentation of the Rococo. Neo-classicism was rationalism in stone, extending the scientific spirit to the built environment. Claude-Nicolas Ledoux was one of its foremost exponents in France, where, until the Revolution, he was employed by the state to design public buildings of a functional rather than a grand type – offices, factories and housing. It was just these sorts of public buildings, along with prisons, workhouses and asylums, that lent themselves to a sublimity of form: geometrically simple, monotonous, overwhelming and awe-inspiring. (He also designed a utopia.)[15]

Neo-classicism was well adapted to the buildings invented by the industrial city: new kinds of buildings for new and sometimes terrible purposes. There was the factory, which ate up human lives even as it spewed out more goods than the world had ever seen. There were the workhouses, asylums and prisons – for the nineteenth century invented the 'total institution'. Confinement was the archetypal punishment for the age which claimed to cherish liberty before all else. The Panopticon, invented by the philosopher Jeremy Bentham, represented in theory the most perfect form of confinement coupled with surveillance; the ultimate realisation of the institutional sublime, embodying as it did the grandeur of authority in its most unremitting form. By the mid century there would be railways, viaducts, vast terminals; a little later there would be tenements, gasworks, power stations; there were already warehouses, arsenals. Above all, simply the rapid growth of cities was their most sublime aspect.

In *Dombey and Son*, Charles Dickens described the endless restless motion and turbulence of the city; and also the vague, indeterminate regions that the new developments produced at the edge of London, and which were evocative of the sublime in a different and more disturbing way. These regions carried the horror of the sublime – the horror of indeterminacy – which was increasingly to become a feature experienced and noted by writers on the city:

> The first shock of a great earthquake had, just at that period, rent the whole neighbourhood to its centre. Traces of its course were visible on every side. Houses were knocked down; streets broken through and stopped; deep pits and trenches dug in the ground; enormous heaps of earth and clay thrown up; buildings that were undermined and shaking, propped by great beams of wood. Here, a chaos of carts, overthrown and jumbled together, lay topsy-turvy at the bottom of a steep unnatural hill; there, confused treasures of iron soaked and rusted in something that had accidentally become a pond. Everywhere were bridges that led nowhere; thoroughfares that were wholly impassable; Babel towers of chimneys, wanting half their height; temporary wooden houses and enclosures, in the most unlikely situations; carcases of ragged tenements, and fragments of unfinished walls and arches, and piles of scaffolding and wildernesses of bricks, and giant forms of cranes, and tripods straggling above nothing . . . In short the yet unfinished and unopened Railroad was in progress.[16]

In *Les Misérables*, Victor Hugo explored a similar but even bleaker and more sinister marginal region, that of the *barrières* or ramparts on the outskirts of Paris, a region where the city seemed to 'disappear':

It was not a wilderness, for there were inhabitants; not country, for there were streets and houses; not town, for the
streets were rutted like country roads, and grass grew in them;
nor was it a village, for the houses were too high . . . The
place was utterly dismal . . . One was conscious of being
between the Salpêtrière, part women's prison and part madhouse, of which the cupola was visible, and Bicêtre with its
barrier – between the madness of women and the madness of
men. As far as sight could reach there was nothing . . . but
slaughter houses, the wall, and an occasional factory looking
like a barracks or a monastery . . . trees in parallel rows,
featureless edifices in long, cold lines, with the monotony of
right-angles. No accident of terrain, not an architectural flourish, not a bend or curve: a glacial setting, rectilinear and
hideous. Nothing chills the heart like symmetry, for symmetry is ennui and ennui is at the heart of grief . . . But at
nightfall, particularly in winter, at the time when the last light
faded and the wind whipped the last brown leaves off the
elms, when the darkness was at its deepest, unrelieved by
stars, or when wind and moonlight pierced gaps in the clouds,
the boulevard became suddenly frightening. Its straight lines
seemed to merge and dissolve in shadows like stretches of
infinity . . .[17]

Here is the sublime in precisely the terms in which Burke described
it. Yet perhaps Burke would not have recognised it as such. For it has
become above all sinister, and what is absent is the aristocratic,
masculine strength which for Burke stamped the sublime with an
unquestionable authority. Present in its place is that absence of God
which seemed to threaten chaos.

This vision of the sublime was to seem now terrifying, now
strangely beautiful as the industrial period progressed. In the first
years of the twentieth century the French journalist Camille Mauclair wrote of the new suburbs of Paris as 'obscure and tragic
places', which nevertheless had their own beauty, a beauty distinctively modern, the new beauty of the industrial cityscape, summed
up by the spectacle of the plain of St Denis, 'with its thousands of
smokestacks, its smelting fires, its innumerable beacons, its interlaced highways where from all sides spreads the beautiful mother-
of-pearl smoke which the twilight embraces'.[18]

'The sublime' is, therefore, not just an abstract theory, but an
idea that has seeped into the collective consciousness to become one
of the ways in which the experience of urbanism is understood,
re-evaluated and transformed. The search for the meaning of the

city, or for meaning in the city, takes many forms, not the least important of which is to create new forms of beauty.

This new beauty, though, will never be without a kind of unease. For Siegfried Kracauer, 'knowledge of cities is bound up with the deciphering of their dream-like expressive images'. He described Berlin as permeated with 'formless disquiet'; while the Parisian *faubourgs* were 'the huge asylum of ordinary people . . . [communal life takes] the form of an asylum, that is certainly not bourgeois but neither is it proletarian in the sense of chimneys, barracks and *chaussées*'.[19]

Burke's concept of the sublime depended crucially on the way in which he distinguished it from the beautiful. It is as if the classical ideal of symmetry splits into two. It is taken up into an awesome ideal of grandeur, the sublime; in which vastness, suggested by monotony and sameness and devoid of decoration, is also meant to suggest the *irregular* vastness of nature. At the same time beauty comes to be defined in diminished, restrictive and above all *feminine* terms.

For what is so striking about Burke's contrast between the sublime and the beautiful is the totally *gendered* nature of these two aesthetic terms. For sublime we may read manly, and all the attendant attributes of strength, authority, power, domination and magnificence. Beauty by contrast becomes explicitly weak and frail. Burke even argues that where beauty 'is highest in the female sex', it 'almost always carries with it an idea of weakness and imperfection'. Because women are aware of this, he asserts, 'they learn to lisp, to totter in their walk, to counterfeit weakness, and even sickness'. Yet he then says that this is *natural*: 'in all this they are guided by nature'!

For Burke beauty consists in smallness, smoothness and gradual variation, in 'the deceitful image, through which the unsteady eye slides giddily, without knowing where to fix or whither it is carried'. Delicacy and fragility are 'essential' to his idea of beauty. The sublime and the beautiful are, Burke concludes, 'indeed ideas of a very different nature, one being founded on pain, the other on pleasure'.[20]

Mary Wollstonecraft criticised this division along sexual lines, so it did not pass unremarked at the time, but she was in a minority. The philosophy of taste – aesthetics – increasingly made a distinction between the grand style and the particular, associating these with masculinity and femininity respectively. The association of femininity with ornament – and by implication with triviality – was to persist through the nineteenth century.[21]

On the other hand, a sentimentalised rural beauty seemed increasingly desirable by contrast with the sublime of the nineteenth-century industrial city. Adam Smith and Thomas Jefferson had approved the virtuous civic pride of the eighteenth-century cities which were of manageable human size. Many rulers and reformers in the nineteenth century felt that the new, huge metropolis was unmanageable. For the optimistic, familiar, rational world of the Enlightenment, the metropolis substituted a vast, phantasmagoric and unearthly space, in which everything was fearsome and even uncanny because it was wholly strange.

In these cities the intelligentsia divided. Some immersed themselves in the new element of urban life – the *flâneurs* we have already encountered; others aimed to impose order, planning and control; yet others railed against the city altogether, and sentimentalised a lost rural idyll. The first two of these contrasting approaches might be said to correspond to a feminine and a masculine approach: surrender and mastery. The story of the nineteenth- and twentieth-century city is largely of the triumph of intervention and mastery over appreciation and immersion. Perhaps it is time to reverse those priorities.

3

Cesspool City: London

Part of the City might be described as having a cesspool city
excavated beneath it.

John Simon, *Report of the Medical Officer of Health
to the City of London* (1849)

It was a Sunday evening in London, gloomy, close and stale . . .
Nothing to see but streets, streets, streets. Nothing to breathe but
streets, streets, streets . . . Miles of close wells and pits of houses,
where the inhabitants gasped for air, stretched far away towards
every point of the compass. Through the heart of the town a deadly
sewer ebbed and flowed.

Charles Dickens, *Little Dorrit* (1857)

Under the impact of the Industrial Revolution, the cities of Europe
and the United States entered a period of explosive growth. Victorian Britain became the world's first urbanised society.[1] Con-
fronted with this upheaval of momentous proportions, the
Victorians produced a copious literature of city life.

Many different kinds of writing went to make up this 'rhetoric' of
revelation, but much of it aimed to shock its audience and to draw a
picture of urban life in the strongest possible, even in exaggerated,
terms. There were reports and investigations into housing, water
supplies and drains, which were directed at officials and a parliamen-
tary audience. There were novels, essays and articles which aimed to
alert the general reading public to the injustices, hardships and
dangers of city life.

To many readers of this literature, the life of great cities, especially
life in the slums and working-class districts, was as foreign and alien
as descriptions of the life of 'savages' in distant lands, and by the mid
century non-European city dwellers were being described in insult-
ing terms. William Wordsworth had simply commented, in his
autobiographical poem *The Prelude*, on the presence in London of
'negro ladies in muslin gowns' as part of the rich variety of the
capital's street life. By the 1850s black prostitutes were described in
terms of their 'ugliness' as African women, while George Godwin, a
serious campaigning journalist, could write casually of the way in
which the men and women of the London slums were 'as lawless as
the Arab and the Kaffir'.[2]

One of the best known investigative journalists was Henry
Mayhew. He described himself as a 'traveller in the undiscovered

country of the poor', a phrase that echoes Hamlet's description of the afterlife as 'the undiscovered country from whose bourn no traveller returns'. Mayhew's use of the phrase, whether intentionally or not, suggests that the East End was so remote, so mysterious and so terrifying that it was like the land beyond death. For a Victorian to pitch him- or herself (it was nearly always himself) into the warrens around King's Cross, Seven Dials or Saffron Hill was, figuratively, to die, to undergo a rite of passage that would destroy something integral to the Victorian identity: the optimism, the belief in the efficacy of providence, and in the ability of the individual to triumph over circumstances.[3]

Much Victorian journalism was a literature of voyeurism, revealing to its middle-class audience a hidden life of the city which offered not so much grist for reform as vicarious, even illicit enjoyment of the forbidden 'Other' that was so close to, yet so far from, the Victorian bourgeoisie. George Augustus Sala, for example, journalist, novelist and friend of Charles Dickens, recorded with a note of triumph the way in which a secret world was inadvertently to be observed. The writer saw everything from his privileged perch on an omnibus roof, 'surveying the world in its workings . . . The things I have seen from the top of an omnibus! . . . Unroofing London in a ride . . . varied life, troubled life, busy, restless, chameleon life.' He, however, remained invisible. 'Little do you reck that an [observer] is above you taking notes, and, faith, that he'll print them!' he cried to the participants in the miniature dramas he witnessed. The city hid yet revealed its secrets, tantalising and titillating. Sala spied on intimate moments, seeing 'now a married couple, enjoying an animated wrangle in a first floor front . . . now a demure maiden lacing her virgin bodice before a cracked triangle of looking glass at an attic window'.[4] It is, of course, significant that this Victorian voyeur was a man peeking at women. One effect of the new anonymity of the great city was that women became more vulnerable to the 'male gaze'. More generally, the condition of women became the touchstone for judgments on city life.

Throughout the nineteenth century the town versus country debate raged, as the cities, and particularly the new industrial towns, were giving birth to 'a system of social life constructed on a wholly new principle, a principle as yet vague and indefinite but developing itself by its own spontaneous force and daily producing effects which no human foresight had anticipated'.[5] This debate drew on the Romantic tradition with its emotional attachment to nature, and in the first half of the nineteenth century the retreat of the countryside before the advancing industrial towns made it hard to feel that civilisation, the creation of man, was in harmony with nature, the creation of God, as had been the more comfortable Enlightenment belief. Country and city had once appeared to complement each other; now the growth of towns had unbalanced the equation, and ugliness and destruction were the result.

Social reformers tended to support the negative view of urban life. Lord Shaftesbury, for example, one of the most prominent social campaigners of the 1840s and 1850s, drew a heartrending picture of the godlessness and vice of the industrial towns, claiming that: 'I am sure that sexual connexion begins between boys and girls at fourteen to fifteen years old. John Stubbs of the police force confirms the above testimony: "We have a deal of girls on the town under fifteen." '[6]

A contrasting view of the 'condition' of the urban labouring classes was put forward by the nonconformist liberals of the north of England. They identified with and took pride in the new cities and the new way of life that was being created. Edward Baines (brother of the radical editor of the *Leeds Mercury*) was forced to concede that:

> the manufacturing districts have a repulsive exterior. The smoke that hangs over them – their noisy bustling and dirty streets – the large proportion of the working classes seen there, many of whom have their persons and clothes blackened with their occupations – the hum and buzz of machinery in the factories – the flaming of furnaces – the rude earnestness of the 'unwashed artificers' – and their provincial dialect are little calculated to gratify 'ears polite' or to please the eye.[7]

But he flung back the accusation of immorality, citing the reports of the Poor Law Commissioners on rural areas – including reports of Dorset, where Lord Shaftesbury's estate lay. Typically, it was the behaviour of women that was at stake, with rural women described as immoral, incompetent and uneducated.

Robert Vaughan, another defender of the new urban order against its detractors, echoed the ancient prejudice in favour of cities as against nomadic life:

> The picturesque . . . may be with the country, but the intellectual . . . must be with the town . . . Man makes the country where Art makes the town . . . When the Almighty placed the Hebrew tribes in possession of the cities of Canaan, he recognised man as a citizen, an improvement upon man as a wanderer.[8]

For him, too, the condition of women was the touchstone of the state of civilisation and progress: only in the modern city were the 'milder sentiments natural to women . . . suffered to make their just impression on man'. In Vaughan's 'great city' the cult of privacy and domesticity in the bourgeois interior permitted women's distinctive contribution its full flowering, and made possible the full development of the sexual division of labour to the benefit of all. Thus the industrial city, which emancipated the working class, was to confine middle-class womanhood within a private enclave, and arguments in favour of 'progress' were given a conservative twist.

Given the filth, noise and overcrowding of the cities, it was not surprising that many reformers wished to bring something of the countryside into the towns. Both in the United States and in Britain the second half of the nineteenth century saw movements to create parks, squares and children's playgrounds. Octavia Hill, one of the most important woman reformers of the nineteenth century, made the bringing of a glimpse of country life to the slum dwellers an integral part of her work. With the financial help of John Ruskin, she refurbished and managed slum properties. Her work did not end with the collection of rent and the encouragement of thrift, for she regularly arranged country outings for tenants – describing how on these occasions they had to be steered away from public houses. She also used to bring them bunches of flowers from the country whenever she could. Her enthusiasm for the countryside led at the end of the century to the founding of the National Trust. Octavia Hill believed not just that the countryside was healthier than the foetid courts and alleys of the city centres; for her there was a direct moral link between 'the quiet influence of nature' and the sober and virtuous life.[9]

Such views were widespread, and flourished partly because the life of the new urban street disturbed many bourgeois Victorians. The noise and dirt of city streets were bad enough. Horse-drawn transport meant that dung mingled with mud and often rain to create a liquid manure that spread filth on pavements and even clothing. The noise of traffic created a fearful din. The smells from tanneries, slaughter houses, glue factories and other industries were often unbearable. Street traders and entertainers plied their wares or begged in a wholly unregulated fashion.

More frightful than all that, however, was the crowd – the promiscuous mingling of classes in close proximity on the street. The gentleman and, worse still, the gentlewoman were forced to rub shoulders with the lower orders and might be buffeted and pushed with little ceremony or deference. This disorder created uncertainty, disorientation and alarm. Popular literature was filled with tales of encounters between the respectable and the rough. Journalists and reformers (Josephine Butler, for example) wrote of occasions when respectable women were mistaken for prostitutes, with alarming consequences such as arrest and detention. The very fact that such mistakes could occur undermined ancient beliefs in the 'natural' distinctions between ranks, or, in more modern nineteenth-century parlance, classes. In the same way, the possibility that a virtuous woman could be mistaken for one who was 'fallen' made the barriers of convention and respectability seem fragile indeed. No wonder that women began to withdraw from the street.

Many believed that the family in its rural, or at least suburban, retreat was the ideal solution or antidote to the horrors of the city. Women of the bourgeoisie had already begun to withdraw from commerce and other employments in the eighteenth century. Now the trend accelerated. It became undesirable and even indecent for a lady to walk in the streets unless she was accompanied by a husband, father or brother, or at least by a male servant. These rules were strictly enforced so far as young, unmarried women were concerned. Once she had passed the age of thirty, the marginal, single woman might gain a small measure of freedom, but this was double-edged, as it signalled that she was 'on the shelf', and had dropped out of the marriage market. Governesses, too, were granted this rather humiliating freedom – a kind of sexual invisibility, and a condition of lessened worth.[10] The freedom to adventure in the city could, however, appear intoxicating to those women compelled by necessity to travel alone. Lucy Snowe, heroine of Charlotte Brontë's *Villette*, revelled in an opportunity to explore London unaccompanied:

> Elation and pleasure were in my heart: to walk alone in London seemed of itself an adventure . . . Prodigious was the amount of life I lived that morning . . . I went wandering whither chance might lead, in a still ecstasy of freedom and enjoyment; and I got – I know not how – I got into the heart of city life. I saw and felt London at last . . . I mixed with the life passing along; I dared the perils of crossings. To do this, and to do it utterly alone, gave me, perhaps an irrational, but a real pleasure . . . my spirit shook its always-fettering wings half loose; I had a sudden feeling as if I, who had never yet truly lived, were at last about to taste life.[11]

Even in the intimidating environment of a foreign hotel, Lucy Snowe was able to hold her own:

> I made my way somehow to what proved to be the coffee-room. It cannot be denied that on entering this room I trembled somewhat; felt uncertain, solitary, wretched; wished to Heaven

I knew whether I was doing right or wrong; felt convinced it was the last, but could not help myself . . . There were many other people breakfasting at other tables in the room; I should have felt rather more happy if amongst them all I could have seen any women; however, there was not one – all present were men. But nobody seemed to think I was doing anything strange; one or two gentlemen glanced at me occasionally, but none stared obtrusively.[12]

Charlotte Brontë was no ordinary woman, and we cannot treat her experience, on which *Villette* was based, as representative. Yet there has perhaps been an over-emphasis on the confinement of Victorian womanhood to the private sphere. The women of the London-based, reformist professional classes – a relatively small group, with many links of friendship – do not conform to this stereotype. Jane O'Meara, for example, the wife of John Simon, the pioneering doctor, was 'highly intelligent and well informed; well able to hold her own in debate on religious and philosophic matters. She was an accomplished raconteuse and letter writer.' As a young woman she had been known to violate 'the conventions of a genteel young lady and daringly travelled in a public conveyance [a train] accompanied only by unknown men'.[13]

The wives and lovers of the Pre-Raphaelite group of painters (formed in 1848) were not typical either. Yet as a group they and their friends confound the crude myth of Victorian women as 'exquisite slaves', and, with however great difficulty, some of them did strive for independence both in work and in sexual relations.

Just as some exceptional women travelled in foreign lands, so some middle-class women explored the urban environment in the nineteenth century, most often in their guise as philanthropists. Octavia Hill came from the progressive professional class to which the Simons also belonged. Her grandfather, Thomas Southwood Smith, was a Christian socialist and, like John Simon, an important medical reformer. Her mother brought up her family largely unassisted by her husband, who suffered from chronic mental disturbance following financial failure. In no way did this upbringing conform to our stereotype of the Victorian lady. Moreover, the family was so poor that Octavia Hill had to earn her own living from the age of fourteen.

Throughout her life she not only played her part as a public figure, lecturing to large audiences, for example, but in her work as a housing manager she ventured fearlessly into London slums. Her female co-workers were equally intrepid. One of these, Emma Cons, would, if necessary, intervene in street fights, 'and forcibly separate combatants, men and women who slunk away from her indignation like whipped hounds'.[14] Yet although Octavia Hill supported the reform of married women's property rights, believed in education for women and encouraged them to play a public role, her vision for ordinary women was deeply conservative: the working-class wife was to be confined to the domestic sphere, creating a traditional home for husband and children.

Josephine Butler was equally unafraid to go among the poor of the great cities. When her husband became headmaster of Liverpool College she went among the pauper women of the workhouse, sharing their work in the oakum picking sheds. Her investigations into unemployment and prostitution among working-class women led her to the opposite conclusion from that reached by Octavia Hill: she believed passionately in the importance of proper work, training and education for all women.

The growth of the city seems to have made the condition of poor women – like that of their homes – more obvious and less acceptable to a small but increasingly confident middle class. During the Chartist demonstration of 1839 in Birmingham, Emma Cadbury and her family watched apprehensively from behind the closed Venetian blinds of their imposing house in the centre of the city. Emma was struck by 'the very coarse hard-featured women'.[15] It was not long after this incident that the Cadburys moved out to the suburb of Edgbaston.

Working-class women as well as men came to work in the towns, as they had always come to London. In the north of England and in industrial towns generally they found employment in the factories. In the Lancashire textile towns the spinners and weavers had a reputation for independence, but in general the picture was of a narrowing of opportunities. Domestic service was the destiny of many.

The nineteenth-century discussion of women's work was overwhelmingly negative, either because those concerned disapproved of women working at all or because they wished to highlight the frightful conditions and pay that were the rule rather than the exception. Conditions were indeed shocking, and women were crowded together in a pitifully narrow range of occupations. The agricultural workers of nineteenth-century Britain were impoverished when the great landlords seized common land by a repeated process of enclosures, and this pushed them to the towns; but they were also positively drawn to the cities by the opportunities for higher wages, and perhaps escape from the restrictions of rural life. In the cities, for example, women could avoid, if need be, some of the social consequences of a fall from virtue.

London was not an industrial town like Bradford or Manchester, remaining to a much greater extent a craft and commercial centre. George Dodd, writing in 1843, noted that several of the most important of the London trades, tailoring and dressmaking, and shoe-making, were not organised along factory lines at all, but were 'handicraft employments which can be carried on at the home of the workman'. The manufacture of clothing was developed 'to an extraordinary extent', and 'tailors and dressmakers are to be reckoned not by thousands but by tens of thousands'. By the 1840s sewing was one of the few trades still open to women:

> In what manner female labour is bestowed in making articles of dress is too well known to need recital. Here, from the Stepney seamstress who wears out life by making shirts at a 1d a piece to the court milliner who is surrounded by the luxuries of life, all produce their results by the slender needle and the supple thread, by dexterity of finger, patience and endurance, and by such lengthened hours of labour as men would rebel against.[16]

The plight of the seamstresses became one of the scandals of the 1840s, publicised by Henry Mayhew, but public outcry did not lead to any significant improvement in the condition of female workers.

This was in part because the belief that the factory system was destroying the family really took hold.[17] The employment of mothers in particular was held to be an evil, partly because it was thought to contribute to the high infant mortality rates. Therefore, for most reformers the solution was not in better employment for women, but in their confinement to the home, and the reconstruction of the patriarchal family. Sir John Simon (husband of Jane O'Meara) was unusual in that he advocated factory nurseries as well as a ban on the sale of the opiates so frequently given to pacify fretful babies.[18]

The working-class family in the city was held to be in danger of complete disintegration, 'turned upside down', according to Friedrich Engels, because 'the wife supports the family, the husband sits at home, tends the children, sweeps the room and cooks'. He regarded this as an 'insane state of things', and although he acknowledged that the previous 'rule of the husband over the wife must have been inhuman too', his attack on the conditions of working-class life in the industrial towns reflected conventional dismay at the 'independence' of the factory woman.[19]

The real or imagined autonomy of the working-class woman in the factory town was often discussed in terms of the natural and unnatural. Urban life overturned a symbolic natural order; and the linchpin of this natural order – the family – was the woman. The role of the wife and mother was then, and has continued to be, a focus of alarm. When James Callaghan, then Labour Prime Minister, spoke in 1977 of the importance of placing the mother 'at the centre of family life', he was essentially voicing anew these nineteenth-century anxieties. To the extent that it released women from the patriarchal family, the nineteenth-century city could be viewed as 'unnatural'; and ideas about nature and the natural shaded into metaphors of disease.

Cities were frequently associated with physical disease. William Cobbett, radical and chronicler of the condition of England in the early years of the century, likened London to a 'great wen' – a growth wherein gathered all the poisonous humours of the social organism. The medical metaphor was also a metaphor for moral disease. Edwin Chadwick, a utilitarian and one of the great reformers of the 1830s and 1840s, cited overcrowding 'as one of the causes of ill health . . . but the overcrowding is also frequently noticed as a cause of extreme demoralisation and recklessness and recklessness again as a cause of disease'.[20]

Perhaps the workers who came to the towns were less horrified than their masters by conditions of life in the cities, because rural slums existed and rural housing in the pre-industrial and industrial period was of a very low standard.[21] The growth of the medical profession, however, coincided with the growth of cities, and this was one reason for the greater concern over ill health. In addition, with the development of the statistical societies in the 1830s, evidence began to be collected on a more scientific basis and this was difficult to ignore.[22]

One source of information came from the investigations into the working of the Old Poor Law, and, after the passing of the Poor Law Amendment Act of 1834, the further investigations of the New Poor Law Commissioners. The dominant force behind the New Poor Law was Edwin Chadwick, who then turned his attention to problems of public health. In his wake, a group of reforming doctors was active in the investigation of the conditions of the fast-growing cities, among these being Sir John Simon and Thomas Southwood Smith, the grandfather of Octavia Hill.

One of the most important documents produced at this time was Chadwick's 1842 *Report on the Sanitary Conditions of the Labouring Classes*. This report was informed both by the environmentalist desire to improve urban conditions, and by the 'disciplinary' or 'tutelary' aims which interested Chadwick so much. For Chadwick was not interested simply in the improvement of health; much more ambitiously, he, and other reformers, wished to regulate, discipline and order the disorderly chaos of the cities. Reform, for Chadwick and his supporters, always contained an element of control, a wish to curb the excesses of the mob and the crowd, and to bring them within the pale of civilisation.

Chadwick's report teemed with examples of the demoralisation which resulted from overcrowding. Workers of both sexes sleeping as many as fourteen to a room were frequently described. The consequent 'impropriety' was sometimes at the level of a young man changing his shirt in front of a young woman, or, perhaps more shockingly, a young woman dressed only in a chemise throughout the visit by the inspectors. At other times 'unutterable horrors' were mentioned:

> In the houses of the working class brothers and sisters and lodgers of both sexes are found occupying the same sleeping rooms with the parents and consequences occur which humanity shudders to contemplate. It is but three or four years since a father and daughter stood at the bar of the Leeds Quarter Sessions as criminals, the one in concealing, the other in being accessory to concealing the birth of an innocent child, born on the body of the daughter by the father.[23]

(Incest itself became a criminal offence in Britain only in 1908.) Incest and promiscuous sexuality were perceived as the bestial result of the frightful conditions which reduced the workers to the condition of animals. It was not usually, in these reports at least, understood as the result of coercion and violence by men, but was simply a manifestation of the animality of the working class of both sexes.

Some contemporary commentators recognised that housing conditions made it impossible for working-class women to create a decent domestic environment. George Godwin, for example, maintained that 'there are hundreds and thousands of dwellings that ultimately beat every occupier and transform the tidy housewife into the slatternly shrew, and the industrious home-loving husband into a disorderly drunkard'.[24]

The 1842 report, on the other hand, blamed women for the demoralisation of the working class:

> The improvidence of which we are speaking is to be traced in very many instances to extreme ignorance on the part of the wives of these people. The females are from necessity bred up from their youth in the workshops, as the earnings of the younger members contribute to the support of the family. The minds and morals of the girls become debased and they marry totally ignorant of all those habits of domestic economy which tend to render a husband's home comfortable and happy, and

this is very often the cause of the man being driven to the alehouse to seek that comfort after his day of toil which he looks for in vain by his own fireside. The habit of a manufacturing life being once established in a woman, she continues it, and leaves her home and children to the care of a neighbour or of a hired child, sometimes only a few years older than her own children, whose services cost her probably as much as she obtains for her labour.[25]

Such a judgment was a total denial of the appalling domestic difficulties that working-class women daily faced. Even to obtain drinking water was often a major undertaking. The eventual provision of a supply of fresh drinking water and the construction of sewage systems in the major towns of Britain were magnificent achievements. Yet in the 1850s Sir John Simon, in his annual reports as Physician to the City of London, and George Godwin, in his magazine *The Builder*, were still describing the provision of water in the metropolis and other large towns – or, rather, the lack of it – in horrific terms.

Water was provided in casks. These, filled once or twice a week, were often located near dustbins or refuse – a potent source of contamination. Many families and individuals had no vessels for water in their rooms. John Simon described water butts made of decayed wood, filled three times a week. A 'black sooty scum' formed on the surface of the water.

The burden of obtaining water bore particularly harshly on women:

The system of supplying water usually adopted by companies is to turn it on to the several districts of the town at certain periods of the day, generally two to three hours three times a week. The houses of the wealthier portions of the community are furnished with cisterns to receive and retain the water.

The poor have to collect water from the butt when it is turned on and those who are engaged in occupations from home necessarily lose their chance of getting a supply. This inconvenience is particularly felt in districts where women and children have much employment.[26]

Even when women were available to carry the water it was an exhausting task:

The labour of carrying water upstairs is felt as a grievous evil. To mothers especially who are often debilitated, the carrying of water upstairs is a very great exertion; mothers not daring to leave a child in the room have to carry the child in one arm and the vessel of water in the other.[27]

The scenes in the queues crowding and shoving round the pumps can be imagined:

> Quarrels which ensue during the water collection are very injurious to the morals and peaceable disposition of the poorer classes; so much so . . . that the Police Magistrate states that a large proportion of the cases of assault brought before him are traceable to the disputes engendered by this mode of supply.[28]

Like so many of his contemporaries, Simon drew a direct connection between deprivation and morality, and morality always meant particularly that of women:

> There is a great advantage in the removal of the assemblages round the public pumps . . . Where young girls are brought into contact with every description of characters the effect is highly objectionable.[29]

Efficient sewage systems were as desperately needed as adequate water supplies. In both cases, morality was inextricably entwined with cleanliness, disorder with filth. For the Victorians excrement became a metaphor and a symbol for moral filth, perhaps even for the working class itself, and when they spoke and wrote of the cleansing of the city of filth, refuse and dung, they may really have longed to rid the cities of the labouring poor altogether.

The medical metaphors of disease, degeneration and filth coalesced in the rhetorical creation of 'cesspool city', about to be submerged in a tide of excrement:

> The entire excrementation of the Metropolis . . . shall sooner or later be mingled in the stream of the river, there to be rolled backward and forward around the population; . . . at low water for many hours this material shall be trickling over broad belts of spongy bank which then dry their contaminated mud in the sunshine exhaling foetor and poison . . . Sewers which under better circumstances should be benefactors and appliances for health in the several districts . . . furnish chambers for an immense faecal evaporation; at every breeze which strikes against their open mouths, at every tide which encroaches on their inward space their gases are breathed into the upper air – wherever outlet exists into houses, footpaths and carriage-way . . . From the polluted bosom of the river steam up, incessantly though unseen, the vapours of a retributive poison.[30]

The stench of sewage caused special horror because the prevailing theory of epidemic disease held that it was passed via the 'miasma' – the poisonous exhalations from undistributed excrement. The fear was all the greater because cholera, which had first struck in 1833 and then returned in 1848, was a new disease, and it attacked indiscriminately, as dangerous to the rich as to the poor. In fact, it caused fewer deaths than typhus, typhoid and TB, but those illnesses were much more likely to affect the working classes.[31]

The middle classes made forceful attempts to police and control the enjoyments of the working masses as a way of controlling the moral cesspool. Secular pleasures were always rife with the danger of immorality. Hence the many attempts to impose strict observance of the Sabbath – for most ordinary people their only day of rest. At the Cremorne Gardens in Battersea the entertainments to be seen during the week were, in fact, banished on the Sabbath: 'the strong minded lady in the glittering tights balanced by a ponderous pole, will not this evening make her terrific ascent on the rope'. However, this did not make for more orderly behaviour, since 'decorous hard drinking is the order of the day'. The respectable artisan families sitting outside were in danger of contamination from the less salubrious characters seated in the spacious saloon. There, 'swells' and unaccompanied women drank and flirted. At one table:

> were seated four young ladies attired in silks and satins with bonnets half off their heads, bad bracelets and cheap rings innumerable adorning their arms, who occasionally helped themselves from two decanters on the table to port and sherry and were asking two fast men conundrums.[32]

Meanwhile, outside, 'teaspoons full of gin and water administered to children by indulgent parents seemed quite to have exhilarated the juveniles'.

Nineteenth-century campaigns to curb the unsuitable enjoyments of the lower classes were inextricably linked to attempts to restrain and domesticate disruptive sexuality. Sir William Wilberforce, most famous for his campaign against the slave trade, had argued that failure to observe the Sabbath, and the spread of obscene and blasphemous publications, had led to the increase in prostitution at the end of the eighteenth century. The Society for the Suppression of Vice had begun its campaign against pornographic literature in 1802.

Prostitution, the 'great social evil' of the Victorians, generated its own literature of investigation. In the 1830s and 1840s clergymen and doctors inspired by evangelicalism campaigned against what they saw as its horrors, and many rescue organisations sprang up. These campaigners adapted a radical theme of the period – popular resentment of the exploitation of working-class women by middle- and upper-class men – and gave it a conservative twist.[33]

Michael Ryan, an evangelical doctor, linked vice and depravity with the pernicious ideology of the French Revolution, although he was well aware that the main reason women resorted to prostitution was 'the insufficiency of wages'. Ryan also wrote *The Philosophy of Marriage*, in which, like the utopian socialists, he argued against the 'double standard' of sexual morality. Ryan argued for a return to the patriarchal order and the clear sexual division of labour within the family, with women assigned an entirely domestic role. Ryan's vision of the importance of this tradition of marriage, and its link with nature and natural harmony, led to a view which, implicitly at least, condemned urban life as inherently vicious. He wrote with horror of:

> the present dreadfully immoral state of the British metropolis . . . Scarcely a street can be passed through without meeting some storehouse of obscenity. Agents are employed for the purpose of entrapping the unwary . . .[34]

He sometimes appeared to confuse organised prostitution with a general profligacy of the working class. For example, he described how brothels were situated in the East End:

> in the midst of a dense and ignorant population. The scenes of vice exhibited in these houses beggar all description . . . Men, women and children of all ages were there associated for the vilest and basest purposes. After perambulating all parts of London during the day, begging, thieving and committing every description of crime, they congregated at night in these houses, revelling in debauchery and licentiousness, bidding defiance to all laws and spreading a moral miasma around.[35]

The idea of the 'moral miasma' must have terrified the Victorians. According to the miasma theory of the spread of disease, you could catch an illness by breathing in the noxious smell of sewage. Could you not also then become literally infected with depravity merely by coming close to the 'contagion' itself?

In the great city the moral miasma was spreading everywhere. A young man, wrote one evangelist, 'cannot pass along the street in the evening without meeting with and being accosted by women of the town at every step', and another claimed that 'his path is beset on the right hand and on the left, so that he is at every step exposed to temptation from boyhood to mature age, his life is one continuous struggle against it'.[36]

Women, too, were constantly exposed to temptation, and, once 'fallen', a woman was doomed, many reformers believed, to a life of increasing degradation and an early and tragic death. Charles Dickens, for example, regarded the fall from virtue as so disastrous that the only solution was for former prostitutes to emigrate to colonies such as Australia, where a surplus of men offered the possibility of marriage and a return to respectability. Many other reformers advocated the emigration of 'fallen women' for similar reasons.

Dickens and his friend, the heiress and philanthropist Angela Burdett Coutts, set up a refuge for fallen women, Urania Cottage. It was opened in 1847, and by 1853 fifty-six women had passed through. Dickens did not wish Urania Cottage to be 'too grim or sorry', nor did he want the young women to be 'hectored' and 'driven'. Yet because the consequences of a 'fall' were so fearful, the regime of reclamation was necessarily strict. 'The design', wrote Dickens, 'is simply . . . to appeal to them by means of affectionate kindness and trustfulness – but firmly too. To improve them by education and example – establish habits of the most rigid order, punctuality and neatness.'[37]

The inmates of Urania Cottage were expected to *internalise* the middle-class view of them – but Dickens's letters to Angela Burdett Coutts contain descriptions of the way in which the young women rebelled against the self-definitions they were under so much pressure (however kindly applied) to accept. When ordered to her room (as a prelude to being ejected altogether) one young woman 'danced upstairs . . . holding her skirt like a lady at a ball'. Dickens caught sight of another, just expelled, 'walking in a jaunty way up Notting Hill and refreshing herself with an occasional contemplation of the shop windows'.[38]

In 1857 the physician William Acton published his major work, *Prostitution*. Acton is best known today for his statement (in a work on gynaecology) that women were 'not much troubled by sexual feeling of any kind'. This belief reinforced his view that prostitution was above all an economic transaction, since pleasure could not be a motive. He therefore took issue with the 'catastrophic' evangelical view of prostitution of the 1840s and 'the notion that the career of the woman who once quits the pinnacle of virtue involves the very swift decline and ultimate total loss of health, modesty and temporal prosperity', as he expressed it. He pointed out that, on the contrary, prostitution had a number of advantages for the working-class woman:

> If we compare the prostitute at thirty-five with her sister who perhaps is the married mother of a family or has been a toiling slave for years in the over-heated laboratories of fashion, we shall seldom find that the constitutional ravages often thought to be necessary consequences of prostitution exceed those attributable to the cares of a family and the heart-wearing struggles of virtuous labour.[39]

Prostitution, he insisted, was in any case not a permanent condition, but rather 'a transitory state through which an untold number of British women are ever on their passage'.

Acton's approach was cooler, more worldly and more 'scientific' than that of the evangelists. Commonsense replaced outrage; science replaced religious fervour; regulation replaced the utopian project of the total elimination of prostitution.

Acton did, nonetheless, view prostitution as a menace to health and morals. Although he demonstrated that relatively few prostitutes actually died of VD, their bodies were 'spreading about a loathsome poison'. It was precisely *because* 'by far the larger number of women who have resorted to prostitution for a livelihood, return sooner or later to a more or less regular course of life' that this pollution was so invasive and alarming. Even more intolerable was the ambiguity: 'the shades of prostitution . . . are as numberless as those of society at large and may be said to blend at their edges'. The horrifying end result was that 'the great substitution of unchastity for female honour has run through and dislocated the whole system'.[40]

The urban scene was therefore tainted, uncertain and disorientating because it permitted or even created this 'blending at the edges'. Who was and who was not a prostitute? 'Who are those fair creatures, neither chaperones nor chaperoned, "those somebodies whom nobody knows", who elbow our wives and daughters in the parks and promenades and rendezvous of fashion?'[41]

The very facts of urban life, according to Acton, made prostitution inevitable. It would always be 'attendant upon civilised, and especially close-packed population'. Nor was it an accident that prostitutes were referred to as women *of the streets*, streetwalkers. For the open street with its lack of boundaries and its freedom for all to use was precisely what created 'promiscuity' in every form.

At the same time, the pursuit of pleasure, as Acton described it, had a mechanical quality. This was consistent with a general Victorian tendency to use metaphors of machinery to indicate the psychological effect upon them of the industrial city. There is a bleak joylessness in Acton's description of the parading crowd in Cremorne Gardens: 'an almost mute procession, not of joyous revellers, but thoughtful, careworn men and women, paced round and round the platform as on a horizontal treadmill'.[42] It was as if the industrial work ethic or performance principle had invaded even the sphere of pleasure.

The regulation of prostitutes and the building of drains were not the only Victorian solutions to the 'moral miasma' of city life. Although housing reform was slow to develop, the middle class found its own solution, while reformers created in their imagination what could not be built on the ground.

In the first half of the nineteenth century there appears to have been a convergence between utopian thought and practical town planning.[43] Many utopian communities were founded, especially in the United States, and both these and utopian writings influenced reformers.

In addition, some factory owners attempted to build 'perfect' towns for their workers. In the United States, Amoskeag, Massachusetts, was the site of one such experiment.[44] Harriet Martineau's description of Lowell, another 'utopian' or philanthropic Massachusetts factory town, alerted British reforming industrialists to the possibilities of environmental engineering.[45] Industrialists in the north of England were genuinely horrified by conditions in the factory towns. They were environmentalists, who believed that if living conditions were improved workers would not only be more contented and more healthy, but would as a consequence become more productive. They also believed that the '"better life" would be secured only in a retreat from urbanity'.[46]

In the 1850s Sir Titus Salt built a model factory town, Saltaire, just outside Bradford. It was zoned, the residential area separated from industry. The houses, built in a neo-Renaissance style, were larger than the usual workman's cottage and not back to back, as in Leeds. The town was equipped with a steam laundry which took care of the whole washing and drying cycle in one hour (and which survived until the 1960s). Like other model towns, and like the early garden cities, Saltaire was a 'dry' town, without alcohol or pubs, but Sir Titus provided recreation rooms at the Saltaire Educational Institute in order to 'supply the advantages of a public house without the evils'.[47] (In the late 1980s another northern industrialist, a clothing manufacturer, bought the disused Saltaire factory with the intention of turning it into a shopping mall, and in 1990 it housed two art galleries.)

Although Saltaire was one of the most complete model towns, the ideas that inspired it had effects on already existing towns such as Halifax, where the factory owner John Crossley (one of three brothers) redeveloped much of the town centre, replacing the hovels and mean courts with a town hall, mechanics' institute, hotel and other public buildings. Many like-minded philanthropic industrialists were determined to create towns that were not only healthier, but were places of beauty and rest.

Utopian ideas had already drawn close to the ideas of the group of reformers influenced by utilitarianism. In 1828, J.A. Roebuck, MP, gave a speech to the Utilitarian debating society in which he outlined a programme of town planning in accordance with Benthamite principles. In his ideal towns there would be tree-lined boulevards, lawns, parks and flowers, and the towns would be surrounded by tracts of common land, which in effect anticipated the twentieth-century 'green belts'. He also advocated the municipal acquisition of land.[48]

The ideas of Robert Owen, who had founded socialist communities both in Scotland and in the United States, influenced another Utilitarian MP, James Silk Buckingham. He had visited the excavations of the ancient cities of Babylon and Nineveh, and also the Shaker and Rappite utopian communities in the United States. The socialistic ideas embodied in some utopian communities did not, however, attract him; on the contrary, he 'wished to avoid the evils of Communism and retain the benefits of association'.[49]

In 1835 Buckingham 'introduced a Bill to enable the local authorities in all towns to provide public walks and gardens, public baths, institutions and museums for the promotion of the health, enjoyment and instruction of the labouring classes'. In 1849 he published *National Evils and Practical Remedies and the Plan for a Model Town.*

In this book he described the city of Victoria, a utopia made of iron and built in concentric squares, sectioned off by eight radial streets. The outermost square was to consist of workers' housing, so that the inhabitants should be near to green open space and also near their work, for Victoria, like the majority of utopian cities, was strictly zoned, industrial activity being separated from the residential quarters of the town. (This form of zoning was to become a key feature of twentieth-century town planning.) As the centre of the town was approached, the housing became grander, and at the very centre were the public buildings. In between were covered shopping arcades.

This was to be an open city. It illustrated clearly the nineteenth-century obsession with the regulation of urban life:

> From the entire absence of all wynds, courts and blind alleys, or culs-de-sacs, there would be no secret and obscure haunts for the retirement of the filthy and the immoral from the public eye – and for the indulgence of that morose defiance of public decency which such secret haunts generate in their inhabitants.[50]

There were also to be 'no beer shops, gin palaces, dram shops, cigar divans, pawnbrokers, gambling houses or brothels'.

As Buckingham himself pointed out, the design of the city was similar to the plans of Sir Christopher Wren for the rebuilding of the City of London after the great fire of 1666. Wren's plans (which proved too expensive to implement) had marked the transition from the medieval city to the secular city of commerce: he planned a city for financiers and merchants, for an oligarchic, not a democratic, form of government. Edwin Chadwick had also mentioned Wren's plans with approval in his 1842 report. When today Prince Charles and the architect Leon Krier once more cite the Wren plans, as an ideal for London in the 1990s, we should note that the tradition they endorse is authoritarian rather than democratic, and has links, as well, with Chadwick's reformist regime of regulation and surveillance.[51]

Buckingham's attitude to women was central to his plan. Like the majority of Victorians he strongly emphasised the natural difference between the sexes. On the other hand, like Robert Owen, he believed that this could be harmonised with a commitment to equality for women. He did not envisage that working–class women, at least, would be withdrawn from the public world of work, and he endorsed John Stuart Mill's belief that all women had the right to an independent income. He pointed out, however, that Mill had never suggested that women should do the *same* work as men. Rather, he suggested, women would undertake work 'better suited to the delicacy of their physical constitutions and more in harmony with the refinement of their feelings'. No women were to be employed in 'laborious occupations, such as carrying heavy burdens, or working at any employment requiring great muscular strength, suited only for men, nor ever to be engaged in any outdoor labour, except in ornamental gardening, and assisting, as required, to gather in the harvest'.

Victoria was, however, to have collective laundries and refectories. A system of collective childcare (apparently residential) would provide high-quality care by trained workers for children, thus sparing them 'the unavoidable contamination which arises from their being brought up, as they now often are, with several of both sexes sleeping in the same room by night', but parents might visit their children at any time, 'or have them at home when desired'.

Buckingham, like John Stuart Mill, was sensitive to the legal inequalities suffered by women in marriage. Accordingly, in Victoria, 'female purity is to be protected by the arm of all'. Adultery and fornication were to be punished equally in both sexes.

In 1876 Benjamin Ward Richardson published another utopian work, *Hygeia, City of Health*. This was dedicated to Edwin Chadwick, of whom Richardson was an ardent disciple. *Hygeia* had begun as an address to the Health section of the Social Science Congress, illustrating how close utopian thought and practical reform had become at this period. *Hygeia* anticipated twentieth-century planning in a number of ways. The houses were without basements, for example – then rather unusual. Instead, the space under the houses was to be used for the disposal of rubbish and for the transmission of water and gas to each house. There was a system of central heating, and glazed tiles were to be used as a labour-saving form of interior decorating.[52]

The philanthropic movement to improve towns was one response to urban conditions in the first half of the nineteenth century. Another was the middle-class suburb, to which the professional and business classes began to transplant their families. The suburb certainly embodied an anti-urban longing for the imagined stability and security of the lost rural past. It was also utopian. One of the earliest suburbs was John Nash's Park Village West, adjacent to Regent's Park, and it has been suggested that this development was influenced by Claude-Nicolas Ledoux's utopian city plan. The influence of the Romantic movement and of the ideal of the picturesque were also strong in Park Village, where the houses were irregular and built along winding culs-de-sac, rather than in the straight terraces of the eighteenth-century ideal.[53]

Although suburbs were later to become the focus of criticism, and indeed hatred, in the mid nineteenth century they seemed to embody all that was most desirable. The detached or semi-detached house surrounded by a garden was a new version of the Englishman's castle. Within it, an elaborate ideal of domestic comfort and consumerism was developed, and at the centre of this enlarged zone of civilised privacy was the woman. It is this middle-class wife who has survived as an image of all that was most restrictive in Victorian ideals of femininity. The wife and mother in the prosperous suburbs of Bayswater or Edgbaston was hedged about with rules of etiquette and dress, forced to take charge of a large household of dependants and servants, and often, of course, had to maintain an appearance of gentility on an income insufficient for the task.

Central to any discussion of urban life and anti-urbanism must be a recognition of the crucial role that women were supposed to play. While working-class women were to be regulated in the model towns envisaged by industrialists and politicians, the role of the middle-class woman was to preside over a semi-rural retreat, which was the opposite in all particulars of the noisy, bustling city which her husband had to negotiate each day. Rest, peace and comfort were the ideals. The very squares of London resembled the private garden of the country house. Even in the central London residential districts, 'the layout of the London street and the pattern of development that informed the Victorian metropolis encouraged withdrawal and seclusion . . . The life of London lay hidden in its drawing rooms,

inside its clubs.'[54] Women could play an important role in the
private, formal world of entertaining, the dinners, balls and soirées,
but the gentleman's club was a male world to which the head of the
family repaired alone, leaving his wife at home. This pattern of life
was, as we shall see, very different from the Parisian.

Architecture, planning and social custom combined to create this
familiar, oppressive ideal of Victorian family life. An essentially
bourgeois ideal, it was extended to the working-class family as well.
By the last quarter of the nineteenth century there were many
reformers who wished to decant the working classes to their own
suburbs. Hitherto, the unskilled and casual labourers, hired on a
daily basis, had needed to live near their work, but with the
introduction of cheap 'workmen's' fares (also used by female
workers) on the railways, it was – in theory at least – easier for them
to live further from the centre. The newer suburbs, however, were
developed primarily for the expanding lower middle class of white-
collar workers and for the better-off sections of the working class,
many of whom aspired to a more exclusive and comfortable way of
life. For the poorest, the suburban ideal remained beyond their reach
and was not necessarily desired at all. Opportunities of employment
for married women (and for children) were fewer in the suburbs,
food prices were higher, and credit harder to obtain,[55] but to many
middle-class reformers it appeared as an ideal solution to the
overcrowding and lawlessness of the slums. Many also shared
Octavia Hill's belief that the place for the proletarian wife and
mother was in the home, and the suburban way of life assisted this
ideal.

Women in cities were perceived as the objects of both regulation
and banishment. It was recognised that women would continue to
work, and could not be entirely excluded from the public sphere, and
for these the policed city, cleansed of temptation, was to be created.
At the same time, the suburban ideal always acted ideologically to
debase and delegitimate the pleasures and possibilities of urban life.
Victorian rhetoric created two opposed types, Angels and Victims,
both in their way idealised, both born from the giddy waves of city
life. These stereotypes to some extent obscured the variety in the
lives and work of women. They were in part creatures of fantasy,
who decorated Victorian literature much as statues of the female
form decorated nineteenth-century architecture. They were living
metaphors of the double nature of the nineteenth-century city.

4

The City of the Floating World: Paris

I shall . . . only think of amusing myself; a business never performed anywhere with so much ease as at Paris . . . this gay, bright, noisy, restless city – this city of the living.

Mrs Frances Trollope, *Paris and the Parisians* (1836)

Meanwhile the restaurants were closing and their lights began to go out. Under the trees of the boulevards there were still a few people strolling to and fro, barely distinguishable in the gathering darkness. From time to time the shadowy figure of a woman gliding up to Swann, murmuring a few words in his ear, asking him to take her home, would make him start. Anxiously he brushed past all these dim forms, as though among the phantoms of the dead, in the realms of darkness, he had been searching for a lost Eurydice.

Marcel Proust, *Swann's Way* (1913)

Paris became 'the capital of the nineteenth century', the capital in terms of pleasure, excitement and consumption. Other European cities, Vienna, for example, cultivated an expansive public life, in promenades, cafés and theatres – unlike gloomy, reclusive London. Yet it was Paris that became the byword for everything that was enchanting and intoxicating about the urban scene.

The centralised nature of French life encouraged this especially rich and varied culture. Everything was drawn to Paris, which became the overheated source of all social, intellectual and artistic expression. The Goncourt brothers, Jules and Edmond, viewed this centralisation with alarm:

We talked about the absence of intellectual life in the French provinces, compared with all the active literary societies in the English counties and second or third-class German towns; about the way Paris absorbed everything, attracted everything, and did everything; and about the future of France which, in the circumstances, seemed destined to die of a cerebral haemorrhage.[1]

Above all, Paris was the city sexualised. Poets sometimes likened Paris to a prostitute, but more often sang her praises as a queen.[2] Either way, the city was inescapably female.

Some of the nineteenth-century anti-urbanists saw cities as harbingers of death. On the other hand, the 1881 Census of Paris appeared to support the opposite view: that nineteenth-century urban civilisation was essentially 'erotic' because the age of the metropolitan population was skewed in the direction of the young and fit: there were fewer children and old people, and more adolescents and young adults. Therefore, the city's 'marriage and birth rates and its productive force should be greater . . . the population is of an age at which vigour, mental and physical activity and productive force, and consequently all the appetites and sexual needs are at their height'.[3]

This cannot, though, explain the gaiety of Paris, since other cities experienced the same population patterns without gaining a similar reputation; 'erotic' was hardly the adjective that mid-nineteenth-century London called to mind, despite its prostitutes, nor was it a city of pleasure.

Paris the capital of pleasure was also Paris the city of revolutions and uprisings. For a century, France was periodically racked by revolution, interspersed with periods of political repression, and not until the Third Republic was thoroughly established in the 1880s were the competing spectres of monarchy and anarchy laid to rest.

These two aspects of Paris – pleasure and revolution – were closely linked. According to Victor Hugo's account, two of the first casualties of the 1848 uprising (which toppled Louis Philippe, the 'bourgeois' constitutional monarch, from his throne) were prostitutes, 'beautiful, dishevelled, terrible'. They mounted the barricades, raised their skirts to their waists and dared the National Guard to fire 'into the belly of a woman'. Both were shot down.

This account is probably inaccurate. A London journal of the period, reporting what is likely to have been the same incident, described the women as advancing respectably dressed and throwing stones at the soldiery. Hugo's embellishment of the incident is significant as an example of the way in which revolutionary activity was sexualised – to the nineteenth-century bourgeoisie the 'red whore' was one of the most frightening spectres of urban life.[4] Conservatives linked the political excesses of the 1789 French Revolution to sexual freedom and anarchy. And, if Paris was the crucible both of sexual freedom and of political revolution, the link that joined them was the female form. A woman was actually the symbol of the French Revolution.

During the Revolution, women had taken part in public pageants playing the part of the Goddess of Reason, and the spectacle that was Paris repeatedly assigned women a representational or symbolic role, which placed them firmly within a realm of pleasure for the most part devoid of real power. Statues of women, for example, adorned the often severe buildings of Paris in astonishing numbers, and from all periods. Sometimes they represented grandiose abstractions: Victory, Justice, France herself; but they might as easily appear to signify sheer lust and hedonism. The female form might even stand for such mundane enterprises as the telephone system,[5] and by the turn of the century the art nouveau posters of Alphonse Mucha had introduced the commercialised seduction of womanhood into advertisements for cigarettes and railway travel.

Meanwhile, the lot of most working-class Parisiennes was, as in other cities, one of relentless toil. The main reason for prostitution, which was widespread, was poverty; many young women, and particularly those on their own without a family, were more or less starving.

As in London, men were usurping what had traditionally been women's work. In 1873 a detailed investigation of women's work in France revealed that women were crowded into the least skilled and most poorly paid sectors of employment, and that since a survey of 1847, women's employment opportunities had narrowed, and the number of woman workers had actually declined, proportionately. One consequence of this was that there were 68 per cent more female than male paupers. Although some women were still to be found in every kind of work, the author of the survey described woman roofers, for example, as 'deviations from the natural order of things, abnormal protestations against the physical weakness of the frail sex'.[6]

Also as in London, the majority of women were employed in the needlework trades. Another important source of employment was in retail. Saleswomen formed an indeterminate class, and it was hard 'to decide whether they are workers, servants or clerks'. These young women put the finishing touches to goods for sale – decorating, wrapping and sometimes delivering. The author of the report noticed that some of these women were among the best dressed working women – in fact, their appearance in shops was part of the sales pitch – but were less well paid than many factory workers.[7]

The social ambiguity of the salesgirl would have been impossible anywhere but in the huge and anonymous city. This ambiguity was a source of alarm to the moralist, and, as in London, the forces of order and reform sought ruthlessly to regulate the lives of women in the city. Prostitution was the subject, in France as in Britain, of persistent debate and moral outrage, and it was in fact from Paris that the first major investigation of prostitution emerged: Dr Parent-Duchâtelet's work *On Prostitution*, published in 1836, upon which many of the later English surveys were modelled.

Parent-Duchâtelet was a member of the Paris Board of Health, and voluntarily undertook a series of general reports on the consequences of urban growth. He investigated the sewers (Victor

Hugo based his famous description of the Paris sewers in *Les Misérables* on Parent-Duchâtelet's reports), and drew a parallel between the study of drains and the study of prostitutes:

> If I have been able to creep into the sewers, handle putrid matter, spend some of my time on muck heaps and in some sort live in the midst of all that is most abject and disgusting . . . without scandalising anyone . . . why should I blush to approach a sewer of another kind (a sewer I admit, fouler than the rest) in the well founded hope of doing some good . . . If I engage in research on prostitutes, must I necessarily be sullied by my contact?[8]

Officialdom saw prostitutes as simply a conduit of filth.

Parent-Duchâtelet returned again and again in his treatise to the 'disorder' that prostitutes caused, a disorder which he linked directly to the political disorder of the French Revolution. It was to inaugurate a form of surveillance to control the 'disorder' that 'in 1796 the municipal authorities ordered a new census of all prostitutes. From 1816 all prostitutes were supposed to be officially registered, and after 1828 each had to produce a birth certificate, and had her own 'dossier'.' Parent-Duchâtelet argued that this individualisation of each woman was necessary because the better the authorities knew the women in question the more successful the surveillance would be.

Michel Foucault has discussed this insistence on the accumulation of facts and information in *Discipline and Punish* and other works, and has argued that it was (and is) a means of controlling the individual through knowledge. He sees it as a pervasive feature of nineteenth- and twentieth-century life. It appeared necessary because of the way in which urban life was breaking down the rigid distinctions between the classes, to create a disorientating confusion as to who was who. In such an ambiguous world, no wonder, wrote Parent-Duchâtelet, that working girls were drawn to prostitution out of vanity and because they wished to shine on this brightly lit stage:

> When simplicity of dress and even more strongly shabbiness of any kind are a source of absolute opprobrium, is it surprising that so many young girls slide into seduction for the sake of a costume they long for, and even more to the extent that this outfit enables them in a manner of speaking to escape from the station in life to which they were born and permits them to mingle with a class by which they might otherwise think themselves despised?[9]

This perception accurately linked the importance of dress with the uncertainty and anonymity of urban life. The city was a spectacle, and in the right costume a woman – or a man – could escape into a new identity. Such, at any rate, was a widely held belief about the great nineteenth-century city. To what extent individuals were really able to escape their origins is less certain,[10] but undoubtedly many reformers believed that anonymity not only made it possible, but also presented an insidious challenge to law and order.

Paris in the 1830s and 1840s was still a medieval city. Each neighbourhood was a maze of winding streets and hidden court-yards. Eugène Sue described the Ile de la Cité near Notre Dame Cathedral, a notorious haunt of criminals, as 'a labyrinth of obscure crooked and narrow streets . . . wretched houses with scarcely a window, and those of worm-eaten frames without any glass; dark, infectious looking alleys [leading] to still darker staircases'.[11] The lack of through roads meant that it was difficult to move freely from one's own *quartier* to another part of town.

The 1830s and 1840s in Old Paris were the great decades of the bohemians. Bohemian Paris was a Paris of students and artists, of poverty and desperate ambition. The students were wanderers (bohemians – gypsies) in their rejection of bourgeois stability, but they clung like limpets to the attics and cafés of the Latin Quarter.

Bohemian Paris sheltered many young women who lived outside the bounds of bourgeois respectability. Arsène Houssaye, who was a bohemian in his youth, but became director of the Comédie Française under Napoleon III, described the gaily dressed '*grisettes*' as 'janitors' daughters in rebellion, dressmakers' apprentices who had snapped their needles, chambermaids who had thrown their bonnets over the rooftops, governesses who had tasted too fully of the tree of knowledge, actresses without a theatre, romantics in search of Prince Charming'.[12]

Jules Vallès, another bohemian, but a leftwing one – he played an active role in the 1870 Commune – painted a grimmer picture of the life of the *grisette*: 'If she flourished in the Latin Quarter it was certainly not in my time', he wrote. He described how one, Pavillon, who was said to have been mistress to a whole circle of well-known bohemians (including Henri Murger himself, the author of the bestseller *La Bohème*), broke down completely, physically and mentally, and ended her life in an asylum.[13]

Flora Tristan and George Sand, both of whom were feminists and also revolutionary socialists, represented a different model for eman-cipated womanhood in the romantic Bohemia of the 1830s and 1840s. George Sand openly took lovers, occasionally wore male dress and smoked in public. According to one (rather hostile) account, she inspired a generation of bohemian women, who showed 'disdain of what became their sex, and a pursuit of glaring eccentricity'. They were called Les Lionnes (the lionesses – as in 'literary lion'). They 'affected to disdain the feminine graces' and went in for sports, drinking and cigar-smoking.[14]

Whereas the dominant progressive trends in Britain were utilitarian reformism and evangelical Christianity, Frenchwomen were more likely to be influenced by utopian or revolutionary socialism. Both Flora Tristan and George Sand lived independent lives in the leftwing culture of Paris, although the existence of a strong socialist tradition did not mean that the equality of women was high on the agenda. The attitudes of socialist groups varied. The Saint-Simonians believed in the equality of women, but the followers of Charles Fourier were less egalitarian.[15]

George Sand was one of the most successful of nineteenth-century French writers, yet is most remembered – and was famous at the time – for her love affairs and flouting of the conventions. She described how, disguised as a man, she could experience the pleasure of being a *flâneur* – a stroller, that quintessentially Parisian way of relating to the modern industrial city of the nineteenth century: 'no one knew me, no one looked at me . . . I was an atom lost in that immense crowd'[16] – an experience denied most middle-class women.

As industrialisation proceeded and the bourgeoisie expanded and prospered, Paris became yet gayer. Café concerts, for example, which offered entertainment and refreshment in a sheltered yet open-air environment, became more and more popular. The French middle class lived in much more overcrowded circumstances than its London counterpart, in cramped apartments rather than large houses. Whole families were therefore more likely to go out together, to enjoy the vibrant street and café life offered by the capital. The Goncourts viewed this with disapproval. 'Social life is beginning to undergo a great change', they wrote in 1860. 'One can see women, children, husbands and wives, whole families in the café. The home is dying. Life is threatening to become public.'[17] Yet Frances Trollope had observed similar scenes in the 1830s, when she reported that, 'It is rare to see either a man or a woman of an age to be wedded and parents, without their being accompanied by their partner and their offspring. The cup of light wine is drunk between them; the scene that is sought for amusement by the one is also enjoyed by the other'; after Mass on Sunday the whole population was to be seen eating and drinking in the many cafés and restaurants in the city.[18]

In the mid century, under the 'Second Empire' (1851–70) presided over by Louis Napoleon, Napoleon III, Paris was reinvented. The Second Empire was a hysterical spectacle of luxury borne aloft on a bubble of stockmarket and property speculation, yet it produced the very solid monument of a magnificently rebuilt city. Ironically, or

perhaps appropriately, Georges Haussmann, the agent of this transformation, financed the whole enterprise by means of floating debts
which led ultimately to his downfall.

Napoleon III had long cherished a dream of rebuilding Paris in a
suitably imperial style, as his uncle, the great Napoleon, had planned.
It seems possible that he was influenced by utopian socialist plans for
ideal cities of the future, plans that were usually highly rationalistic
and symbolic; the plan for the new Paris also incorporated a revival of
Renaissance town planning.

In 1853 he appointed Georges Haussmann as Prefect of the Seine,
and within the space of sixteen years Paris was transformed. Haussmann and Louis Napoleon drove wide new streets and boulevards
through the densely crowded quarters of central Paris, connecting east
to west and north to south. In place of the slums of the Ile de la Cité
there rose uniform, imposing offices and apartment blocks. Les
Halles, the old central markets (removed in the 1970s), and the rebuilt
Opéra were among the most ambitious constructions. The Bois de
Boulogne was designed on the 'romantic' English model of Hyde
Park, and became the parade ground of high society and the demi-
monde.[19]

Napoleon and Haussmann devised new building regulations pre-
scribing the heights of buildings, the harmony and uniformity of the
new frontages and rules regulating the maintenance of the exteriors.
Behind the high façades of the new buildings, however, overcrowding was as bad as ever.

Many condemned the ruthless thrust of the boulevards as counter-
revolutionary: in the old narrow streets it had been relatively easy to
throw up barricades and for insurrectionaries to melt away and escape
arrest. Permanent barracks were indeed built at strategic points, yet
even more significant were the railway stations and railway lines that
brought thousands of visitors and migrants to the city. New streets
created a 'circulatory and respiratory system' for modern traffic and
movement. In this way Haussmann, by means of the physical changes
he wrought, enhanced the 'modern' quality of the nineteenth-century
capital, with its constant flux and movement.[20]

Haussmann was also accused of having built a second, industrial
Paris in the plain of St Denis – what one writer described as a Siberia
'crisscrossed with winding unpaved paths, without lights, without
shops, with no water laid on'. Whether or not there was a deliberate
attempt to banish artisans and workers to the industrial suburbs, the
classes in the city began to be more segregated. A further paradox of
the 'modern' city was that even as its inhabitants experienced it as
more fragmented and disorientating, the regulation of the new mass
society tightened.[21]

During the Second Empire political repression perhaps even, ironically, added to the gaiety of the capital. Jacques Offenbach's popular operettas, which incorporated veiled social satire, distilled the glittering hedonism of the 1850s and 1860s. Government censorship and repression created a depoliticised bohemia, in which opposition was stifled, or at least displaced, reappearing as frivolity and moral nihilism, and yet enriching the artistic atmosphere.[22]

As the Parisian middle class grew rich, the classic bohemia went into decline. The growth of industry impoverished the artisan and petty bourgeois families from which many of the students and clerks of bohemian circles had come, and by the late 1840s the *flâneur* had replaced the bohemian of an earlier period.

The *flâneur* lived on the boulevards, and made the streets and cafés of Paris his drawing room. Like the bohemian, the *flâneur* often lived on his literary wits: the turbulence of the fast-expanding cities gave birth in Paris, as in London, to a whole new journalistic literature of vignettes, anecdotes and 'travellers' tales'.

The difference between the bohemian and the *flâneur* was that while the bohemian had been passionately emotional, the *flâneur* was a detached observer. He caught the fleeting, fragmentary quality of modern urban life, and, as a rootless outsider, he also identified with all the marginals that urban society produced. In particular he empathised not so much with the organised working class as with the down and outs: the ragpickers, the semi-criminal and the deviant.

The ragpickers were one of the most abject and notorious groups in Parisian society. They lived like nomads in shanty towns near the *barrières*, the areas close to the city limits and town gates; and of all the bizarre kinds of work that the growing urban scene produced at this period of early industrial capitalism, none was more symbolic than theirs.

In Paris, as in London, refuse, dirt and dust threatened to overwhelm the gaudy edifice of urban civilisation. Rubbish was the inevitable end product of the whirl of sensual fulfilment in the restaurants, concerts and brothels; and at the same time formed the foundations upon which the city of pleasure was built. The dust heap was the unspeakable aspect of the city of charm and light.

The ragpickers in their hovels represented the 'Other' of Paris, the underside of the city of gaiety and pleasure. Writers such as Charles Baudelaire and Gérard de Nerval were particularly drawn to these outcasts, because just as the scavengers searched the dust heaps for hidden silver cutlery, accidentally thrown away,[23] so did Baudelaire and de Nerval, as writers of the city, seek out the forgotten or unnoticed treasures of urban life to record and embellish.

For Baudelaire, both writers and ragpickers were outcasts to some extent. The writer understood the inner meaning of the city and revealed it in his poetry or prose; the ragpickers symbolised this inner meaning. Karl Marx, by contrast, detested the marginals, whether ragpickers or *flâneurs*, as counter-revolutionaries. He likened the anarchists – double agents and agents-provocateurs of the Parisian underworld – to prostitutes, whose painted faces concealed duplicity and evil.[24] He saw them as the political rubbish thrown up by urban society. What is interesting about this much harsher and strictly political judgment is the way in which Marx nevertheless uses metaphors similar to those of Baudelaire: prostitution remains at the heart of the city's meaning.

Baudelaire, indeed, believed that poets resembled prostitutes. They had something to sell – their writing. Since this expressed their soul, their truest self, in selling it they were in a sense prostituting themselves.

They resembled prostitutes in another way, for if prostitutes were women of the streets, the poet in his guise as *flâneur* or dandy also walked the streets. Indeed, Baudelaire saw the essential condition of Parisian city life as a kind of universal prostitution created by consumerism, circulating 'securely in the city's clogged heart'.[25]

So, just as the *flâneur* was a prostitute, perhaps also the prostitute could be said to be the female *flâneur*. There were, of course, important differences, but both shared an intimate knowledge of the dark recesses of urban life. They understood, better than anyone, the pitiless way in which the city offered an intensity of joy that was never, somehow, fulfilled. The spectacle melted away just as you felt you had reached its centre; the bubble burst when you touched it. That was the source of the melancholy which lay at the heart of the city of pleasure. None felt this more keenly than Gervaise, the heroine of Emile Zola's novel of Parisian working-class life, as she touched rock bottom, crushed by what seemed like the insatiable appetite of the city itself:

> She walked slowly on. The gas lamps were being lit in the misty darkness, and the long avenues which had gradually disappeared into the shadow reappeared blazing with light, stretching out and slashing a way through the night as far as the vague darkness of the horizon. There was a great breath of life . . . This was the hour when from end to end of the boulevards pubs . . . [and] dancehalls flared up with the fun . . . of the first round of drinks . . . And the night was very dark, still and freezing . . . broken only by the fiery lines of the boulevards stretching to the four corners of heaven.[26]

In recent years feminists have argued that there could never be a
female *flâneur*. They have gone further, to suggest that the urban
scene was at all times represented from the point of view of the male
gaze: in paintings and photographs men voyeuristically stare,
women are passively subjected to the gaze. The public arena – cafés
and places of public entertainment such as the Folies Bergères –
offered a '*mise en scène*', or setting where men of the bourgeoisie
could meet and seduce or purchase working-class women. Middle-
class women were restricted to certain limited public spaces designated as respectable: parks and the opera, for example. This division
is reflected in the subjects chosen by the Impressionists, painters who
devised new techniques to capture the glittering visual fragmentation
of the urban scene; Manet, Degas and others painted backstage
scenes, bars and brothels, but Berthe Morisot's choice of locations
and subject matter was necessarily much more restricted; she often
painted domestic scenes.[27]

There has perhaps been a tendency for this argument to be
overstated. Women did participate actively as well as passively in the
spectacle, and the whole Parisian atmosphere of pleasure and excess,
both sexual and political, did create an environment in which women
were able to gain certain freedoms – even if the price of this was their
over-sexualisation and their participation in what was often a
voyeuristic spectacle. In this it was unlike London. There were, of
course, important English woman writers – and of these, George
Eliot lived with a man who was not her husband. There were also
English demi-mondaines. Yet the whole atmosphere of mid-
nineteenth-century London was worthier and more serious, and
there was much less public life in the shape of concerts and
spectacles. This difference was illustrated at the great 1867 Paris
Exhibition, when the British pavilion, amid a riot of exotic and
luxurious displays from other nations, consisted of 'a Bible Society
kiosk, a Protestant church, agricultural machines, a model farm and
a school'.[28]

In March 1862, the Goncourt brothers went to the Opéra:

A dazzling audience . . . The balcony was resplendent with
demi-mondaines and the corridors were crowded with those
handsome men wearing foreign decorations who fill the corridors of the Opéra on ball nights. In the boxes there was quite a
pretty array of prostitutes. It is wonderful what a centre of
debauchery the theatre is. From the stage to the auditorium,
from the wings to the stage, from the auditorium to the stage
and from one side of the auditorium to the other, invisible
threads criss-cross between dancers' legs, actresses' smiles and

spectators' opera glasses, presenting an overall picture of Pleasure, Orgy and Intrigue. It would be impossible to gather together in a smaller space a greater number of sexual stimulants, of invitations to copulation. It is like a Stock Exchange dealing in women's nights.[29]

The metaphor of the stock exchange symbolised the linked obsessions of frenzied speculation and sexual experience that gripped the Second Empire. On an unstable financial basis was built a society of consumerism and erotic illusion.

A whole class of demi-mondaines – financiers, entertainers and above all courtesans – occupied a central position in the society of the Second Empire. The courtesans played a directly economic role in two ways. They were the ultimate objects of conspicuous consumption; and they also intervened directly in the economics of speculation, often acting as agents for brokers and financiers, working on a commission basis among their clientele.[30]

Emile Zola based the heroine of his novel *Nana* on several of the most notorious courtesans of the Second Empire. Nana represented disorder itself. She was less a human being than a conduit through which everything flowed – money, jewellery, food, wine, and any and every sensual and violent experience. The folly with which she flung her money around when she had it – fortunes from men who ruined themselves and their families on her account – was just one particular facet of the general and insensate disorder of Second Empire life.

In the opening scene of the novel, Nana's appearance on stage, naked save for a gauze veil, signalled her as the incarnation of sexuality, a sexuality as threatening as it was desirable:

Nobody laughed any more . . . A wind seemed to have passed over the audience, a soft wind laden with hidden menace . . . the woman stood revealed, a disturbing woman with all the impulsive madness of her sex, opening the gates of the unknown world of desire.[31]

Nana's life was brutally cut short by smallpox – surely Zola's euphemism for syphilis – and gloomy intimations of decay, disease and mortality lurked beneath the hysterically gay surface of the demi-monde.

If Nana represented female sexuality as uncontrolled disorder, an alternative and equally alarming image of the courtesan was the Goncourt brothers' description of the most successful of them all, La Païva, as a mechanical doll:

She was coming forward between the chairs like an automaton, as if she was worked by a spiral spring, without a gesture, without expression . . . [a] rolling puppet from a danse macabre . . . [a] Hoffmannesque mummy . . . a vampire with the blood of the living on her purple mouth while all the rest was livid, glazed and in dissolution.[32]

Although the new urban world was a Saturnalia, paradoxically the machinery of the Industrial Revolution appeared to have infected the whole of life with a machine-like quality. We have already seen how, to William Acton, human beings in search of pleasure at Cremorne Gardens appeared like unreal, clockwork figurines; so too La Païva, who seemed to the Goncourts like the sinister doll from the macabre *Tales of Hoffmann*, a doll who preyed on the living.

Despite these sinister undertones, Paris displayed as its charming everyday self the society of the spectacle in all its glory. Napoleon III inaugurated the Paris Exhibitions, the first held in 1855. The 1867 International Exhibition in particular was 'the apotheosis of the Second Empire'. The display reached new heights with Chinese tea pavilions, Brazilian temples and Turkish tents: it was a dazzling dream world.

In Paris as in other great cities a more permanent form of the exhibition had also appeared: the department store. The department store was a public space pretending to be a private interior, just as the public street and the cafés became a kind of salon for the *flâneurs*.

Emile Zola's novel *Au bonheur des dames* (*The Ladies' Paradise*) used the creation of a great department store as the image of this new consumerist yet mechanised society. The Ladies' Paradise is erected as a temple of dreams based on commerce: this is the floating world of the bourgeoisie. As described by Zola, the creation of the building itself is accomplished only at the cost of the destruction of the surrounding neighbourhood, including the livelihood of the artisans and small shopkeepers with their old-fashioned goods and sales methods – the 'Old Paris' that was menaced by Haussmann's plans. The new shop, more like a palace, is a phantasmagoric experience, and above all an erotic one.

On the opening day, one bourgeois lady, trying on gloves, seems to be involved in a seduction scene as, almost lying across the counter, the young male assistant holds her hand, 'taking her fingers one by one, pulling on the glove with a long caress . . . while he looked at her as if waiting to see her swoon with voluptuous joy'. Meanwhile, in the hall, silks and satins are displayed:

streaming down like a bubbling sheet of water falling from above and broadening out on the floor. Pale satins and tender silks gushed out first . . . renaissance satins with the opalescent tones of spring water, silks transparent as crystal, eau de Nil,

Indian sky, spring rose, Danube blue. Then came the heavier stuffs, satins and duchess silks in hot shades, flooding in great waves. At the bottom, as if it were the basin of a fountain, lay the stiffest materials, damasks, brocades, lamé and silks embroidered with pearls, slumbering in a bed of velvet – every kind of velvet, black, white, coloured, hollowing out with glancing folds a still lake in which reflections from sky and countryside seemed to dance. Women pale with desire leant over as if to see their reflections. All, faced with this cataract pouring itself out, were thunderstruck at such luxury and seized with an irresistible desire to throw themselves in and be lost in it.[33]

Behind the scenes, however, the young woman shopworkers sleep in cells like a nuns' dormitory, and are fed in relays with machine-like precision.

The department store created an 'aesthetic demi-monde' for the bourgeoisie in which beauty was for sale as a commodity. Consumption became a substitute for virtue. The department store offered the customer an imitation *vie de château*: shopwalkers and assistants were as if footmen and ladies' maids; the shop was as if an upper-class interior. Yet ultimately this masquerade was a dream, because the bourgeoisie, or at any rate its men, had to work for their wealth, yet longed to be like the leisured aristocracy who owned the ultimate luxury of consumption: time.[34]

The hotel was similar to the department store or the café, for it too was both public and private, and yet neither. Like the department store, it was an intermediate, amoral zone in which appearances – however fictitious – and the ability to pay were all that counted. The New York Waldorf Astoria, for example, described by Henry James at the turn of the century, was, like the Ladies' Paradise, a mirror world, which operated by laws of its own in which money replaced morality; and in 1920s Berlin, Siegfried Kracauer chose the hotel foyer as the perfect metaphor for the experience of the modern city. It was a pseudo home for anonymous individuals, in which the twentieth-century equivalent of the dandy, the private detective, could watch this world of deceptive identities and purchased grandeur.[35]

The presence of women created a special and ambiguous atmosphere in these zones, which were public, yet aimed at the intimacy of the private interior. The bourgeoisie, it is true, idealised the woman in the bosom of her family, and bourgeois culture made possible the immense elaboration of the private sphere – after all, what middle-class ladies purchased at The Ladies' Paradise was for the embellishment of themselves, their children and their homes. At the same time, bourgeois consumerism invaded the public sphere, and the very spaces that were permitted to respectable women were in many cases devoted to purchase and sale rather than to morally more elevated activities. There, women looked, as well as being looked at; in any case, it was above all the appearance of respectability that counted. In a sense, respectability itself was just another mask.

Despite the elaboration of the private sphere, women formed an essential element of the crowds in the streets, at the theatre and in the parks. Department stores in their seduction of women created zones such as restaurants, rest rooms and even reading rooms where they could, towards the end of the century, go unchaperoned or certainly free of men's protection. The carriages of fashionable women rolled along the promenades of the Bois de Boulogne, and, of course, women teemed through the *faubourgs*, or outlying working-class districts of Paris.

Not surprisingly, the Second Empire witnessed the development of fashion to an astonishing degree. Charles Frederick Worth (actually an Englishman) invented *haute couture* (high fashion) in the modern sense of the named designer, and created fabulous gowns for the Empress Eugénie and her court. The mad extravagance found everywhere else appeared at its most dazzling and most ephemeral in the adornment both of the ladies at court and of the great courtesans.

Baudelaire and his contemporaries experienced the sensations of the new metropolis as 'modern', yet the changes already taking place in Paris generated the beginnings of a sensibility of nostalgia. As Paris was transformed architecturally, the surviving districts of 'Old Paris' became picturesque. This nostalgia became the 'charm' of Paris.

The charm of Paris combined overpowering melancholy at the loss of the past with the loneliness of the 'atom in the crowd'. It was the charm of the alleyways and courtyards lapped in shadow, the bridges and quays of Paris, which were beautiful especially *because* they seemed doomed to crumble before the developer's demolition squad. Shabby, forgotten corners of the city inhabited by the marginals became precious and magical.[36]

After the end of the Second Empire, in 1870, Paris lost much of its gaiety, but by the 1890s, the capital was re-established as the city of pleasure. Pleasure now, however, was more fully commercialised, as Paris was becoming a tourist and consumerist mecca in the twentieth-century sense. As part of this, the charm of Paris' could itself be commercialised as a myth.

The cabarets and dance halls of Paris now offered the tourist a spectacle which consciously represented an image of 'gay Paree'. By the 1890s the famous Moulin Rouge cabaret was attracting nightly crowds and the Montmartre district, once a charming, semi-rustic backwater, had long since been brought within the city boundary. At the Moulin Rouge tourists crowded to the raucous, sweaty music-hall shows, whose dancers are still familiar today because the painter Henri de Toulouse-Lautrec drew them on his posters for the cabaret and in his paintings of Montmartre low life.[37] What had once been spontaneous working-class entertainments were now reworked for the consumption of a class of spectators.

Quite apart from prostitution, urban life made possible the emergence of other forbidden sexualities, and in particular a 'gay subculture', first for men and later for women. Homosexuals had known places of rendezvous in the 1830s, and it was claimed that homosexuality was widespread among the dandies of the 1840s.[38] Baudelaire wrote some of his poems to lesbians; he addressed them as 'disordered souls', as sterile yet noble, devout satyrs, feverish and desiccated. He saw them as bachelors like him, and like him searching for the unattainable. Walter Benjamin, writing about Baudelaire, saw the 'mannishness' of the lesbian as a consequence of industrial work and urban life; this mannishness was part of the 'heroism of modern life'. It was also, nonetheless, another indication of the 'unnaturalness' of city life.[39]

By the time that Marcel Proust was describing Parisian lesbian and gay circles during the *belle époque* (the period 1890–1910), 'gay identities' were well established. Homosexuals were now a 'race apart', one of the mysterious and, many felt, sinister groups that inhabited the endless labyrinth that was a great city.

A sexualisation of the spectacle of all aspects of life both degraded women and sometimes offered them the escape of wealth and the freedom of depravity. Toulouse-Lautrec often depicted his singers and prostitutes as lesbians. By 1900 *belle époque* 'pleasure guides' alerted readers to the existence of specialised brothels in which lesbian love played a special role.

At the same time, Paris provided a suitable environment for the growth of a genuine lesbian subculture. The American heiress Nathalie Clifford-Barney opened a lesbian salon. The poet Renée Vivien and the writer Colette lived in this world – which was both condoned and suppressed. Exploited as a titillating perversion, lesbianism was not acceptable as an open way of life. Colette described it as a 'marginal and timorous life, sustained by an out-of-date form of snobbishness'. Although Colette lived with her lesbian lover 'Missy', the Marquise de Belboeuf, for eight years, her recollections are rather mocking:

How timid I was, at that period when I was trying to look like a
boy, and how feminine I was beneath my disguise of cropped
hair. 'Who would take us to be women? Why, women.' They
alone were not fooled. With such distinguishing marks as
pleated shirt front, hard collar, sometimes a waistcoat, and
always a silk pocket handkerchief, I frequented a society
perishing on the margin of all societies . . . The clique I am
referring to . . . tried, trembling with fear, to live without
hypocrisy, the breathable air of society. This . . . sect claimed
the right of 'personal freedom' and equality with homosexuality, that imperturbable establishment. And they scoffed,
if in whispers, at 'Papa' Lépine, the Prefect of Police, who never
could take lightly the question of women in men's clothes.[40]

According to Colette, her lesbian friends were afraid of appearing
openly in public in male attire. They wore long trousers and dinner
jackets at their private parties, but in the street they covered them
with a long cloak, 'which gave them an excessively respectable look'.
They did, however, have their own 'dives' – neighbourhood cinemas, basement restaurants, a Montmartre cellar run by a woman
who was a lesbian herself.

The charm of Paris now began to be enshrined in the '*chanson
réaliste*', the popular songs of working-class life which were being
sung in the café concerts of Montmartre, and these too could be
commercialised: explored in the French films of the 1920s, 1930s and
1940s (for example, René Clair's *Sous les toits de Paris*); but above all
in the performances of stars such as Georges Brassens, Edith Piaf and
Yves Montand, who became famous after the Second World War.[41]

The songs of Piaf and of the less famous Fréhel sentimentalised the
poor women of Paris. The heroines of their songs were often
prostitutes and always marginal – waitresses, failed singers in cheap
bars – but seldom or never ordinary working-class women like those
of Belleville or Ménilmontant. Their melancholy and plaintive songs
were of lost illusions and doomed love:

Never the hope of an evening to come;
Hullo, good evening
Farewell the one I adore;
No tomorrow, nothing that lasts,
That's been my life forever more.[42]

Thus even poverty and sorrow were aestheticised in the myth of the
'charme de Paris'.

After the Second World War the Latin Quarter again became the
centre of an influential counterculture. St Germain des Prés became

the haunt of the real and imitation Existentialists, headed (willingly or unwillingly) by Jean-Paul Sartre and Simone de Beauvoir. Some of the women in the postwar existentialist circles had been active in the resistance – the writer Marguerite Duras, for example. Others, such as Simone Signoret, who became a star of the postwar French cinema, were communists or close to the Communist Party.

Simone Signoret's first starring role was in *Casque d'or* (*The Golden Marie*). This film re-created the world of the criminal fringe in the cabarets of the 1890s. Central to the plot was the tragic love that so often – in the myth, at least – lurked beyond the whirl of noise and pleasure. Marie, the heroine, brought catastrophe to the men who adored her: in the erotic myth that was Paris, pleasure and danger lay close together. The figure of the free woman was always ambivalent. The alternative to being a victim in the vein so successfully exploited by Edith Piaf was to be a destroyer of men like Nana or the great courtesans.

Most of the women associated with St Germain des Prés were highly sexualised figures. Juliette Greco, the *chanteuse* of existentialism, shocked French (and international) society with her informal clothes, lack of make-up and unconventional life, but her role was a familiar one in bohemian terms. In early films by Claude Chabrol and other New Wave directors, Left Bank young women appeared faithless and frail – in Jean-Luc Godard's famous first film, *A bout de souffle* (*Breathless*), for example, Jean Seberg's heroine is responsible for the anti-hero's death. Like Greco, these film characters were sexually and (perhaps even more important) emotionally free, yet otherwise locked into traditional stereotypes.[43]

Yet it was this Left Bank movement that provided the context for Simone de Beauvoir's pioneering feminist work *The Second Sex*. Simone de Beauvoir had from the beginning been passionately a Parisienne. Not only was she brought up in Paris, but the personal drama of her intellectual and sexual emancipation seemed inseparable from its setting in the hotels and cafés of Montparnasse and St Germain. In her autobiographies, her assignment to teaching posts in the provincial towns of Rouen and Marseille appear as forms of exile. She enjoyed the conquest of nature when she climbed the Alpes-Maritimes near Marseille, or took skiing holidays, but real life was Paris. The city provided a world in which you could dispense altogether with the trappings of bourgeois privacy; for years her home was a hotel room; her base was a café; there she wrote her books, ate her meals, met her friends and lovers. The terraces of Les Deux Magots and Le Flore provided her with a role and a setting which de-emphasised her position as merely the partner of a well-known male writer. Unlike the wives and lovers of the

American Beats and the English bohemians of 1950s Soho, a well-established public urban world offered her a stage on which she could appear in her own right. For Simone de Beauvoir, Paris *was* freedom:

> The most intoxicating aspect of my return to Paris in September 1929, was the freedom I now possessed . . . From my fifth floor balcony I looked out over the Lion of Belfort and the plane trees on the rue Denfert-Rochereau . . . I was free to come and go as I pleased. I could get home with the milk, read in bed all night, sleep until midday, shut myself up for forty-eight hours at a stretch, or go out on the spur of the moment. My lunch was a bowl of borsch at Dominique's, and for supper I took a cup of hot chocolate at La Coupole.[44]

So, in a perhaps unexpected way, Paris, the capital of sexual pleasure, gave birth to the most influential feminist text of all.

5

Cities of the American Dream

Chicago . . . here it was again, westward from this window, the gray snarled city with the hard black straps of rails, enormous industry cooking and its vapor shuddering to the air . . . and the different powers and sub-powers crouched and watched like sphinxes.

Saul Bellow, *The Adventures of Augie March* (1953)

A skinny lad was . . . offering her arbutus in a basket . . . Through the scent of the arbutus she caught for a second the unwashed smell of his body, the smell of immigrants, of Ellis Island, of crowded tenements. Under all the nickelplated, goldplated streets enameled with May, uneasily she could feel the huddling smell, spreading in dark slow crouching masses like corruption oozing from broken sewers, like a mob.

John Dos Passos, *Manhattan Transfer* (1925)

In no city in the western world were beauty and cruelty, hope and despair so closely associated as in the 'Babylons' of New York and Chicago. For women especially, the intensity of contrast was immense. The great nineteenth-century cities had initially appeared as menacing environments, too dangerous for middle-class women to negotiate by themselves, while threatening working-class women with loss of virtue or even of life. By 1900 economic and technological developments were beginning to provide new forms of female employment: clerical, office and shop work as an alternative to factory and domestic employment. The bicycle and the growth of suburban railway networks brought women increased mobility.

Women were still closely supervised within the family, and the most likely destiny for middle-class women was marriage and domestic cares. The lives of working-class women were often a hard, bitter struggle, both in the home and in waged labour. Yet urban life created a space in which some women could experiment with new roles. Alternative sources of support existed which only the great cities could provide. For middle-class women the most likely alternative to marriage was a career and spinsterhood, but in the bohemias of western capitalism, 'free women' – even if with difficulty – claimed the right to heterosexual experience outside marriage, or sometimes to lesbianism, and they fought for a place alongside men in artistic and political life. Meanwhile, working-class women were joining trades unions and struggling for better conditions, and this struggle had more than 'just' an economic significance: when women joined forces against the harsh bosses, they found both an unaccustomed autonomy as individuals and the comradeship of the group, and their militancy extended to protests against the way they were treated as women. Rose Chernin, the daughter of Russian–Jewish immigrants, who became a communist organiser in the 1920s and 1930s, remembered, for example, how women in the sweatshops attacked bosses for sexual harassment.

Both European theories of urban development and the actual development of European cities influenced the growth of cities in the United States. In turn, American cities increasingly appeared to Europeans as prototypes of what was at once most inspiring and most terrifying about the process of urbanisation. In the twentieth century both the skyscrapers of New York and the decentred urban sprawl of Los Angeles seemed to prefigure the urban future.

In the United States, as in Europe, there was a dialogue between the pro- and anti-urbanists. Both the countryside and the small town embodied enduring images of virtue to set against the evil that was life in the great city, but this contrast was altogether more extreme than any presented to Europeans. American cities of the nineteenth century grew even more swiftly and intensely than their European counterparts, but, chaotic and terrifying as they were, they stood in contrast to another reality equally or more lonely, vast and engulfing: the wilderness. In England the contrast between rural and urban was the contrast between the soot-smoked industrial towns and the tamed rural scene of the country landowner's park; in America the wilderness seemed much more like that region of chaos and formlessness outside the human boundary altogether.

Anti-urbanism was possibly even stronger in the United States than in Europe, yet the building of cities was crucial to the conquest of the American interior and the West: for the white American there was never a period of subsistence agriculture; economic development was always based on trade and a communications network which depended upon the growth of cities.[1] Nor was the frontier mentality ever entirely an impulse to escape civilisation. Indeed, so far as women were concerned, their role in the Old West was to bring a civilising influence to bear on raw mining settlements and lonely prairie hamlets.

Unique to the United States was the influx of immigrants from Europe. The United States also had a larger black population than any European country. Although Africans, Asians and Arabs were to be seen in London and Paris, the relationship of black Afro-Americans to the American city was again unique – and intense.

In America, the first black slaves had been brought to cities, and it was only with the development of the cotton plantations in the southern states in the eighteenth century that there was more extensive use of rural slave labour and much tighter control of this labour force. At first, slaves had been allowed to build dwellings for themselves as they wished, and they had tended to follow the African pattern of the village compound cluster. Later, the plantation owners were much more likely to insist on the building of uniform rows of slave cabins. Even then, some artisans managed to preserve concealed elements of African traditions of construction. Some, for example, used a framework of hand-joined wood filled in with wedged-in stones.[2]

After the end of the American Civil War in 1865 industrialisation came rapidly to the United States, and Afro-Americans began to migrate to the industrial cities. With the arrival of the European immigrants, blacks were pushed further and further down the social scale. The influx of Afro-Americans into the rapidly developing American cities around 1900 was one factor in renewed fears about the 'evil city'.[3] Like women, blacks did not have a perceived right to be on the city streets at all.

Chicago was the American 'schlock city' of the late nineteenth century. In his novel *Sister Carrie*, published in 1900, Theodore Dreiser described the impact of the Chicago of 1889 by likening it to a 'giant magnet, drawing to itself from all quarters the hopeful and the hopeless'. Dreiser emphasised its size, its raw vitality, its optimistic anticipation of future growth. 'Its streets and houses', he wrote, 'were already scattered over an area of seventy-five square miles', and he described how, in the wake of industry, 'the huge railroad corporations which had long before recognised the prospects of the place had seized upon vast tracts of land', while 'streetcar lines had been extended far out into the open country in anticipation of rapid growth, [and] the city had laid miles and miles of streets and sewers through regions where perhaps one solitary house stood out alone'. As in Paris and London, there were amorphous regions on the outskirts, 'open to the sweeping winds and rain, which were yet lighted throughout the night with long, blinking lines of gas lamps fluttering in the wind. Narrow board walks extended out, passing here a house and there a store at far intervals, eventually ending on the open prairie.'

To Dreiser's heroine, Carrie, the activity of the city was utterly strange and bewildering: 'the great streets were wall-lined mysteries to her. The vast offices, strange mazes which concerned far-off individuals.' The city appeared to have a life force which moved, controlled and determined the destinies of its inhabitants, who were will-less in the face of its blind energy. So Carrie, too, 'was again the victim of the city's hypnotic influence, the subject of the mesmeric operations of super-intelligible forces'.

It was not that Carrie had no active desires; on the contrary, walking through a glittering department store in search of work, 'there was nothing . . . which she did not long to own'. Clothes were more than an end in themselves, however. Without them Carrie could not become a participant in the spectacle of urban life; her desires were for the *prerequisites* of visibility, and therefore of existence itself:

> Not only did Carrie feel the drag of desire for all of this which was new and pleasing in apparel for women, but she noticed, too, with a touch at the heart, the fine ladies who elbowed and ignored her, brushing past in utter disregard of her presence.[4]

Later, translated to New York with her lover, the erstwhile bar manager Hurstwood, she felt again, and more intensely, the urban truth that only by becoming a part of the spectacle can you truly exist in the city. Parading with a friend along Broadway:

> She noticed . . . that [her companion's] manner had rather stiffened under the gaze of handsome men and elegantly dressed ladies, whose glances were not modified by any rules of propriety. To stare seemed the proper and natural thing. Carrie found herself stared at and ogled . . . With a start she awoke to find that she was in fashion's throng, on parade in a showplace – and such a showplace.[5]

Carrie took command of this society of consumption by becoming an object of (vicarious) consumption herself: a theatrical star. Only when she had become an image, by having her photograph in the papers and on posters on public walls, did she finally feel that her existence was real.

In the excited, headlong development of Chicago and New York as Dreiser described them, there was a moral ambiguity, or, rather, a disorientating amorality. Whether it led to triumph, or, as in the case of Carrie's lover, Hurstwood, to disintegration and suicide, seemed a matter more or less of chance. Like Zola's Nana, Carrie embodied the flux and disorder of the escalating city, and Dreiser's characters were 'carried away' by the city, the endless flow of which carries everything away.

By the end of the nineteenth century the conditions of extreme poverty and overcrowding in the rapidly expanding North American cities led to a new determination to reform civic life. The attempt to replace the 'evil city' with more civilised conditions took a number of different forms. The Progressive Era in the United States (from around 1890 to 1910) saw the movement to create parks and parkways, the movement to provide playgrounds; the Settlement movement; and the City Beautiful movement. Some reformers aimed to improve the conditions of life for ordinary people; others believed that the lives of the city masses could be transformed by architecture.

The City Beautiful movement embodied the view that architecture and planning can, of themselves, change human behaviour and revolutionise human society. In this it resembled the Garden City movement, then developing in Britain, although the leaders of the City Beautiful movement were not interested in the garden city, but looked for inspiration to Haussmann. The architectural style they favoured was neither the functional 'modern' style already being used in downtown Chicago, nor the medievalism of Parker and Unwin, the architects of the first garden city at Letchworth. Rather, they looked to the French-inspired 'Beaux-Arts' style, based on Renaissance or Neo-classical models.

The concept of the City Beautiful was first exposed to the public at the Chicago World's Fair of 1893. Daniel Burnham, the Superintendent of Construction to the Exhibition, collaborated with the leading New York architects of the day to produce a White City for the exhibition, based on the ideal of the city as a unified public, civic space. Its effect was stunning; it gave those who visited the exhibition faith that a new kind of urban life could be created, and the World's Fair was seen as inaugurating the era of modern city planning.[6]

Developing from this, Daniel Burnham's *Plan for Chicago* was published in 1909. He and his associate, Edward Bennett, claimed to be building on the ideas not only of Haussmann, but also of his forerunners: Louis XIV, his minister Colbert and his architect Le Nôtre. The *Plan for Chicago* was also in the tradition of Ledoux's early-nineteenth-century plans for Washington, DC, and the Capitol.

Burnham and Bennett sought to translate Haussmann's vision of Paris to Chicago, and they also closely followed the seventeenth-century view in their emphasis on the public aspects of town planning. (Relatively few aspects of the *Plan for Chicago* were carried out, although the lake front was developed largely as Burnham had imagined.)

The *Plan for Chicago* resembled the plans of many of the utopians in its emphasis on order, beauty and the magnificence of public buildings. It was beautifully illustrated with watercolours by Jules Guérin, which showed a well-dressed and orderly throng of men and women strolling at leisure, and gracious and elegant thoroughfares rather dwarfed by huge civic edifices. Although Burnham and Bennett were dedicated urbanists who understood that it was precisely the variety of opportunity and the profusion of pleasure that made city life exciting, they, like the utopians, desired to eliminate all excess from city life. They did not confront the possibility that this would destroy precisely what made city life exciting.[7]

In its monumental style of beauty, their imagined city seemed remote from the slums of Chicago at the turn of the century. A more practical reforming effort was the Settlement movement. If the City Beautiful movement sought to solve the ills of urban living by means of civic architecture, the Settlements aimed to do so by means of human example and the organisation of the downtrodden.

Many reformers of both kinds were inspired by the hugely successful utopian novel *Looking Backward*, by the American writer Edward Bellamy. This book, published in 1888, was inspirational, for it spoke to the felt sense of crisis at the close of the nineteenth century, and was an indictment of the teeming, sordid cities of the time. Yet it also conveyed a sense of optimism. There was still then a widespread belief in the ability of technology and planning to revolutionise society without the bloodshed and conflict of an actual revolution; Bellamy transformed this into a vision of a harmonious, technicist, 'socialist' future in which politics had become redundant because centralised planning had solved all political questions.

In some respects Bellamy accurately anticipated twentieth-century developments: the credit card, for example. ('An American credit card', states one character, 'is just as good in Europe as American gold used to be.') In other ways, the book reflected the preoccupations of its time. Bellamy believed in the 'improvement of the race' – the so-called 'science' of eugenics; and, parallel to this, assembly-line efficiency as the key to economic success – ideas that, today, are largely discredited.

Bellamy's description of Boston in the year 2000 was the description of a City Beautiful:

At my feet lay a great city. Miles of broad streets, shaded by trees and lined with fine buildings, for the most part not in continuous blocks but set in larger or smaller enclosures, stretched in every direction. Every quarter contained large open squares filled with trees, along which statues glistened and fountains flashed in the late-afternoon sun. Public buildings of a colossal size and architectural grandeur unparalleled in my day raised their stately piles on every side.[8]

Bellamy acknowledged the oppression of both middle-class and working-class women, and used some feminist ideas in his book. Arrangements were made, for example, for communal feeding. Yet his solutions seem most unsatisfactory today. There was no sense of the liquidation of class differences. Working-class women were to be recruited to the mass 'industrial army', where they were to have equal pay, but there was little sense of an end to their lives of toil. Middle-class women, freed from their imprisonment in the private sphere, were to be given the ubiquitous credit card and the freedom to spend, but Bellamy did not imagine that they would work. The heroine of the novel was entirely a product of 1900, elevated to a pedestal, yet with no calling but to minister to her mate. She remained a consumer, and also an icon. This was partly because Bellamy's socialism, or nationalism as he called it, needed a 'sacred emblem', and women were this emblem. They were the inspiration, the spur and the prize for men in a society which had done away with unbridled capitalist competition.[9]

To be fair, many American feminists of the period held views that were not too different from Bellamy's – or appear similar to us today. Some of these women, with their different blueprints for reform, had been influenced by the early utopian socialists; but not all emphasised the vote and the right to work. They desired to raise the status of women within the home as well as outside it, and to compel society to give a much more central place to domestic reproduction, although there was also a widespread belief towards the end of the century that domestic work, like manufacturing, would shortly be collectivised.[10]

By the last decade of the nineteenth century there was a growing domestic science movement. This emphasised nutrition, and the municipalisation of domestic services in the shape of public kitchens. At the 1893 Chicago Fair a house containing a modern scientific kitchen was on display, and a new National Household Economics Association was actually founded at the Fair. These new fields of endeavour opened fresh opportunities for professional employment for women.[11] Some of their ideas found expression in the Settlement movement.

The Settlement movement had begun in the East End of London. Canon Barnett and his wife Henrietta (who was centrally involved in the development of Hampstead Garden Suburb) were important figures at this time and had their headquarters at Toynbee Hall, Whitechapel.

In 1883 a young American woman visited the slums of the Mile End Road, heard about the 'submerged tenth', as the unemployed were beginning to be called, and later read Andrew Mearns's *The*

Bitter Cry of Outcast London, a campaigning polemic which had aroused the public conscience of the British capital. During a second visit to London she attended a meeting of the striking match girls at the Bryant and May factory, and in 1888 she visited Toynbee Hall.

This young woman was Jane Addams, and in 1889, with the help of her college friend and companion, Miss Starr, she opened Hull House in Chicago. It was to become the most famous Settlement house in the United States, and by 1913 it consisted of thirteen buildings.

Set down in the midst of the immigrant colonies of Sicilians and Neapolitans, Russian and Polish Jews, Germans and Bohemians, Jane Addams and her helpers rapidly became involved in all aspects of the urban problems that beset the majority of the city's working masses. Overcrowding was one of the worst difficulties they faced. Sometimes seven or eight men, women and children found themselves living in two small rooms.

The workers and volunteers at Hull House saw the other side of the immensely successful World's Fair (also known as the Columbian Exhibition) during 'the terrible winter after the World's Fair when the general financial depression throughout the country was intensified in Chicago by the numbers of unemployed, stranded at the close of the exposition', as Jane Addams wrote in an account of her work, *Twenty Years at Hull House*. From its early years the Settlement dedicated itself to the workers' cause.

The work of Jane Addams drew on the traditions of the English Settlement movement, and found itself in the vanguard of a similar movement in the United States. At Hull House both women and men were involved in social work, community work, a soup kitchen, and the organisation of the workforce to agitate for better conditions and pay. In addition, it was a collective living situation for some of the men and women who wanted to dedicate a period, at least, of their lives to this model of the public good. There was a residential building for men, and the Jane Club, a similar arrangement, for women. This was not just for the middle-class Settlement workers; indeed, the idea came first from a group of striking working women:

At a meeting of working girls held at Hull-House during a strike in a large shoe factory, the discussions made it clear that the strikers who had been most easily frightened, and therefore first to capitulate, were naturally those girls who were paying board and were afraid of being put out if they fell too far behind . . . One of them exclaimed: 'Wouldn't it be fine if we had a boarding club of our own, and then we could stand by each other in a time like this?'[12]

The club opened in 1891, and three years later had fifty members.

The first decade of the twentieth century was one of female industrial militancy in the United States; unionisation and industrial unrest ran parallel with the increasing mechanisation of trades such as garment-making. The most famous strike of the period was the 1909 shirtwaist strike, when 20,000 garment workers came out, but this was not an isolated incident. Nor were militancy and radical ideas confined to the factory floor; cooperative boarding clubs were being formed by working women in New York, and students were designing original communal building projects. In 1919 the International Ladies Garment Workers Union established Unity House in New York as just such a cooperative.[13]

Some of the most important work undertaken at Hull House was the support of groups of strikers and the organisation of campaigns against the sweated labour of women and children. In the first years, 'we came across no trades-unions among the women workers, and I think, perhaps, that only one union, composed solely of women, was to be found in Chicago then – that of the bookbinders', wrote Jane Addams. At a later date, 'the women shirt makers and the women cloak makers were both organised at Hull-House as was also the Dorcas Federal Labour Union, which had been founded through the efforts of a working woman, then one of the residents'. Jane Addams records, in addition, that 'the first officers of the Chicago Woman's Trades Union League were residents of Settlements, although they can claim little share in the later record the League made in securing the passage of the Illinois Ten-Hour Law for Women and in its many other fine undertakings'.[14]

Another campaign in which the Hull House residents became involved was the Consumers' League. Like similar organisations in France,[15] the League aimed to use 'consumer power' to place pressure on retailers not to sell sweated labour goods, and to mitigate the incredibly long hours of work endured by salesmen and women.

Hull House, therefore, was a truly radical endeavour, and could not be dismissed as the interference of Lady Bountifuls or as a form of social policing. Jane Addams believed, for example, that it was 'stupid . . . to permit the mothers of young children to spend themselves in the coarser work of the world', and this was an understandable view, given the almost unbelievable hardships faced by women both at home and at work. Yet, sensitive to their actual circumstances – many mothers *had* to work – she tried to create childcare, feeding and educational opportunities that matched these needs.

Jane Addams displayed, in her writings at least, an ability to cross this gulf and a strong empathy with working women and the poor.

She seems to have been able to see life from the point of view of those whom she wished to help:

> Never before in civilisation have such numbers of young girls been suddenly released from the protection of the home and permitted to walk unattended upon city streets and to work under alien roofs . . . As these overworked girls stream along the street the rest of us see only the self conscious walk, the giggling speech, the preposterous clothing. And yet through the huge hat, with its wilderness of bedraggled feathers, the girl announces to the world that she is here . . . she states that she is ready to live, to take her place in the world.[16]

She recognised that to return to the ways of the 'old country' – arranged marriages and the chaperoning of girls – was inappropriate and in any case impossible, and that therefore 'by all means let us preserve the safety of the home, but let us also make safe the street in which the majority of our young people find their recreation and form their permanent relationships'.

The Settlement drew together the new movement for cooperative living, as it was called, and the old tradition of the utopian communities of the 1830s and 1840s. The first resident at Hull House was an old lady who had once lived at the famous utopian community Brook Farm, and who 'wished to live once more in an atmosphere where idealism ran high'.

To a greater extent than in Europe, housing forms developed to suit the needs of those not living in the traditional family. Hotel and boarding-house life were particularly prevalent in American cities. Although criticised as a danger to morals and a threat to the family, the fashionable boarding house extended throughout all classes in American society from the mid nineteenth century. Married couples as well as single persons lived in them, and they were important architecturally as well as socially. Purpose-built blocks such as Astor House in New York City and Tremont House in Boston were early examples, and by the last quarter of the nineteenth century innovative middle-class apartment blocks continued this tradition of semi-communal living. Blocks of 'French flats' such as the Hotel Pelham in New York (which had a steep mansard roof in the Haussmann style) were provided with the 'modern', 'labour-saving' luxuries of elevators, central heating and bathrooms with hot and cold water. In some cases, central vacuum-cleaning systems were even installed. These had nozzles in each room which were connected to a large pump in the basement and were either used to suck out the dust, or, reversed, could be used as hair dryers. There were communal laundries and public dining rooms – so that in some ways these apartment blocks were reminiscent of Edward Bellamy's Boston of the year 2000. Not all were luxury blocks, however. There was a working-women's hotel in New York, and in the early years of the twentieth century there was a special hostel for black women in Harlem. These hotels were often cramped, and apartment life did have a slight aura of moral laxity. In her novel *The House of Mirth* Edith Wharton described hotel society as a rootless demi-monde, and when her heroine sank even further down the social scale, the working-women's hostel in which she found herself was bare and dreary. On the other hand, they offered independence and companionship, and the American feminist writer Charlotte Perkins Gilman was an ardent advocate of apartment living.[17]

In the 1920s another form of experimental housing appeared in the Bronx. At this time Rose Chernin was organising successful rent strikes there, and there was also a communist cooperative housing block:

> People put their money together, borrowed from the bank, rebuilt the building, and lived together . . . They had everything there – a shopping centre, a nursery . . . There was a wonderful mood in that cooperative . . . [It] was an enclave, a little corner of socialism right in the middle of New York.[18]

During the Progressive Era woman writers and artists were trying their luck at independence in bohemian communities, which were springing up in the great cities. Not all adventurous middle-class women chose the path of Settlement living or a life dedicated to the service of others, although, certainly in Chicago, the philanthropic world and bohemia overlapped.

Paris inspired the American bohemias that sprang up in New York from the 1860s onwards. In the early years one or two women earned the title of 'Queen of Bohemia', but they were exceptional. In the 1890s, a woman was more likely to achieve prominence as the hostess of a literary salon – but in order to hold court in this way you normally had to be wealthy.

In 1866 the beginnings of a bohemian group existed in Chicago too, and by the 1890s the bohemian community was accustomed to gather at the Bohemian Club and the Cypher Club. Women played a crucial role in the Chicago bohemia. One of the most important meeting places was the Little Room, a weekly meeting of men and women writers and artists who formed a community on equal terms. The Little Room began its meetings in 1898, but by 1902 a split was beginning to develop as the men assumed the dominant positions. A few years later some of the most prominent men from the group formed a club for men only. The women then formed their own Cordon Club.[19]

Women ran the little magazines that flourished. In 1912 Harriet Monroe started the periodical *Poetry*. This published the early experimental work of many who later became major modernist writers: Robert Frost, D.H. Lawrence and Yeats, for example. Chicago's other important 'little magazine', the *Little Review*, which was founded in 1914, was also the brain-child of a woman, Margaret Anderson, who 'at times had to escape creditors in a tent on the wintry lakeshore. She moved her piano and her friends there, together with manuscripts and galley proofs of the next issue'.[20]

It was possible for women to make their way in the world without going to the lengths of openly rejecting convention. The influence of bohemianism and the existence of avant-garde artistic circles gradually opened up opportunities for women in journalism and other semi-artistic callings.

Eleanor Stoddard, one of the characters whose fortunes John Dos Passos traced in his panoramic novel *USA*, started her adult life working as a sales assistant in the interior-decoration section of Marshall Fields department store in Chicago. She then took the opportunity to branch out as a freelance interior decorator in partnership with her friend Eveline Hutchins. By the early 1900s it was acceptable for unmarried women to live alone or with women friends in an hotel or an apartment. The *Chicago Post* reported that:

> the ladies of bohemia are not without their fascinations, and are usually women of any age between twenty-five and thirty. They have usually passed through more than one love episode and are valuable contributors to the story writing departments of papers of the New York *Mercury* or *Ledger* type. They are neither unprotected females, strongminded women or lorettes, but women who have learned to take life as they find it, and living out their existence in their own free way, they are careless of what the world says.[21]

Yet it remained an anxious, ambiguous existence. Relationships with men were fraught with unease and disappointment. If Eleanor Stoddard was a little in love with Eveline, Eveline in her turn fell for Maurice; but Maurice moved into Eric's studio apartment, and 'seemed to be thoroughly happy. They slept in the same bed and were always together. Eleanor used to wonder about them sometimes, but it was so nice to know boys who weren't horrid about women'.[22]

In the late 1920s, Chicago's bohemia still existed in 'Towertown', so called because it clustered round the old Chicago watertower. Bohemia then was 'a place of transition, a place in which life is adventurous . . . but often very lonely . . . a place where everything is loose and free but everything is problematic'.[23]

Frank Zorbaugh, a member of the important Chicago School of Sociology, carried out a study of Chicago's bohemia. By the 1920s the creative artists of the original bohemia had left, and what remained, according to Zorbaugh, was sterile rebellion, 'Russo-French teapots, battered candle sticks. Exotic drawings, a few "daring" books, and not too many brooms or dust pans.' Perhaps he sneered at and devalued this world because it was dominated by women:

> Of late years, in New York and Chicago, with changing mores and the emancipation of the younger generation of American women, Greenwich Village and Towertown have become women's bohemias. It is the young women who open most of the studios, run most of the tearooms and restaurants, most of the little art shops and book stalls, manage the exhibits and little theaters, dominate the life of the bohemias of American cities. And in Towertown the women are, on the whole, noticeably superior to the men.[24]

What Zorbaugh seemed most to dislike was the lesbian and gay element – for bohemia was one of the few places where it was at all safe for homosexuals to be open about their sexuality.

Dos Passos's Eleanor and Eveline had moved to New York before the First World War; by 1910 Greenwich Village was coming to seem a more exciting centre of bohemian living than its Midwestern counterpart. In New York – as in Paris much earlier on – a whole urban district was coming to be identified with the alternative way of life. For a period, studios and apartments could be rented cheaply and the low dancing halls and French wine shops in the vicinity of Washington Square were transformed into cafés, restaurants, tearooms and clubs where artists and intellectuals met. As early as the 1890s successful woman artists, sculptors and architects had their studios in the neighbourhood. In 1895–6 *Godey's Magazine* ran a series of articles describing and illustrating the studios, with their jazzy cushions and avant-garde pictures. Their bright colour schemes and modern furniture were at least twenty years in advance of the times.

Between about 1910 and the end of the First World War, Greenwich Village was a centre not only of artistic and personal experimentation but also of serious political agitation. Henrietta Rodman, for example, who lived and worked there, was:

> a high school teacher, a protester, a leader of demonstrations, and ever new factions, a blazer of trails . . . a suffragist; she stood for the rights of married teachers; she explained sex to her high school girls; she agitated for simpler and saner dress. She

wore a loose flowing gown that looked like a meal sack and yet
did not conceal the trim lines of her body. She wore sandals on
her small, shapely feet, making the queer brown socks visible.
Her hair was cropped years before the other Village girls dared
bob theirs.[25]

In 1914 Henrietta Rodman founded the Feminist Alliance, which
campaigned on a number of issues. Her most ambitious project was a
feminist apartment house, but this never materialised.

Bohemian life flourished on the West Coast as well. The group of
artists and writers that settled in Carmel, south of San Francisco,
included several women. In southern California, Pasadena and the
Arroyo Seco, a nearby canyon close to the 'wilderness', witnessed
the growth of a high-minded colony at the turn of the century.
Influenced by the Arts and Crafts movement, its members married
their ideals to the culture of the Navajo. This community, too,
boasted a number of gifted women, including Mary Austin, who
wrote of the beauty and mystery of the desert lands.[26]

Mary Austin's life was a troubled one, for she had an unhappy
marriage and a handicapped child. Bohemian life may have seemed
especially attractive to women of an independent turn of mind and to
those for whom conventional marriage had proved a disappointment, but the bohemian life itself brought further difficulties. One
woman journalist asked in 1898: 'Is feminine Bohemianism a failure?'
As she pointed out, a man could pass through bohemia, sow his wild
oats and then 'select the purest woman for his wife and the most
sequestered nook for his home', but the same option did not exist for
the female bohemian, who had no wish to retire to the suburbs with
a man who was her intellectual inferior. In addition, the women of
bohemia were talented and refined, but most of them found it almost
impossible to earn a living salary. No wonder that this writer had
herself been tempted to pose in the nude, which paid almost as much
as her job as a journalist.[27]

In the 1920s the bohemias of America went into decline, as, despite
an economic boom, political reaction gripped the country. Greenwich Village was still booming, but now tales of 'free love' and
supplies of prohibition liquor drew tourists and dilettantes. Rich
women came looking for artist lovers and rich men installed their
mistresses in arty apartments. Bohemia actually supported the
growing consumerism of American society. Fashions, furniture,
interior design and entertainment could all be sold with the help of a
Greenwich Village gloss.

Harlem became an alternative mecca for the sightseers and sensation seekers of the 1920s. Although there had been black Americans

in New York since the seventeenth century, until the end of the nineteenth they lived in small pockets, although always in impoverished and marginalised sections of town. Well before the First World War there were approximately sixty thousand Afro-Americans in New York. In the mid to late nineteenth century they were clustered in the 'tenderloin' district, and there was an important Negro community on West 53rd Avenue between 6th and 7th Avenue. At the turn of the century the major black cultural institutions were to be found there; the district attracted a black bohemia, particularly of theatrical workers, and the black churches, the YMCA, black hotels and fraternal societies had their headquarters in that area.[28]

At this time Harlem was a fashionable suburb for upper-middle-class white families. During a hectic real-estate boom, large brownstone houses and apartments were built because it was expected that the extension of the rapid-transit system would make the whole neighbourhood more accessible. Instead, more and more property speculation resulted in the collapse of the market in 1904–5, and from then on Afro-Americans began to move into the area. By 1910 many of New York's most prominent blacks lived in Harlem, and at the same time all the major black cultural institutions were relocating from the West Side.

During the Progressive Era reformers became interested in the life of American blacks as they moved into the cities. Mrs Victoria Earle Mathews, herself black, founded a Negro Protest and Women's Rights Society in New York and delivered lectures on 'the awakening of the Afro-American woman'. She was shocked by the way in which young black women coming to the city, often from the rural South, were cheated by extortionate employment agents into paying premiums to get low-paid jobs, and were sometimes drawn into prostitution. In 1897 the White Rose Working Girls' Home had been opened, and in the early years of the twentieth century the National League for the Protection of Coloured Women was founded.[29]

Then and later black women in New York outnumbered black men: in 1890 there were 1000 black women for every 810 black men; in 1910 the ratio was 1000:850. This was partly because, although economic opportunities for all blacks were restricted, women could more easily than men obtain work of some sort, however menial. Black women did laundry, became maids, did cleaning and cooking.

Black men found it difficult to get work. College graduates found themselves forced to accept manual employment, and to be a Pullman porter was the most they could aspire to. A tiny black elite lived in Harlem, but most middle-class blacks were clerks, actors, musicians and music teachers or small businessmen. In the whole of

Harlem there were only forty-two black doctors and twenty-six black lawyers; between twenty-five and thirty black nurses employed by the New York visiting nurse service managed to make 30,000 visits a year.[30]

Yet this was the period of the 'Harlem Renaissance'. One of the outstanding black writers of the Renaissance, Langston Hughes (who was also gay), wrote cynically that most ordinary Afro-Americans had never heard of the Harlem Renaissance, 'and if they had it hadn't raised their wages any', but the upsurge of black writing and artistic creativity on the stage and in music was tremendously important. The black writers of the period acted as the voice for a growing sense of identity which came in part from the increasing visibility of blacks and their growing political awareness and determination. It was not surprising that this should have occurred in the first huge 'black metropolis' within a metropolis, with its concentration of black cultural institutions and the added stimulus of blacks from countries outside the United States, particularly the Caribbean.

Although black writing became fashionable among white intellectuals in the 1920s, the white men and women who came to the nightclubs were not interested in the Harlem Renaissance. They came for the spectacle to be found at the Cotton Club or Connie's Inn, where big-name black entertainers played to exclusively white audiences; or they could go to the little dives, where the entertainment was in watching the black customers, 'like animals in a zoo' as Langston Hughes put it.

Ordinary Harlemites invented the 'rent party' in order to get away from these white intruders, who wanted to leer at 'high yallers', 'tantalising tans' and 'hot chocolates' – an obsession with every variation in colour was part of the racism of the Harlem spectacle. Guests at the rent parties paid an entrance fee of 25 cents, and for this price it was possible to enjoy bootleg liquor, good food and impromptu music and singing as well as dancing.[31]

The search for pleasure brought further exploitation to Harlem. Whites went to Harlem in search of an erotic utopia of sexual thrills, and black women and men often had little option but to provide them with what they wanted. Through the eyes of Malcolm X, who escorted white clients to Harlem for sexual rendezvous during the Second World War, the exploitation and tension of these taboo encounters was ugly and the source of mutual contempt:

> In all of my time in Harlem, I never saw a white prostitute touched by a white man. White girls were in some of the various Harlem specialty places. They would participate in

customers' most frequent exhibition requests – a sleek, black negro male having a white woman. Was this the white man wanting to witness his deepest sexual fear?[32]

Even in the 1920s Harlem was becoming a slum, and after the Crash it deteriorated still further. Much of the original housing stock was solid and spacious, but Afro-Americans, since they could not afford the very high rents – much higher than for comparable sections of the white community in other parts of the city – sublet, took in boarders and lodgers, and many of the dwellings became multi-occupation rooming houses.

In addition, the very low wages and salaries, and the relative lack of black capital within the community, meant that poverty, over-crowding, health problems and high crime rates became endemic. As well as the prostitution and pimping, there was hustling, number-running and other forms of gambling, dope-dealing and all forms of petty – and less petty – crime, all of which formed the daily life of a sizeable proportion of the Harlem population, excluded by racism from all the better paid jobs.[33]

The vogue among white intellectuals for all things 'Negro', like the influx of tourists, did not outlast the 1929 Wall Street crash. Many, although not all, the writers of the Harlem Renaissance stopped writing at the end of the 1920s; some of the social stars of the period did not physically survive long into the 1930s. A'Lelia Walker, the most famous black hostess of the Renaissance period, and the daughter of Madame Walker, who became a millionaire by inventing a successful hair straightener, died in 1931.[34]

Yet the vibrant, harsh existence of New York's Harlem and Brooklyn inspired black woman writers to record their lives in some of the most memorable novels of the mid twentieth century. Paule Marshall found a beauty in the monotonous streets of brownstones in Brooklyn:

> In the somnolent July afternoon the unbroken line of brown-stone houses down the long Brooklyn Street resembled an army massed at attention. They were all one uniform red-brown stone. All with high massive stone stoops and black iron-grille fences staving off the sun. All draped in ivy as though mourning, their somnolent façades indifferent to the summer's heat and passion . . .
>
> Glancing down the interminable Brooklyn Street you thought of those joined brownstones as one house reflected through a train of mirrors, with no walls between the houses but only vast rooms yawning endlessly one into the other.[35]

For Rosa Guy, Harlem and the whole of Manhattan glittered with excitement that 'drives me like a fire, day, night, day, night'. Even though life was dangerous and hard, her heroine fell in love with New York:

> Lights running around the Times Building, smoke coming from the billboard cigarette smoker's mouth, water falling down the sides of buildings, splashing out onto the avenue, sparkling in the lights. Electricity had changed night into day, and folks stood out enjoying it. In such numbers! Talking, laughing, crowding streets and eating places, lining up to enter glittering showplaces. Coloured folks too! Right out there in that brightness – wearing bow ties, boaters, slick-looking spats, sporting canes – laughing, talking loud, belonging – and sounding free.[36]

But in *The Street* Ann Petry described a different world – the bleak district that Harlem had become by the 1940s:

> There was a cold November wind blowing through 116th Street. It rattled the tops of dustbins, sucked window blinds out through the top of opened windows and set them flapping back against the windows; and it drove most of the people off the street in the block between Seventh and Eighth Avenues except for a few hurried pedestrians who bent double in an effort to offer the least possible exposed surface to its violent assault.[37]

Despite the bitterness of the city's poor, the decade of the 1940s was perhaps the golden age of New York. Although it was not the political capital of the United States, it was the 'capital of capital', the headquarters of American industry and finance, and the hub of communications and culture. To many it seemed an ugly place, but that was part of its vitality. Its tremendous concentration of manufacturing and commerce, however, exacerbated the housing crisis.[38] In any case, beneath the bright, brash façade lurked an emptiness and melancholy, pictured so hauntingly in Edward Hopper's paintings – a city of yawning windows, empty rooms; and of women spied unawares, nude or in déshabille as they gaze speechlessly at nothingness, or wait in evening offices for the boss to leave – or to seduce them.[39]

For the more privileged, New York in the 1940s remained a magical and romantic place. Elizabeth Hardwick described this city, in which some of the black entertainers still played in the remaining nightclubs: 'their worn, brown faces, enigmatic in the early evening, their coughs, their split lips and yellow eyes'. Billie Holiday was there:

> She was fat the first time we saw her, large, brilliantly beautiful, fat . . . She was glittering, sombre and solitary . . . stately, sinister and determined. The creamy lips, the oily eyelids, the

violent perfume – and in her voice the tropical l's and r's. Her presence, her singing created a large, swelling anxiety . . . Sometimes she dyed her hair red and the curls lay flat against her skull, like dried blood.[40]

Yet it was as if Manhattan was no longer the centre of things. Now its charm resided in its marginality, which became haunting and made possible another kind of urban experience: the surreal, the fragmentary:

We lived there in the center of Manhattan . . . No star was to be seen in the heavens, but the sky was always bright with the flicker of distant lights. No tree was to be seen, but as if by a miracle little heaps of twigs and blown leaves gathered in the gutters. To live in the obscuring jungle in the midst of things: close to – what?[41]

The anthropologist Claude Lévi-Strauss arrived in New York in 1941. It was, he wrote, not 'the modern metropolis I had expected'. Instead it was 'an immense horizontal and vertical disorder attributable to some spontaneous upheaval of the urban crust rather than to the deliberate plans of builders'.

Strata from different epochs emerged, and 'despite the loftiness of the tallest buildings and the way they were piled up and squeezed together on the cramped surface of an island . . . on the edges of these labyrinths the web of the urban tissue was astonishingly slack'.[42]

In these hidden or uncertain places he found extraordinary shops selling Renaissance treasures or ethnographic curiosities for a few dollars; behind the skyscrapers were still to be found decrepit cottages with gardens similar to those of Balzac's Paris. 'Like the urban fabric, the social and cultural fabric was riddled with holes. All you had to do was pick one and slip through it, if like Alice, you wanted to get to the other side of the looking glass and find worlds so enchanting that they seemed unreal.'[43]

6

Architecture and Consciousness in Central Europe

As I was walking, one hot summer afternoon, through the deserted streets of a provincial town in Italy, which was unknown to me, I found myself in a quarter of whose character I could not long remain in doubt. Nothing but painted women were to be seen at the windows of the small houses, and I hastened to leave the narrow street at the next turning. But after having wandered about for a time without enquiring my way I suddenly found myself back in the same street, where my presence was now beginning to excite attention. I hurried away once more, only to arrive by another detour at the same place yet a third time. Now, however, a feeling overcame me which I can only describe as uncanny.

Sigmund Freud, '*The "Uncanny"*' (1919)

Until 1918 Vienna was the heart of the Habsburg Empire of central Europe. Although by the mid nineteenth century this empire was in decline, the Habsburgs continued to improve and beautify their capital. In 1859 work began on the Ringstrasse, a broad street which encircled the inner city and was built on what had previously been the fortifications. The Ringstrasse was a 'vast, continuous circular space', lined with public buildings, parks and apartment blocks. In the fashionable districts these were based on the Baroque prototype of the nobleman's palace and were known as 'rent palaces'. In the outer, poorer districts, monotonous, multi-storey blocks were built for the working class. These too looked back to a Baroque building form – the army barracks – and were in fact referred to as 'rent barracks'.[1]

Public social life was important in Vienna. The Corso section of the Ring saw the daily promenade of Viennese society, and the Viennese cafés were centres of intellectual discussion (exclusively for men, if illustrations from the turn of the century are anything to go by).

Viennese intellectual circles were small, but between the turn of the century and 1918, some of the most significant and influential currents of twentieth-century thought developed there. Vienna in the 1900s nourished Sigmund Freud and Adolf Hitler; Ludwig Wittgenstein, the philosopher (who actually attended the same school as Hitler for a time); Robert Musil and Karl Kraus; Gustav Mahler and Arnold Schoenberg; Otto Wagner and Adolf Loos; and Gustav Klimt and Oskar Kokoschka. It was a centre of Jewish life and of anti-Semitism; it was a centre of avant-garde creativity yet had not cast off its pre-democratic authoritarian form of government. Its pioneers of modernist architecture aimed to create a rational style fit for the machine age, but, simultaneously, the philosophies and art of Vienna explored the irrational sources of human emotions, and its frantically pleasure-seeking lifestyle expressed those emotions in almost hysterical fashion – so much so that the Viennese waltz, at one level an obvious symbol of *joie de vivre*, seemed to the French composer Ravel something closer to a *danse macabre*.[2]

Although Vienna's artists and writers did not all place urban life explicitly at the heart of their concerns, what emerged was an investigation of urban consciousness and experience. Femininity and the figure of the woman played an important yet extremely ambiguous role in Viennese urban life and thought.

The paradoxical opposition between the 'modern' building or city expressive of 'scientific' rationalism on the one hand, and the irrational and dislocated consciousness that it produced on the other, was cast as the opposition between the male and female principles. In this disorientating city the hero of modern life appeared, his psyche assaulted by its clamour, shock and speed, his identity shattered and problematic. The introspective, autobiographical novel was an ideal vehicle for the examination of this fractured modern identity, and Robert Musil's *The Man without Qualities*, set in early-twentieth-century Vienna, explored its peculiar alienation.

The novel was never finished, and – suitably, given that it is an exploration of the dissociation of urban life – lacks a traditional narrative. Ulrich, the main character, offers the reader a subjectivity through which to view the strangeness that is modern city life. Indeed, Ulrich is himself a stranger, somehow outside the Viennese social circles in which he mingles. An attitude of irony appears as the only possible stance to be taken in the face of the glittering disorientation of the urban spectacle:

> Motor-cars came shooting out of deep, narrow streets into the shallows of bright squares. Dark patches of pedestrian bustle formed into cloudy streams. Where stronger lines of speed transected their loose-woven hurrying, they clotted up – only to trickle on all the faster then and after a few ripples regain their regular pulse-beat. Hundreds of sounds were intertwined into a coil of wiry noise, with single barbs projecting, sharp edges running along it and submerging again, and clear notes splintering off – flying and scattering.[3]

The discrepancy between what we see and a hidden reality is not confined to the physical properties of the world; it permeates social reality as well:

The fact is, living permanently in a well-ordered State has an out-and-out spectral aspect: one cannot step into the street or drink a glass of water or get into a tram without touching the perfectly balanced levers of a gigantic apparatus of laws and relations, setting them in motion or letting them maintain one in the peace and quiet of one's existence. One knows hardly any of these levers, which extend deep into the inner workings and on the other side are lost in a network the entire constitution of which has never been disentangled by any living being. Hence one denies their existence, just as the common man denies the existence of the air, insisting that it is mere emptiness; but it seems that precisely this is what lends life a certain spectral quality – the fact that everything that is denied reality, every-thing that is colourless, odourless, tasteless, imponderable and non-moral, like water, air, space, money and the passing of time, is in reality what is most important.[4]

The hero's relationship to feeling is affected by his sense of a double reality. After a quarrel with his mistress, they make love, but this interlude seems to have nothing to do with what came before and afterwards:

This erotic metamorphosis of consciousness was only a special case of something far more general; for nowadays all mani-festations of our inner life, such as for instance an evening at the theatre, a concert, or a church service, are such swift appearing and disappearing islands of a second state of consciousness temporarily interpolated into the ordinary one.[5]

At the same period, Freud, also a citizen of Vienna, was working to investigate this very sense of psychic dislocation. He emphasised its roots in the *unconscious*, and looked to what he called 'the refuse of the phenomenal world' – that is, the trivial, the fragmentary, the disregarded and marginalised aspects of daily experience – for the key to its meaning. Both the new aesthetic and the new psychology displaced every traditional assumption about what was important and central. They made a virtue of what the critics of metropolitan life most feared: the indifference, the transience, the confusion and the profusion, the ugly, the trivial, the eccentric and the strange. Freud may therefore be said to have produced a theory of human subjectivity that was itself essentially urban – although his work reflects the ambivalence towards city life that was so common.[6]

The anxiety or even torment that haunted many male writers and their heroes was clearly associated with the idea of sexuality:

experienced as both an infinite possibility and a fearful danger in the urban environment. Freud and others from the close-knit group of intellectuals in Vienna before the First World War placed sexual difference at the heart of their theories of modern life. Woman represented feeling, sexuality and even chaos; man was rationality and control. Some valued the excess of experience to which femininity opened the way; some writers developed a vision of the possible harmony between the gender opposites; for others femininity was threatening and horrifying, and the antagonism between female sensuality and male intellect an eternal source of conflict and threat.

The sharp differentiation between the feminine, with its suggestion of eroticism and bacchanalia, and the masculine, with its perhaps excessive control, paradoxically went hand in hand with a 'homosexual reawakening'. Sexuality was ambiguous. The art of Gustav Klimt, for example, with its androgynous women and men, was ambivalent; it suggested a sexuality that was both decadent and liberating, an erotic life both hidden and blatant. Masculinity and femininity were eternal opposites, yet could coexist in one body: the androgynous man and the phallic woman.[7] The female figures of Salome, who cut off John the Baptist's head (castration), and of Lulu or Pandora, who out of mere childish, amoral curiosity let loose all evils on the world, were key symbols of womanhood in the art and literature of the period.

Freud's case histories presented a detailed picture of the frustration of Viennese women's (and men's) lives at the turn of the century. Freud himself expressed a doubt whether it was worthwhile to cure his female patients of their neuroses when reality was so constricting. Marriages were often business partnerships. The bourgeois pattern of late marriage prevailed, and condemned unmarried middle-class women to celibacy, their future husbands to sex with prostitutes. Sexual encounters were likely to be tainted with guilt and disgust, and writers such as Arthur Schnitzler and Stefan Zweig later recalled the foetid sexual atmosphere of pre-First World War Vienna, with its suffocating bourgeois hypocrisy and enormous population of prostitutes.[8] As in the literature of nineteenth-century Paris, the prostitute often appeared as the heroine of modern life. Karl Kraus, the Viennese satirist, romanticised her as a natural force posed against the falsity of contemporary civilisation, which with its technology enforced a separation between male thought and female beauty.[9]

Freud, who was the most influential, perhaps, of all Viennese thinkers, based his theory of sexual difference on his knowledge of the lives of his Viennese patients, many of whom were women. It was a theory which emphasised the fragile nature of sexual balance. In his novella-like case histories women struggled with their sexual inferiority, while men fled from the fear of castration. There was an at times compulsive emphasis on sexual difference, yet everywhere there was ambiguity, bisexuality and perversity. With a leap of the imagination, Freud incorporated this sexual alienation into a theory of male and female sexuality which both acknowledged and tried to overcome the sexual uncertainty of modern urban life. In his essay on 'The "Uncanny"', sexual disquiet is specifically linked with the city, characterised by unforeseen yet repeated encounters and coincidences, and populated by 'painted women'. The seemingly unorganised and uncontrolled nature of public life rendered sexual encounters ambiguous and uneasy.

The novels and letters of Franz Kafka, who lived in Prague, another capital of the Habsburg Empire, were filled with a similar disquiet originating from the indeterminacy and strangeness of the urban environment. Sometimes the disquiet of K, hero of *The Trial*, appeared to arise from the alienation of poverty. Even when the atmosphere of the working-class districts was friendly, it constituted an assault on the lonely hero:

> Windows were piled high with bedding, above which the dishevelled head of a woman would appear for a moment. People were shouting to one another across the street; one shout just above K's head caused great laughter . . . Women were thronging into and out of [the] shops or gossiping on the steps outside. A fruit hawker who was crying his wares to the people in the windows above, progressing almost as inattentively as K himself, almost knocked K down with his push-cart. A phonograph . . . began stridently to murder a tune.[10]

More typically, poverty appeared horrific and threatening:

> This was an even poorer neighbourhood, the houses were still darker, the streets filled with sludge oozing about slowly on top of the melting snow . . . there was a gaping hole out of which, just as K approached, issued a disgusting yellow fluid, steaming hot, from which a rat fled into the adjoining canal. At the foot of the stairs an infant lay belly down on the ground bawling, but one could barely hear its shrieks because of the deafening din that came from a tinsmith's workshop at the other side of the entry . . . K . . . wanted to get out of the neighbourhood as quickly as possible.[11]

These passages suggest a bourgeois horror of the working class and the poor, but Kafka's unease was also associated with sexuality. In a letter he described an encounter with a young woman who worked in a shop opposite his apartment, and whom he watched from his window:

> We came to an understanding by sign language . . . but when I came down in the evening someone else was already there – well, this didn't make any difference . . . she . . . signed to me that I should follow them . . . we walked, I following slowly, to the girl's apartment . . . there the man said goodbye, the girl ran into the house, I waited a while until she came out again, and then we went to a hotel . . . Even before we got to the hotel all this was charming, exciting and horrible, in the hotel it wasn't different. [12]

The film *Metropolis* (1927) explored similar themes, depicting a paranoid realm in which hordes of workers swarmed like ants in a second, underground city beneath the skyscrapers of the rulers' utopia. The masses were roused to revolt by the evil woman – an image of the 'red whore'. She took the form, however, of a mechanical double of the pure and passive heroine. Woman, in other words, was a double figure with sinister associations: the pure woman and the seductress appear as one and the same, and the double could only be destroyed by being burnt at the stake, like a witch. [13]

At their most paranoid these fears could end in the rabid anti-Semitism of Hitler's *Mein Kampf*. Hitler spent impoverished years as an unsuccessful artist in Vienna, where he loathed the prostitutes, the Jews and the decadence of the urban scene.

For others, urban life opened the way to sexual exploration, and the fulfilment of fantasies. In Berlin during the Weimar Republic (1919–33) the carnivalesque and transgressive impact of city life reached a new intensity. Christopher Isherwood in *Goodbye to Berlin* (on which the film *Cabaret* was based) presented himself as another outsider, who observed the homosexual night-clubs, the good-time girls, the latent fascism of the underclass and the white-collar workers, and likened himself to the mechanical eye of the camera, there simply to record without making any moral judgment. In this choice of metaphor he alluded to the feeling of being, as an intellectual, and/or artist, reduced to the status of observer. At the same time he evaded acknowledgment of his commitment, as a homosexual, to the liberating aspects of the life he described. His friend Stephen Spender, also a poet, was franker about the opportunities that Berlin and other great German cities such as Hamburg offered for the exploration of 'forbidden' sexualities during the Weimar period:

During these months I discovered a terrifying mystery of cities . . . This is that a great city is a kind of labyrinth within which at every moment of the day the most hidden wishes of every human being are performed by people who devote their whole existence to this and nothing else . . . the hidden life of forbidden wishes exists in extravagant nakedness behind mazes of walls.[14]

Part of Hitler's growing appeal during Weimar was his denunciation of a sexual excess that he, at least, associated with the Jews. The threat of the dirty Jewish prostitute was one particularly and repulsively racist image used by Hitler to excite the prejudices of his growing following. But the leftwing, radical critics of Weimar also viewed the prostitute in an ambivalent light. In the caricatures of George Grosz and the paintings of Otto Dix she appeared as a horrific figure, and although their works ostensibly attacked the institution of prostitution with its exploitation of working-class women, they also betrayed a horror of female sexuality itself. The 'big city' (title of one of Dix's paintings) was the setting for a repulsive orgy of bestial purchased sex.[15]

The counterpart to the search for sexual pleasure, which was always more or less forbidden, was the sexual crime. Or perhaps the sexual crime was fatally linked to the freedom of women in the city. An inescapable link certainly appeared in the work of several writers, between women's freedom and sexual violence. In Wedekind's play *Pandora's Box*, Lulu, the heroine, was cast in a fatal relationship with Jack the Ripper. The only major character in Robert Musil's novel of Viennese life who was capable of responding spontaneously to experience was Moosbrugger, a madman convicted of the brutal murder of a woman he had desired. Biberkopf, the 'hero' of *Berlin-Alexanderplatz*, Alfred Döblin's panorama of the German capital as it slid downwards towards slump and Nazism in 1929, had killed his mistress.

At the beginning of *Berlin-Alexanderplatz*, Biberkopf has just come out of prison after serving a sentence for this crime, and almost the first thing he does is to visit a cinema where a lurid sex melodrama is being shown. In the cinema, 'the long room was packed full, ninety per cent men with caps on'. These poverty-stricken individuals, it is implied, were offered in the mechanical entertainments of the metropolis an impossible fantasy of sexuality.[16]

More generally, although the tumult of city life as Döblin's Biberkopf experienced it in 1929 was unremittingly harsh, the city created a space in which an alternative approach to life could bloom. The cacophony of traffic, the tempting shop windows, the cafés, the milling crowds, proposed an alternative to the work ethic and the clockwork factory routine; and offered alternative identities of aesthete, criminal or revolutionary.

The modernity of early-twentieth-century city life appeared, then, as possibly seductive, but ultimately as a threat to the very survival of the male identity. At the same time, Viennese artistic and intellectual life was straining towards the creation of a style appropriate to contemporary urban consciousness. The generation of artists and architects who were working shortly before the First World War became founders of modernism and the Modern movement, desiring a functional architecture, revolutionary in its approach, to replace the elaborately recycled Renaissance and Gothic styles of the Ringstrasse, which represented the official establishment of the Habsburg Empire. They spoke of the house as a 'machine for living' and used the analogy of the factory.[17]

Modernism extended to all design. Adolf Loos, an Austrian architect and critic, wrote in 1908 that 'the evolution of culture is synonymous with the removal of ornament from utilitarian objects'. The position Loos took was an elitist one, in which the (spiritual) 'aristocrat' represented the most advanced stage of human evolution. 'So immensely strong is his individuality that it can no longer be expressed in articles of clothing. Freedom from ornament is a sign of spiritual strength', wrote Loos. By contrast he considered the child, the 'savage' and the woman to be at a lower level of civilisation, since they still took pleasure in self-ornamentation. He recognised, however, that women were forced to adorn themselves, because the average woman could ensure an economic future for herself only by winning the love of a man, and she had to do this by seduction:

> But we are approaching a new and greater time. No longer by an appeal to sensuality, but rather by economic independence earned through work will the woman bring about her equal status with the man . . . Then velvet and silk, flowers and ribbons, feathers and paint will fail to have their effect. They will disappear.[18]

In the first decade of the twentieth century, artists all over Europe took up the call to modernism. The Italian Futurists expressed ideas similar to those of Adolf Loos, embracing the 'machine age' future even more enthusiastically, if that were possible. They wholeheartedly rejoiced in the excesses of urban life. The *Futurist Manifesto of Architecture*, written in 1914, welcomed all the elements that reformers found so disturbing: the noise, the tumult, the ugliness, the inhumanity:

We must invent and rebuild the futurist city: it must be like an immense, tumultuous, lively, noble work site, dynamic in all its parts; and the futurist house must be like an enormous machine. The lifts must not hide like lonely worms in the stairwells; the stairs, become useless, must be done away with, and the lifts must climb like serpents of iron and glass up the house fronts. The house of concrete glass and iron, without painting and without sculpture, enriched solely by the innate beauty of its lines and projections, extremely 'ugly' in its mechanical simplicity, high and wide, as prescribed by local government regulations, must rise on the edge of a tumultuous abyss: the street, which will no longer stretch like a footpath level with the porters' lodges but will descend into the earth on several levels, will receive the metropolitan traffic and will be linked, for the necessary passage from one to the other, by metal walkways and immensely fast escalators.[19]

They perceived that the modern was making possible the 'creation of a new ideal of beauty, still obscure and embryonic, but whose fascination is already being felt even by the masses'. 'We are no longer the men of the cathedrals, *the palaces*, the assembly halls', they wrote, 'but of big hotels, railway stations, immense roads, colossal ports, covered markets, brilliantly lit galleries, freeways, demolition and rebuilding schemes.'

For the Futurists, the solution to the problems of the great cities was not the relocation of whole populations from the slums, nor the reorganisation of whole districts according to picturesque principles. Instead, the observer should change his consciousness and his conception of beauty. Then he would find a beauty in the utilitarian uniformity of the modern city.

The architect Otto Wagner was another uncompromising modernist. He believed that the huge city – the metropolis – offered its inhabitants a guarantee of democracy, because of their anonymity in its endless warrens. He also emphasised the virtues of uniformity. 'Our democratic essence, which is imposed upon us by both the call for cheap and healthy houses and the enforced economy of our lifestyles, has the uniformity of our dwelling houses as its consequence', he wrote. It was useless to retreat into the past; the challenge must be met 'by raising uniformity into monumentality'.[20] In his designs he elevated the Viennese 'rent palace' and 'rent barracks' into the ideal modern living form.

During the Weimar Republic the Bauhaus design school explored the possibilities of modernism as an ideal stylistic form for twentieth-century life: a strictly functional style. Superfluous ornamentation was rejected; the form of every object for daily use, from the teacup to the apartment block, must suggest its purpose. The wider relationship between art and technology, art and industry, came to the fore; modern science had made available the means whereby useful, well-designed objects could be mass-produced:

> The stadium has carried the day against the art museum, and physical reality has taken the place of the beautiful illusion. Sport merges the individual into the mass . . . The standardisation of our requirements is shown by: the bowler hat, bobbed hair, the tango, jazz, the Co-op products, the DIN standard size and Liebig's meat extract . . . The folding chair, roll-top desk, light bulb, bath tub and portable gramophone are typical standard products manufactured internationally and showing a uniform design . . . the unqualified affirmation of the present age presupposes the ruthless denial of the past . . . architecture has ceased to be an agency continuing the growth of tradition or an embodiment of emotion.[21]

'A modern building', wrote Walter Gropius, director of the Bauhaus, 'should derive its architectural significance solely from the vigour and consequence of its own organic proportions. It must be true to itself, logically transparent and virginal of lies and trivialities, as befits a direct affirmation of our contemporary world of mechanisation and rapid transit.'[22]

The efforts of the Bauhaus came under increasing attack as leftwing and subversive because its architects rejected tradition, a national style and craft ethos. The 'International style', as it came to be called, was associated with politically progressive views and socialism between the wars. This association seemed confirmed when the Bauhaus was finally forced to shut down by the Nazis after they came to power in 1933.

Since the 1960s, there has been a decisive turn against the International style. Its critique of the fussiness and over-ornamentation of bourgeois nineteenth-century taste was nevertheless perfectly valid. Purity and minimalism are recurrent themes in design; the simple and labour-saving interiors of the Dessau houses and the restrained and sober lines of the architecture were refined examples of one particular approach to design. The International style claimed, however, to be more than that; the designers who promoted it believed that it embodied 'universal' laws of design, which were unchanging and ahistorical. What is more, they believed that this style could change the world. In this respect their claims were utopian and overreached the possibilities of modernism.

The Russian writer Yevgeny Zamyatin criticised it in his novel

We, published in 1924, as a form of 'Taylorism'. This was a reference to the American who invented the assembly line, and Zamyatin implied that the International Style could degenerate into emptiness, repetition and monotony. It rapidly grew in popularity throughout central Europe, nevertheless; modernist blocks of workers' flats, such as the famous Karl Marx Hof in Vienna, sprang up,[23] while in the Soviet Union there was immense interest in modernist experiments. There was therefore a strong ideological association at this time between modernism and socialism.

The International Style might seem to prefigure a classless utopia, but it had less to say about relations between the sexes and today some women reject it as 'male'. It changed the shape of the house and everything in it without actually challenging the functions of the domestic unit. In the United States a few women architects in the 1920s were designing labour-saving or even 'kitchenless homes'. In Hollywood, Irving Gill built the Dodge House, a beautiful modernist structure which contained a central vacuum-cleaning system with hose outlets in the skirtings. (It was demolished in the 1960s.[24]) Also in California, Alice Constance Austin constructed a utopian plan for a 'socialist feminist city'. Houses would be provided with built-in furniture to eliminate dusting and sweeping, and she imagined an underground residential delivery service of cooked foods for the whole town. The architect Rudolph Schyndler built a 'co-operative dwelling' for himself and his wife, Pauline Gibling (a former Hull House resident) and their friends Clyde and Marion Chase. Cooperation was limited, however: all four individuals had private studios, but those of the women were situated next to the kitchen, connecting it with the entrance halls, so that the only indoor circulation was through the women's 'private' studio spaces.[25]

No such experiments for living were envisaged by the Bauhaus. On the other hand, the School designed a prototype house, and one of the students, Marcel Breuer, devised for it a revolutionary functional kitchen, inventing the concept of wall cupboards and floor cupboards separated by a continuous work surface – a labour- and space-saving plan we have come to take for granted in kitchens today. Yet there seems to have been little criticism in the Bauhaus of the traditional division of labour within households along male/female lines. Although women designers worked at the Bauhaus, in theory equal to the men and free to specialise as they wished, they tended to gravitate to the textiles department, traditionally a women's field.[26]

Yet the efficient house as a 'machine for living' was in women's interests, and in fact interested women designers and architects between the wars. In Britain, for example, women architects were guided towards the design of houses. This was partly because domestic design appeared to offer male architects few rewards in terms of money or prestige, and partly because it was stereotyped as a 'suitable' area for women, in line with their 'natural' domestic interests. There evolved a tradition of modernist 'social' architecture, with holiday camps and nurseries, many designed by women.[27]

Another prominent pioneer of modernism in architecture was Le Corbusier. Le Corbusier rejected equally the Garden City, the suburb and the actually existing metropolis. Paris, with its '*îlots insalubres*' (unsanitary districts) and lack of overall plan, seemed to him to be in danger of imminent disintegration, a decay he described in the medical terms that were popular with many reformers at this time, and he wanted large areas of the historic centre of Paris to be flattened in order to make way for modern skyscrapers; these would contain the administrative life of the nation.

In the 1920s and 1930s Le Corbusier developed his plan for the Radiant City, a vision even more utopian than that of Edward Bellamy or William Morris. Le Corbusier argued that the most serious problems of twentieth-century urban living were due to the mismatch between modern technology and its location in pre-machine-age cities, which had been designed for life and transport before the automobile had been invented. In *The Radiant City* he described the horrors of commuter living from the point of view of his secretary, who told him that 'all the trains are packed solid, morning, noon and night. And sometimes the men aren't too pleasant, we're all squashed together like in the subway and you have to look out!'[28]

Le Corbusier had thought that life was cheerful, bright and amusing for 'these little Paris birds, so trim, with their heads in the air and their chic, miraculously made out of nothing'. Now he realised that they suffered 'the martyrdom of suburbanites. And something else again: the terrible solitude in the crowd of that vast urban agglomeration.'

Le Corbusier's plans envisaged a complete revolution in everyday life. He called for the elimination of unnecessarily long hours of work, denounced suburban living and commuting, and equally the disease-ridden slums, lacking trees, fresh air and sunlight. He solved the travel problem and problems of overcrowding at one stroke by designing tower blocks surrounded by parkland. These were not to be the isolated blocks with which we have become familiar on municipal housing estates; a series of towers would house a whole city. Workplaces, offices and shops would be situated on the first six floors of the buildings to minimise the time taken to get to work, and the working day could be cut to five hours. The separation of the pedestrian and the automobile was to be complete. Le Corbusier wanted to 'destroy the corridor street', and replace it with pedestrian walkways completely separated from motorways, loopways and roundabouts, which would siphon traffic safely away.

The parkland would be used for the sports and physical recreation Le Corbusier considered essential for health. (Siegfried Kracauer took exactly the opposite view of the cult of sport and physique. For him it was yet another example of the standardisation of mass society.[29])

Functional interiors would necessitate the abolition of the stuffy knicknacks of the bourgeois home: 'Home life today is being paralysed by the deplorable notion that we must have furniture. This notion should be rooted out and replaced by that of *equipment*.'[30] Le Corbusier deliberately emphasised the way in which collectivity and individuality would harmonise in this new form of living space: the counterpart to the extensive public services was the privacy of family life.

The communal restaurants and/or prepared food sent to individual homes, and the other facilities, including play areas and nurseries, were not intended to do away with the woman's domestic role. Nurseries would diminish the level of domestic drudgery (a five-hour working day was to be the norm for women as well as for men), but their main role was to ensure eugenic standards of childcare – 'scientific child rearing'. Le Corbusier objected to the fact that modern life had 'made woman a worker too and uprooted her from her former position at the centre of home and family life'. The correct solution was to return women to the home, since 'the result would be less industrial unemployment'. Le Corbusier, in fact, eulogised nature and a system of dualities in which male and female differences corresponded to other natural and eternal forms of difference – man equals sunlight, woman water. His city, seemingly so futuristic, therefore was built on the most conservative philosophical foundations.

Moreover, although for Le Corbusier, as for the Bauhaus, modernism in design appeared to signify the coming of a egalitarian society, his ideas were supremely elitist, and his utopia would have been administered by a small group of planners who were 'above politics'. He was always casting about for a government that would finance his grandiose schemes, and he was willing to flirt both with socialism and with fascism if they would support him. He undertook experimental designs in the USSR in the 1920s. (Sound-proofing problems plagued a Moscow apartment block he designed, as a result of which some of his Soviet colleagues dismissed his ideas as part of an H.G. Wells fantasy world.[31]) For a short period in the 1930s he hoped that Mussolini would make him the architect of the New Italy.

Architecture played an important role in the USSR, in Nazi Germany and in Mussolini's Italy, as the expression of their shared belief in the importance of the state. Both modernism and Neo-classical styles seemed fit to represent the grandeur of the socialist or fascist state – although as Albert Speer, the architect of Nazi Berlin, noticed, Neo-classicism was characteristic of new public buildings in American and western European cities as well.[32]

In the Soviet Union in the 1920s planners attempted not merely to meet the severe housing shortages, but to devise the ideal socialist living space. There had long been a tradition under the Tsars of a form of town planning that took account of a perceived need for surveillance and control. St Petersburg had been built in the eighteenth century as a spectacular public monument, rationally designed and segregated. In the second half of the nineteenth century, Russia was extending its grip on Turkestan, and building colonial cities abutting on the old Islamic cities such as Bukhara and Kazakhstan. The traditional design of these cities, with bazaars, mosques and residential quarters with a cellular structure and homes built round courtyards, gradually ceded to a European model.[33]

In the early twentieth century both Garden City and City Beautiful philosophies were popular in Russia. After the 1917 Revolution, artists and architects dedicated themselves to the vision of building the 'new society'. Established styles of building, whether Neo-classical, Renaissance or Gothic, seemed doomed relics of the oppressive society that had been overthrown, and there was therefore a strong theoretical commitment to modernism. Despite the hardships of the early years, and the backwardness of the country to which socialist revolution had come, in a sense unexpectedly, planners and architects in the 1920s were striving towards wholly new forms of existence, which rejected alike the traditional patriarchal family and, in many cases, the traditional city as well. There were plans, many of which were never executed, for communal living arrangements, factories, arts centres and collective farms.[34]

What form the Soviet city should take was hotly debated. There were de-urbanists, who proposed to abolish the 'contradiction' between town and country by distributing the population evenly all over the country. Urbanists devised a variety of plans. Volgograd (Stalingrad) and Magnitogorsk were built as 'linear' cities, based on complete zoning. In the 1920s all such plans favoured communal living, in order to break down the nuclear family, and to abolish the differences between rural peasants and urban workers.[35] Under

Stalin, the cultural ferment of the 1920s was gradually crushed. From 1932 onwards modernist architecture began to be condemned as 'formalist' – decadent or western – and socialist realism became the only approved form. In practice this meant the return of a pompous City Beautiful style. Debates about the ideal form of cities and experiments in communal living ceased. Stalin decreed that the Soviet Union was now a socialist country, and therefore further innovations were unnecessary.

Soviet planners had nevertheless internalised the belief that a dwelling is a 'machine for living', and this led to the view that it should be constructed along the lines of a factory, that houses could be mass-produced in the same way as cars, watches or cameras. This, unfortunately, was like saying that everyone in the socialist state should wear a uniform, and had disastrous results for the appearance and amenities of many central European cities.[36]

During Weimar, the rebuilding of Berlin was strongly influenced by modernism. The architects Ludwig Mies van der Rohe and Ludwig Hilberseimer described utopian cities. Hilberseimer in particular envisaged modern man as a hotel-dwelling nomad – the coming of socialism seemed to imply the abolition of domestic life altogether. Woman's function and position was never considered in these utopian visions.[37]

In Nazi Germany, the emphasis was on a newly designed Berlin as a public space that glorified the Nazi state. It was perhaps appropriate that Adolf Hitler should have chosen architecture as the highest expression of the Nazi ideology. He had originally wanted to be an architect, and part of his bitterness against Vienna arose from his failure to gain entry to the school of architecture there. At the same time he had been impressed by the elaborate architecture of the Ringstrasse.[38] After he came to power he chose Albert Speer as his architect – indeed, Speer was intended to be the Haussmann to Hitler's Napoleon:

> Hitler remembered everything about the Ringstrasse, and wanted the new Berlin to surpass both it and Haussmann's Paris. For years he had kept sketches he had made of the monumental buildings he planned to erect along a magnificent wide tree-planted avenue running through the centre of Berlin. He regarded Haussmann as the greatest city planner in history, but hoped that I would surpass him.[39]

Hitler and Speer designed plans for a whole new Berlin, most of which was never built. The Chancellery, which was completed, was destroyed in 1945.

Speer's Berlin would have been an extreme expression of the city as work of art and as the glorification of authority. Speer himself concluded in retrospect that it would have been 'stamped by monumental rigidity'.[40] The central vista in Hitler's redesigned Berlin was to have been crowned with an enormous domed hall. Speer likened it to a building designed during the French Revolution for the glorification of the Goddess of Reason. If Speer had succeeded in building the Nazi version of the City Beautiful in Berlin it would surely have been a nightmare of order, its aim the repression by an irrational political regime of all the uncontrolled impulses released under Weimar – inflation, unemployment, erotic experimentation. In Nazi Berlin neither women nor men, neither heterosexuals nor homosexuals, were intended to have access to any zones of freedom. This was the logical conclusion of the city seen not as a space for human congregation, but as a frozen, deathly, political work of art. In practice this vision was never fulfilled – even lesbians and gay men managed to maintain some form of illicit social scene during the Third Reich,[41] and of course the attempt to impose perfect order led in practice to cruelties infinitely worse than anything witnessed by Dickens or Edwin Chadwick. The 'real' Nazi city was the Warsaw ghetto – or even Auschwitz: orderliness run mad in the pursuit of extermination.

The vision of a fascist City Beautiful was the opposite of the frightening fluidity of sensation and experience that writers such as Kafka and Freud had explored. It was as if both the mass-production 'socialist' cities of concrete and glass and the monumental work of art imagined by Hitler and Speer were formed, however unconsciously, in response to the 'uncanniness', the cacophony, of the twentieth-century modernist city. The city experience fractured and threatened human subjectivity; somehow the towers of concrete, glass and steel were to reimpose control, community and order.

7

The Lost Metropolis

The Dwellers in a slum area are almost a separate race of people, with different values, aspirations and ways of living . . . Most people who live in slums have no views on their environment at all . . .

When we are dealing with people who have no initiative or civic pride, the task, surely, is to break up such groupings, even though the people seem to be satisfied with their miserable environment and seem to enjoy an extrovert social life in their own locality.
Wilfred Burns, *New Towns for Old: The Techniques of Urban Renewal* (1963)

Town planning, as it evolved in the twentieth century, often presented itself as a solution to both the social and the physical disorders of the city, but the success of the town-planning movement was a defeat for cities as spontaneously growing and evolving constructs in which there could be diversity and richness of life. Like the Victorian philanthropists they so despised, the twentieth-century planners displaced the general problem of poverty – ultimately of social and economic inequality – on to housing and urban chaos, believing that scientific planning would not only replace the slums but would also purge the disorderly aspects of working-class life, such as gambling, street entertainments, prostitution and unlicensed street trading. Gone for ever would be the wide boys and good-time girls, the foulmouthed viragos and criminal gangs, replaced by a new race of symmetrical families and solid citizens. Strict zoning of use (residential, industrial, commercial) and, particularly in Britain, an obsession with low-density housing, were to bring about this final solution to the 'problem' of the great city.

Town planning after 1945 did not arise in a vacuum, however. It had its roots in earlier efforts, dating from the turn of the century, to transform cities into utopias.

While the modernism of central Europe imagined an architecture suited to the 'machine age', many American and British reformers and planners turned their backs on the future. They were convinced that the answer to the chaos of urban life was to reduce the size and density of cities and somehow to restore the relationship of city dwellers to the countryside. The metropolis must be replaced by a kind of monumental village: the garden city.

In Britain the model town of Saltaire had been followed by other experiments. Two of the most influential were Bournville, founded by the Cadbury family on the outskirts of Birmingham in 1879; and Port Sunlight, Liverpool, built by William Hesketh Lever (later the first Lord Leverhulme) at his Merseyside soap factory in 1888. There were also smaller philanthropic experiments, such as the Shaftesbury Estate in Battersea. Like Octavia Hill's model housing schemes, these were advanced as solutions to slum life, but the houses at Bournville were intended for '"a superior class of quiet and respectable tenant"',[1] and most of the schemes depended on rents that were too high for all but the most well off sections of the working class.

The early Victorian suburb had been part of the increasing separation of the classes, but at a later date new middle-class suburbs were built in emulation of the workers' model villages. The developer of Bedford Park in Turnham Green, west London, begun in 1876, 'proposed to supply for the middle classes that which the Shaftesbury Park Estate had partially done for the labouring classes'.[2] The design of Bedford Park was also influenced by *Hygeia*, Benjamin Ward Richardson's utopia; the houses were built, rather unusually for the time, without basements.

One of the most influential town-planning pioneers of the early twentieth century was Patrick Geddes. Originally trained as a biologist, he was committed to an emphasis on sexual difference, since 'what was decided among the prehistoric Protozoa cannot be annulled by Act of Parliament',[3] but although the differences he perceived have today become clichés of conservative thought – males are active, females passive, men are brainier but women kinder – he was sympathetic to the emancipation of women, since he believed that 'feminine qualities' should have more influence in the world of men.[4] It was partly because he believed that it was essential to harmonise and reconcile masculine and feminine qualities in the environment that he sympathised with the garden-city ideal being developed and popularised by Ebenezer Howard.

Inspired by Bellamy's *Looking Backwards*, Ebenezer Howard published *Tomorrow: A Peaceful Path to Real Reform* in 1898. Howard was not an outright anti-urbanist – he praised the civic virtues and the cultural benefits of cities – but he rejected the extremes and intensity of the huge metropolis, and believed that cities should never grow beyond a certain size. They must be radically separated from yet organically linked to the countryside, and within them different urban functions must also be kept apart. Garden cities were intended to be both more orderly and more aesthetic than the 'teeming metropolis'. Garden cities never teemed.

Central to Howard's garden city was male/female difference,

which became a metaphor in his plan for the reconciliation of town and country:

> Human society and the beauty of nature were meant to be enjoyed together . . . As man and woman by their varied gifts and faculties supplement each other, so should town and country. The town is the symbol of society . . . of science, art, culture, religion . . . The country is the symbol of God's love and care for man . . . We are fed by it, clothed by it, and by it we are warmed and sheltered. On its bosom we rest . . . Town and country must be married.[5]

With the help of Lever and Cadbury, Howard had raised enough funds by 1902 to purchase a site for the first garden city: Letchworth. The architects chosen to design Letchworth were Barry Parker and Raymond Unwin. They had been influenced by William Morris and the Arts and Crafts movement, and sought in their designs to re-create the organic, picturesque qualities of the medieval village. The idea of the stable – and patriarchal – village community suited the views of Cadbury and Lever, too.[6]

At Letchworth, Parker and Unwin attempted to create a harmonious community by dint of providing different kinds of dwelling: single villas for middle-class residents; and workers' cottages grouped round central courtyards or quadrangles with a shared lawn. There were even two small, experimental schemes for cooperative living with communal dining rooms and laundry.[7]

As at Bournville, the workers' cottages at Letchworth were rented exclusively by artisans and skilled workers. When the printing and light engineering plants began to fill the industrial park, the unskilled bicycled to work from lodgings beyond the agricultural belt that surrounded the new town.

In any case, it was far from clear that the ordinary industrial worker wanted to live in rural surroundings. *The Garden City*, journal of the Garden City movement, undertook a survey in 1909, which revealed considerable lack of enthusiasm. One newly established firm reported that its workers were merely 'grumbling less' about the lack of urban amenities than they had twelve months previously.[8]

Letchworth became a haven for radicals and bohemians in its early years. (The same had been true to a lesser extent of Bedford Park.) In the 1950s, the reminiscences by long-standing or former inhabitants often mentioned vegetarians, dress reformers and eccentrics. Although this may have been because such individuals were unusual, and therefore stood out, rather than because they were the norm, Letchworth in its early years certainly had a reputation for attracting cranks and aesthetes. But as Frederic Osborn, a life-long promoter of the garden city ideal, pointed out, 'looking back we can see now that the eccentricities of this Letchworth circle were mostly fashions in advance of their stiff and hidebound time'.[9]

Independent women seem to have found Letchworth a congenial place in which to live in its early years. Ethel Henderson, who arrived in 1905 and spent her whole life there, believed that the 'alternative' interests of the community made for equality between the sexes. She conceded that:

> Of course we were looked on as cranks . . . I suppose we were cranks, but I think we were very nice ones . . . Bare legs and sandals for both men and women soon became quite common-place [most unusual in 1905] . . . We led the way in many things. Vegetarianism was still young enough to cause great amusement.[10]

Women played an important social role in bringing people together. Mrs Barry Parker, for example, formed a group of progressive educationalists who opened a school in the town. Some women even started independent small businesses. Isabelle Linnell first became interested in the garden city when she heard a talk on Ebenezer Howard's ideas at a 'drawing-room meeting' in 1903:

> In 1904 my friend Miss Marguerite Borisson and I cycled down from London to view the estate. The Borisson family took up residence . . . as soon as a house could be built for them . . . Miss Borisson spent much time teaching languages at the adult education settlement. In 1908 I rented a small shop for the sale of leadless glaze crockery . . . Three years later I moved into larger premises.[11]

Hampstead Garden Suburb, founded on garden city principles in 1907, also attracted women of progressive views. Henrietta Barnett was one of its founders, and hoped that it would bring about the much longed for reconciliation between classes. Here too, bohemians were to be found, but radical bohemianism in these projects for rational living was of the worthy rather than the Parisian dissipated kind, and Letchworth and Hampstead were, like Saltaire, 'dry'.

One woman remembered afterwards that she had been:

> full of sympathy for and interest in the ideals of Bournville and Port Sunlight, Letchworth Garden City and the Hampstead Garden Suburb . . .
> Sharing the privileges, opportunities and responsibilities of a

composite community thrilled me from the first. I was born and bred in a Sussex village and had lived in a flat in Westminster. The suburb seemed to me to have most of the advantages of both. Entertainments and social contacts were at one's door, Groups . . . studied, discussed, organised, rehearsed and did propaganda for everything that made life rich and interesting. Above all, there were space, trees, flowers and privacy for all.[12]

Letchworth and the second garden city, Welwyn, were concrete embodiments of the new ideas about town planning and urban living. While claiming to incorporate all that was best of the city, their ideology was essentially anti-urban. After the First World War, at a time of political unrest, country life was even invested with counter-revolutionary properties: the British workman could spend his evenings doing healthy digging and gardening, instead of repairing to the pub or attending seditious political meetings. The garden city was a sanitised utopia, with the obsessional, controlling perfectionism that characterised all utopias. The working classes were to be harmonised with and reconciled to the middle classes by becoming in effect a reduced copy of them.

Perhaps this would not have mattered had the ideas of Geddes, Parker and Unwin been confined to experiments for the more unconventional members of the middle class. In fact, the garden city plan, and the architectural style of Letchworth, were hugely influential, not just in Britain but internationally. The idea of the garden city became a dominant model of how all good cities should be.[13]

Raymond Unwin was a member of the Tudor Walters Committee set up in 1917 to investigate and make recommendations on the design of municipal housing. The Report of the Committee set new, much higher standards for the design and amenities of working-class homes to be built after the First World War. A women's sub-committee, set up in 1918, found, however, that the Committee did not always observe the wishes of the working-class people whose well-being was at issue, especially if they were women – those most concerned with living space. The women's sub-committee argued that women's working conditions in the home should be a primary consideration. They discovered that women would prefer the retention of the separate parlour, which, although used primarily on formal occasions, did also provide a separate space in which they could relax, but the Tudor Walters Committee preferred the single living room, as this achieved a light and airy domestic environment and a high standard of design more economically than the traditional dwelling with kitchen and parlour, and it was this ground plan that often prevailed. In fact, to have a separate parlour was an aspiration of the 'respectable working class', both men and women. Parker and Unwin had already met with opposition at Letchworth when they had attempted to introduce cottages without parlours: '"the workmen and their wives,"' reported *The Garden City*, '"do not take kindly to the innovation; they like the parlour and they mean to have it."'[14] The massive municipal estates, especially those built by the London County Council between the wars, owed much both to the garden city ideal and to the architectural style of Letchworth. They did provide better domestic working conditions for women, but were often remote from shops and other amenities, and were much less friendly than the inner-city streets from which most families had come.

In those slums, life was often violent – women as well as men engaging in fights and petty crime – and people were very poor. Partly because housing was so bad, the locals lived much more of their life in the street, finding their amusements, their friendships and a close collective identity there. The decanting of these populations to a more wholesome environment seemed a social and eugenic necessity to those who perceived them as an affront to bourgeois order.[15]

As part of the attempt to kill the culture of the slums, it was LCC policy to 'break up' communities when they were rehoused, so that the continuation of old friendships was unlikely, and there was only the family for support. On the new housing estates, life, as well as being utterly different, was particularly lonely for wives marooned in the eugenic culs-de-sac. Women rehoused to the Watling Estate, at Burnt Oak, near Edgware in outer London, for example, constantly complained, saying that the place was 'like a desert'. Left alone all day, women were compelled to make new contacts and help one another to some extent, but it was the men who created some kind of formal community life on this estate, since their wives were too overburdened with housework to play a significant part. A higher standard of housing involved families in the beginnings of a more 'consumerist' way of life, with 'luxuries' such as the wireless becoming part of rising expectations. Women were offered a new vision of comfort and family life, yet were increasingly imprisoned in the genteel interior, and the new consumerism also increased the amount of domestic work they had to do.[16]

In the years between the wars privately built suburbs were developed as pale copies of the garden city. There, in the 1930s, the skilled elite of the working class, and clerical and white-collar workers, were beginning to become owner occupiers. Their incomes were rising in real terms, and a semi-detached house could be purchased for as little as £500.

The lives of married suburban women, most of whom did not work, were restrained and isolated. As early as 1909 the campaigning writer C.F.G. Masterman had written that the women of suburbia 'with their single domestic servants . . . find time hangs rather heavy on their hands. But there are excursions to shopping centres in the West End, and pious sociabilities . . . and the interests of home.'[17]

Between the wars, servants were not always easy to find, and there was less sociability than there had been in the larger Victorian and Edwardian families. Private medicine and schooling, and 'keeping up with the Joneses', meant heavy financial responsibilities, so families were small, and an atmosphere of sexual and cultural abstinence prevailed.[18]

The ideal held up to these suburbanites was, by contrast, euphoric. Although the architectural ideal of garden city and suburb was traditional, the new lifestyle was to be based on modern technology, especially electricity, which was represented as almost the spirit of modern living. In the words of Patrick Geddes:

> The fairy godmother is coming . . . year by year now she stands waving her fairy electric wand as the herald of the new era, in the domestic labour and consequently life of woman, ready and waiting to free her from all the old elements of dirt and drudgery, and thus henceforth for good and all. Her future in the adequate neo-technic home, characterised by electricity and its labour saving, by hygiene and by art is thus as true princess, that is, lady commanding assured wealth, effective service, adequate leisure, and thus with no limit to her refine-ment and her influence. As soon as we please, then, we may begin to emancipate Cinderella, no longer depress her through slavery into charwoman or crone . . .
>
> In the incipient domestic order – electric, hygienic, eugenic – the drudging charwoman, the futile fine lady alike disappear, and woman at once elemental and evolved, vigorous yet refined, will reappear within her home, and be at once effective in the kitchen and inspiring in the hall.[19]

Male writers seem to have seen suburbia as an environment created by and for women. The home was woman's sphere, in which she exercised her choice. Writing in 1936, one planning expert described women as more conservative than men, but also 'more open to the appeal of small novelty: aesthetically she has few or none of the makings of a citizen'. The responsibility for the 'bad taste' found in the suburbs was therefore women's alone![20] In fact, new magazines appeared to promote the suburban aesthetic. *Good House-keeping*, for example, was aimed at this readership, and every issue featured illustrated articles about 'ideal' homes set in leafy glades, and ideas for the enhancement of the domestic interior – although the British *Good Housekeeping* in the 1920s also carried a perhaps surprising number of articles on issues such as employment and equal pay, some of them written by well-known feminists.

Suburbia had come to the United States as well, and brought similar problems to women there. As early as 1909 Grace Godwin in the American *Good Housekeeping* had observed that suburban life exiled wives to 'lonelyville': 'The busy men leave on early trains, and are at once plunged into the rush of their accustomed life among their usual associates', she wrote, but the young wife was left behind, 'standing behind the struggling young vines of her brand new piazza'.[21]

As in Britain, the ideal of the garden city rapidly prevailed. Converts to Ebenezer Howard's views, such as Lewis Mumford, dominated architectural and planning circles. (Mumford was in constant touch with Frederic Osborn, an enthusiastic disciple of Ebenezer Howard and the main British campaigner for the garden city.)

The best-known American garden-city project was Radburn, New Jersey. Radburn, which developed a – largely unjustified – reputation for 'communism' and 'socialism' in the 1930s, was perhaps most influential in its total separation of pedestrians and cars, and its siting of small housing neighbourhoods between the traffic arteries. It also had one of the first shopping centres to be equipped with off-street parking. It thus anticipated the shopping malls of recent years, although the intention was very different, as it was part of an overall plan for the city. In both these aspects it demonstrated the way in which the role of the automobile was already crucial in the design of cities – or at least in the way town planning was thought about and discussed.[22]

The devastation of the Second World War created new opportunities for town planning. Paradoxically, in central Europe, where modernism had been so influential, blitzed historic city centres were lovingly re-created and restored (although dreary housing estates often appeared on the outskirts). In Britain, by contrast, bombing was perceived as an opportunity to do away with the Victorian city altogether.

Architects and planners damned the 'Gradgrind' England of the Industrial Revolution as 'gaunt, grimy and forlorn', a dismal region, unplanned and centreless. Some even felt that the blitz had been 'providential' in clearing away so much of the nineteenth-century towns, which had been 'a mere multiplication of that object of

Victorian hate and fear – the workhouse: a hateful prison-workhouse, sordid, brutal, mean'.[23]

The British planners, however, not only hated the Victorian city; they also loathed 'suburban sprawl' and wished to protect the countryside. The garden city therefore seemed the perfect solution, and it was in Britain that the garden-city idea was most fully developed. After Ebenezer Howard's death in 1929, Frederic Osborn had continued to campaign for his ideas, and succeeded in making the garden city part of government planning after the Second World War.

The incoming Labour government planned a number of 'new towns' built on garden-city principles, surrounded by green belts to which the 'surplus millions' of the slums were to be decanted. Stevenage, Harlow, Milton Keynes and others in the south, Cumbernauld in Scotland and Peterlee in the north-east were some of these 'utopias on the ground'. In most of them the architecture favoured was low-rise, undistinguished Anglo-Scandinavian. Peterlee, a mining town, might have gone against this trend, for the architect commissioned to design it was Lubetkin, the distinguished Soviet modernist architect. (Best known for his penguin pool at the London Zoo, he designed a number of innovative buildings in Islington immediately after the war.) Vested interests and general conservatism (from the National Union of Mineworkers as well as from local government officials and others) made so many difficulties over Lubetkin's design for a high-rise miners' 'fortress' that Lubetkin eventually withdrew.[24]

Typical of the new thinking were Patrick Abercrombie's ambitious plans for Greater London. He fully subscribed to the garden-city ideal and regarded London as just an 'amorphous sprawl', containing 'vast areas of inchoate, incoherent housing'. He did like its disparate 'villages', and wished them preserved, but he planned for just over one million Londoners to be decanted to new towns, and, as he said, 'the choosing of sites for new communities is always an exhilarating side of the planner's work'. Whether it was quite so exhilarating for the Londoners who were to be moved was not so certain – there was a whiff of authoritarianism about his solution, which required 'the exercise of methods of social control tempered by insight and forethought . . . the anonymous slightly over one million people must be selected with as little restriction of their freedom as possible'.[25]

The 'new towns' were built on a neighbourhood plan, with the intention of creating localised community feeling. Shops and amenties were all in the centre of town, however, and transport was often poor. One woman resident who settled in Stevenage New Town in the early 1960s remembered how difficult it was to get about, especially with small children, unless you had a car. There was not much to do – only one crowded swimming pool, for example. Class divisions remained, with most of the middle-class families residing in the surrounding country villages. There was quite a lot of vandalism on the working-class estates, partly because the teenagers were so bored.

This mother with young children felt very tied to the house, and began to be depressed after about six months. There was no part-time work for women, and no nurseries for the under-fives, although a child-minding network existed. Only coffee mornings relieved the boredom. There were few entertainments and no feel of history about the place either. Nor were there any old people, for the town was populated almost exclusively by young, white, working-class families. (The nearest sizeable black community was in Hitchin.) On the positive side, new residents were pleased to have clean modern homes and a safe, pedestrian-orientated environment for children.[26]

Yet it was just this way of posing the needs of children against a challenging existence for adults – or, rather, for adult women – that both reflected and reinforced the belief that metropolitan life was incompatible with the satisfactory reproduction of society. The old urban communities had many advantages for women. The close proximity of female kin had eased the problems of caring for the old and for children, and there had usually been better opportunities for at least some kind of work.[27] Now it seemed as if women of all classes must be domesticated and isolated if children were to be reared healthily. The consequences were not only detrimental to women – and perhaps, paradoxically, to children; they also destroyed the life of cities.

It was a great pity that politicians, planners and the many feminists who hoped for so much from the 1945 Labour government failed to capitalise on the experiences of wartime Britain, when many women and men had had to live in novel communal situations: in the armed forces, in evacuated government departments and other relocated offices, factories, schools and hospitals, and in hostels for industrial war workers. By the end of the war, the National Service Hostels Corporation was running approximately two hundred hostels all over Britain. One enthusiast for this form of collective living felt that it provided a needed alternative to the exclusiveness of the family unit. It appears, however, that in the mixed hostels (regarded as rather daring) many couples got engaged, and it was usual for women to do their boyfriends' washing – collective living apparently didn't challenge established gender roles.[28] It must also have been the case that when the war ended many looked forward to a return to 'normality'. The way in which government ministries, civil servants and social-welfare professionals promoted the return to 'traditional family life' nevertheless arose from patriarchalist fears – women had become too free in wartime, and illegitimacy, divorce and venereal disease were the results.[29]

A popular Australian novel of the period, *Come in Spinner*, by Dymphna Cusack and Florence James, expressed the enormous ambivalence of the period in relation to urban life. Published in 1951, it is in many respects a feminist novel. Its heroines are three women who work in the beauty salon of a smart Sydney hotel. The urgent raw vitality of Sydney, with its American GIs and sailors from all over the world, its luxury and poverty, forms the background to the temptations, opportunities and dangers of city life for women. One woman succumbs to the lure of a rich but loveless marriage, so that she keeps the life of luxury – the races, restaurants and jewellery – at the cost of renouncing love. The young sister of another is lured into prostitution. A third woman goes back to the country and her family, and this outcome is symbolically linked to the love of a passionate and masculine man. Although, therefore, the excitement and pleasure of city living are recognised, and indeed exploited to the full, the moral message is of the city as dangerous to women, not only in an obvious sense, but as hostile to women's 'deepest' needs – for the love of a good man, and for children. Other Australian novels of the period concentrated more exclusively on working-class life in the big city. *Bobbin' Up* by Dorothy Hewett and *The Harp in the South* by Ruth Parkes celebrated the survival skills of women battling in a harsh environment, but were much less critical of urban life as such. Their heroines, like the real-life Rose Chernin in New York, seemed to love the city while acknowledging its bitterness and hardship.

The metropolis of the Second World War – New York in Christina Stead's *A Little Tea, a Little Chat*, for example – has often been described as a place of excitement as well as danger. Many have remembered even London during the blitz as convivial and exciting, although in Elizabeth Bowen's novel *The Heat of the Day* there is a sense of endurance, suffering and paranoia. Perhaps the ultimate portrait of a great city suffering the devastation of war (or, in this case, its aftermath) is the Carol Reed film *The Third Man*, in which divided, devasted Vienna mirrors the anguish of the romantic, tragic heroine, who needs, but refuses, the protection of the two men who could help her. She opts instead for the criminal who has caused children to die by his blackmarket peddling in adulterated penicillin, and whose own life ends in the sewers. At one level, the film is a bleak portrait of a war-torn city, but its gender politics takes it beyond this, and with its use of the underground 'cesspool city' motif it returns to the theme of the evil city inhabited by lawless men and destructive to women and children.

The Third Man marked a transition. The cultural climate changed very swiftly after the end of the war, and by the late 1940s the independent woman on her own in the big city was likely to be portrayed in a more negative light than had been the case either before or during the war. Of course, the majority of women who came to the great cities of the western world did so not as radical bohemians, but simply in order to earn a living. That life could be lonely, and even desperate. Hilda Lawrence's New York thriller *Death of a Doll*, published in 1947, shed a paranoid light on the life of the 'single girl' in a hostel for women working in department stores, the telephone company and other hard, rather unrewarding jobs. The lesbian owners of the hostel try to make it homely, but the place as described is stuffy, claustrophobic, infantilising; significantly, the murderer, creepily stalking through the corridors, turns out to be one of the lesbians.[30]

The association of urban life with female sterility and death was not confined to popular culture. Lewis Mumford clearly believed that women could and should be more adequately confined in the new garden cities. In an article on the Abercrombie plan, he revealed the anxieties that led after 1945 to the renewed ideology of the family:

> The sterility of the big city is a purposeful sterility: it is due to the essential failure of this civilisation to arrange the goods of life in a rational order, and to put biological and social purposes above those mechanical and financial achievements – with their complementary 'diversions' – which have become emblems of megalopolitan success. The mischief is not due solely to the physical ills produced by a wasteful and over complicated urban routine: it is due to a growing concern for the inessential, the trivial, the glamorously empty, which Paul of Tarsus found, in a similar period of decay, among the Corinthians and Athenians.[31]

Fortunately (from his point of view), he was able to report that among his most brilliant and promising female students in the United States he had observed 'a radical change in attitude from their mothers' generation: babies and family life have become central again, and the attractions of a professional career . . . have become secondary. If that change has been taking place in England it will set the stage for a positive population policy.'

In the suburb or 'new town', women were to be the guardians of taste. As early as 1948, the influential educationalist John Newsom hailed the housewife as the new consumer. She needed, however, to be educated 'to the point where she rejects the functionally futile and aesthetically inept and demands what is fitting and beautiful . . . Woman as purchaser holds the future standard of living of this country in her hands.' The 'good taste' that Newsom wanted to see was Bauhaus functionalism. He shuddered at cottage teapots and fussy cretonnes.[32]

In the 1950s there seems to have been a partially suppressed struggle between the planners and officials in the British 'new towns' and the people, especially the women, who actually lived in the houses. The houses were often influenced by modernist ideals, and many of them were open-plan. Bureaucrats tried to ensure that the furnishing of the interiors matched the architecture; and designers deplored the way in which housewives and DIY husbands 'spoilt' their homes by dividing up the 'spacious' living areas, and introducing three-piece suites and 'awful' patterned wallpapers. Net curtains were another bone of contention; they gave privacy, but were out of tune with the clean lines of some of the housing designs.[33]

Feminists have recently condemned this aesthetic authoritarianism, and have defended the 'popular' taste of the housewives who came to the 'new towns' in the 1950s on the grounds that the elaborate interiors fulfilled a need for symbolic self-expression. They have argued that the housewife, who was the focus of so much attention, was patronised by conservatives and radicals alike. The former simply indulged their snobbery and sense of threat when complaining about the 'wealth' of those who lived on housing estates (they actually dared to buy cars!) and the vulgarity of their taste in wallpaper and carpets ('loud' colours and 'garish' patterns). To the radical professional middle classes the housewife was the ultimate 'consumer', seduced by 'meretricious' goods and 'phony' advertising; they seemed to feel that she was in turn seducing her husband away from the paths of a 'true' working-class way of life and consciousness.[34]

No doubt Bauhaus design was potentially elitist: although it claimed to be functional, it couldn't be mass-produced but relied on skilled craftsmanship; its rejection of ornament was too austere for many. 'Popular' styles, on the other hand, are not necessarily 'authentic'. In postwar Britain they were largely determined by the mass production and retailing of designs based on bourgeois taste of an earlier age. Like the mock-Tudor exteriors of the suburbs, the mass-market furniture design of the 1950s often reproduced the most conservative design. Producers and retailers might say that they were merely responding to consumer demand, but in practice the purchasers were offered nothing else at a price they could afford. Taste certainly is used to demarcate class boundaries, but that does not mean that there is anything inherently authoritarian about Bauhaus style, or that three-piece suites invariably represent the best solution to the furnishing of a living room.

What was depressing about the planning approach of the 1950s was not that planners liked functionalist design. It was their contempt for the residents of their housing estates, and their assumptions that a rigid sexual division of labour prevailed.

Even more seriously, the rationalistic utopia of the planners rested on a major inconsistency. Local authorities shouldered the burden of redeveloping the 'worst' areas of their cities and providing subsidised housing for ordinary citizens. Yet the right of private developers to reconstruct city centres with private capital was taken for granted. The property developer needed the local authority in order to obtain sites (cleared, for example, by means of compulsory purchase orders issued by the council, if necessary). In return, property developers provided jobs, shopping and entertainment. Yet they gave residents and users little say in what sort of environment was created, or in the uses to which the land from which they profited was put.[35] In addition, the zoning of cities into areas defined by use meant a segregated city. The city-centre shopping precinct was one result. Planners believed that pedestrian areas would create a safe and pleasant environment. Yet these 'precincts' depended on good public transport, which was not always available. They favoured the large chain-stores rather than small shops. Most of all, the 'cathedral close' concept did away with all the unexpected and *un*planned aspects of street life. At the same time, with supreme inconsistency, the planners aimed to create 'neighbourhoods' and 'communities' in the new residential areas they were building, in spite of the fact that they utterly rejected the spontaneous communities of the old working-class neighbourhoods they were pulling down.

In any case – quite apart from the impossibility of planning human waywardness out of existence – the development of 'new towns' and the redevelopment of existing ones did not stop the suburbs from spreading into the countryside, and in the 1950s the attack on suburbia rose to a peak. In Britain, architectural and planning style was the major focus, while in America, the social and psychological consequences of the new suburban lifestyle caused more anxiety.

In Britain, doubts about low rise and low densities crystallised dramatically in the special edition of the *Architectural Review*, *Outrage*, published in 1955. The editor, Ian Nairn, told his readers that, 'the outrage is that the whole land surface is being covered by the creeping mildew that already circumscribes all of our towns. This death by slow decay is called subtopia. Subtopia is the world of universal low-density mess', its atmosphere 'drifting like a gaseous pink marshmallow over the whole social scene'.[36]

Meanwhile in the United States sociologists and novelists described a man in a grey flannel suit, a conformist dragooned by the demands of his bureaucratic workplace, by the competitiveness of his neighbours in the suburbs, and by his domineering wife, into a lifestyle of compulsory 'togetherness' and frantic keeping up with the Joneses. At every level, from lower-middle-class suburbia to the wealthy 'exurbanite' colonies, the suburban way of life posed serious problems for women. In the latter, alcoholism and adultery hinted at the underlying alienation of a world in which ambitious, well-educated, intelligent women renounced (as no doubt Lewis Mumford would have approved) their own ambitions, to become instead 'superior drudges'.[37]

In France too the new suburbia came under attack. In her novel *Les petits enfants du siècle* Christiane Rochefort satirised the working-class monotony of high-rise flats on the periphery, where housing allocation was dependent on raising a *'famille nombreuse'*. Life was bounded by the washing machine and TV, paid for out of the large family allowances with which the state reinforced female domestic servitude. In Jean-Luc Godard's film *Two or Three Things I Know about Her*, made in 1967, bored housewives engage in amateur prostitution in order to augment their incomes.

With Betty Friedan's *The Feminine Mystique*, published in 1963, the critique of the suburbs became overtly feminist. She voiced the boredom of suburban wives, with their formless discontent, the 'problem without a name'. The opening chapter of the book draws a grim picture of the pointless lives of women in the suburbs, driven to changing the bedlinen twice a week and baking their own bread because they have so little 'real' purpose to their lives. The irony was that the super-efficiency of the mechanised ex-urbanite home, far from freeing women to broaden their lives and take up interesting work outside, had simply created more domestic toil. Suburban housewives were victims of an 'everyday life' in which their role was largely to consume commodities intended to symbolise happiness; in practice, the avalanche of things became cloying, suffocating them.[38]

This theme reappeared in the new genre of popular lesbian novels which flourished in the 1950s. The novel sequences of Valerie Taylor and Ann Bannon, in particular (reissued by Naiad Press in the 1980s), expressed the dislike many women seem to have felt for the men their husbands became in the rat race of American middle-class society, a society which, in the suburbs at least, religiously excluded sexual deviance or even single parenthood, not to mention political nonconformity. In these novels, the bohemias and gay subcultures of Chicago and Greenwich Village were posed as liberating alternatives.

By the late 1950s, housing projects in the US, council estates in Britain, and the 'HLM' housing in France (the initials stood for dwellings at moderate rent) were all turning to high-rise building. Tenants in public housing were subjected to cost-cutting experiments in modernist buildings that lacked the lift attendants, porters and social amenities which Le Corbusier, for example, had assumed when he designed his Radiant City.[39] Prefabricated building systems and expensive central heating, which tenants could not afford to run, led to damp, and to rapidly developing structural faults. Long, badly lit corridors and walkways, and windy, pointless open spaces were lonely and dangerous at night. Estates were often further out from the city centre, sometimes right on the outskirts, in which case they were served by neither shops nor transport. The classless utopia of which the modernist architects had dreamed had presupposed a new political order. In its absence, the new architecture merely replaced the dirty, crowded, lively industrial city with icily alienated environments: penitential housing estates and bleak business districts. As a result, modernism came to be equated both with the destruction of familiar streets and street life and with 'totalitarianism' and the 'big brother' state. The political thrust of this was to blame local government, usually for being too leftwing and interfering, although, in Britain at least, it was the Conservatives who continued to build public housing in the 1950s, but kept up numbers only by drastically cutting the cost, which in practice meant cutting standards.[40]

One of the most influential attacks on this kind of 'urban renewal' was Jane Jacobs's *The Death and Life of American Cities* (1961). She perceived that although Le Corbusier and the garden–city ideologues had believed themselves to be poles apart, both had destructively converged on the intimate urban fabric, preferring to replace it with totally planned space. Her critique allowed virtually no place for planners at all, but in her haste to condemn the urban wasteland they were creating, she also left out the effect produced on cities by unfettered capitalist development. Her polemic assumed that the alternative to City Hall was the continuation of things as they were, the spontaneous community of the neighbourhood with its rich class and ethnic variety and diversity of use. She celebrated the street life of Greenwich Village and other 'villages' in metropolitan centres – yet 'her' Greenwich Village of the late 1950s and early 1960s was itself a stage in the evolution of city-centre neighbourhoods whose charms had been discovered first by artists and bohemians, later by the professional classes, and which were ripe for further gentrification. The precondition for this process in Manhattan was the 'de-industrialisation' of New York in the 1950s.

Many of the old industrial buildings, often initially scheduled for demolition, were taken over by artists in the early 1960s, and so began the fashion for 'loft living'. This challenged the conformity and rigid division of sex roles found in the suburbs. Gays and women played an important role in the development of 'art as a way of life' in 1960s Manhattan. Andy Warhol's Factory is the best-known example of this process; the ambiguity of his work and that of his associates derived in part from the fusion of art and commodity, style and lifestyle, that was entailed. Art, conservation, preservation and gentrification were promoted by property developers to maintain control and increase profits. There was a close connection between capital accumulation and cultural consumption.[41]

Meanwhile, urban renewal and property development were actively destroying some of the old white working-class and lower-middle-class communities of greater New York. Robert Moses, the all-powerful utopian planner, drove expressways through the Bronx Jewish community, devastating the area: 'for ten years, through the late 1950s and early 1960s, the center of the Bronx was pounded and blasted and smashed . . . our ordinary nice neighborhood transformed into sublime, spectacular ruins'.[42]

A process similar to the gentrification of lower Manhattan occurred slightly later in the Marais district of Paris. Originally built in the seventeenth century as a quarter of luxury palaces, it had deteriorated by the mid twentieth century to a crumbling slum. It might well have been destroyed altogether in the early postwar years when the French enthusiasm for urban renewal was at its height. There was always opposition to this 'Americanisation' of Paris, however, and in the early 1970s conservation rather than skyscrapers became the fashion.

The historic Marais district now became a major focus of restoration, and this process meant the displacement of the traditional artisans and craftworkers who lived and worked there. This population was, on the whole, very resistant to moving. Fears they may have had of being unable ever to return were fully justified, since after the renovations the area developed into a high-rent, luxury sector, with prestige housing for the rich and new retail outlets not suitable for the former population of craftworkers.[43]

While a new elite was taking over areas such as SoHo and the white working and lower middle classes moved to the suburbs, more and more non-whites were moving into the old city centres of the United States. Racial polarisation was aided by poverty and by directly discriminatory measures in the suburbs, and blacks were trapped in the inner cities.[44]

Governmental concern crystallised in Daniel Moynihan's 1965 report on the issue. He blamed the 'matriarchal structure' of the black community. This, he argued, because 'it is so out of line with the rest of American society, seriously retards the progress of the group as a whole, and imposes a crushing burden on the Negro male'. He claimed that the 'weakness' of the black family structure was the principal source of most of the aberrant, inadequate, or anti-social behaviour that 'did not establish but now serves to perpetuate the cycle of poverty and deprivation'.[45] In other words, black *women* were blamed for the problems of the ghetto, when it might have been more appropriate to praise their strength in the face of unbelievable difficulties.

By the late 1960s parts of New York had become as desolate as a bombed city, where 'row after row of apartment houses . . . have sunk into decay. More than 500 buildings have been completely deserted. Whole blocks are silent; only the sounds of glass crunching underfoot and the gurgle of water from vandalised pipes echo through the burnt out hulks.'[46] Yet despite the rats, fires, vandals and muggings, some women were trying to organise rent strikes, and campaigning for the relocation to public housing of families displaced by yet more urban renewal.

In many cities the ghettoes rose up against the oppression of their lives in the mid 1960s. There was organised political action by militant groups, many of whom engaged their communities in struggles over housing, welfare and the conditions in the ghettoes. There were also riots, and these hastened the decline of the city centres. 'Riot Renaissance' was the cynical name for the architectural 'style' of the 1970s ghettoes – main streets boarded or bricked up and whole blocks burnt down, and it seemed as if the inner city might become 'just one great big poorhouse'.[47]

Riot-torn Watts, Newark and Cleveland seem finally to have become the image of the impossible metropolis in the 1960s and 1970s. By the 1970s it was as if a futurist nightmare had become the present. In Angela Carter's New York:

It was July and the city shimmered and stank . . . I was astonished to see so many beggars in the rank, disordered streets, where crones and drunkards disputed with the rats for possession of the choicest morsels of garbage . . . The skies were of strange, bright, artificial colours – acid yellow, a certain bitter orange that looked as if it would taste of metal, a dreadful, sharp, pale, mineral green . . .

Groups of proselytisers roamed the streets . . . The city was scribbled all over with graffiti in a hundred languages expressing a thousand griefs and lusts and furies and often I saw, in virulent dayglo red, the insignia of the angry women . . . and combat-suited blacks . . . mounted guard with machine guns at every door and window . . . of the university.[48]

By the late 1960s urban community groups were springing up in many cities across the world – groups of tenants, homeless squatters, home owners whose properties were threatened by traffic schemes and redevelopment – who were no longer prepared to see their communities bulldozed into oblivion, and were determined to halt the destruction and the decay. 'Take over the city' was the cry, and community action was an important part of a general political radicalism.

Militancy in great cities was not itself new. Giant cities had always been 'disproportionately proletarian', and issues such as transport and housing were more explosive in the metropolis than elsewhere. Both in Paris and in London, for example, the transport systems were strongholds of unions. The confrontation between tenant and landlord was also a basic feature of urban life.[49]

Women had traditionally always been involved in struggles over housing; they led rent strikes, organised childcare and were also involved in the provision of outings and entertainment and help in times of sickness or special poverty. In the movements of the 1960s and 1970s women were once again prominent. This was partly because more women than men lived in the inner city and mothers and the old were more imprisoned within their localities more than even unemployed men. Thus they were also more reliant than men on public housing and transport. 1977 American figures showed that the ratio of women to men in urban areas was 115:100 as against 108:100 in rural areas; but in the age group of those over 65 the ratio was 157:100.[50] Single-parent families (the vast majority of which are headed by women) were more common in the inner city than elsewhere, and in the inner city both the employment and the unemployment of women were higher, that is to say, women in cities were more likely to enter paid work, but also more likely to be 'officially' unemployed – on benefit of some kind, not 'housewives' supported by a man. Poverty had always attacked women disproportionately,[51] but in the United States it had traditionally been seen as a problem of minorities, in Britain as a problem of class. The rebirth of feminism meant that poverty was gradually acknowledged to be disproportionately a *women*'s problem. For inner-city women, childcare was an important issue, and in the 1970s centres of all kinds sprang up, becoming the focus for political action by women in most of the great cities of the world.

The grassroots struggles of the 1960s and 1970s made a number of advances and obtained real benefits for their constituencies. Although community action often failed to achieve its objectives, it could be argued that it did force public recognition of the many problems women (and blacks) face in the urban environment. Poverty and violence have increased rather than diminished since the late 1960s; on the other hand, as women in cities the world over have become increasingly involved both in paid work and in community struggles, they have not only voiced their grievances more loudly but have begun in some cases to be taken more seriously.

The lesbian and gay community was another urban group that made its presence visible through community action. San Francisco was the most developed 'gay city', but there were gay communities in many other large North American cities and in London, Paris, Amsterdam and Sydney.

Until the 1960s gays, even in San Francisco, were a beleaguered minority subject to constant harassment, but thereafter the San Francisco gay community developed its own street culture – bars, cafés, gay businesses and boutiques and gay housing sprang up around the nucleus of Castro Street. This was possible in part because the gay community was not poor. Many gay men in particular had professional jobs and disposable income. Because of this, an important part of the development of the community was the renovation of housing (often by collective households).[52] Despite the backlash of the 1980s, the lesbian and gay urban communities of many world cities continued to create a space for themselves, a space dependent on urban forms, and the unique chance, offered by the city, to escape from patriarchal social formations. Like black urban culture, lesbian and gay culture in the 1970s and 1980s testified to both the opportunities and the risks of city life.

The collective situation of women in cities is strongly determined by class, although virtually all urban women are vulnerable to a greater or lesser extent to the violence of city life. Poor and working-class women have struggled for a right to a decent life and basic amenities that women from wealthier sections of society have long enjoyed, and no one could deny that the pleasure of the city is most unevenly distributed among women, the dangers likewise. This should not blind us to the pernicious effect of the ideology that has sought to banish *all* women from urban space, and to lock them into an often stifling domestic privacy. That this attempt succeeded only partially does not exonerate those who promoted it from their share of blame for the disastrous effects the ideology of semi-rural domesticity has had on the built environment.

The way in which minority cultures have become more clearly defined in the twentieth century is an example of the ambiguous chemistry of urbanism mixed with prejudice. While women have been shifted away from urban space and *equated* with anti-urbanism, in an often subtle and indeed subliminal way, minority groups have twisted an advantage from being at the interface of urban freedom and ideological repression. Like the existence of bohemian sub-cultures (to which some blacks and gays were always drawn), their emergence was in part the result of prejudice and labelling. It was also the *reaction* to stereotyping; urban subcultures were part of a process of *self*-definition. Lesbians and gay men created communities or 'ghettoes' both for safety and for a sense of identity. Urban life provided the space in which subcultures could flourish and create their own identities, yet the more visible and confident they became, the more vulnerable that made them to surveillance and contain-ment. Ghettoes have usually felt comparatively safe within, yet have been easy to attack from without. This was true for the Jews in Warsaw and in Whitechapel. There was strength in numbers, but at the same time the fascists knew where they were and converged on their stronghold. Self-exposure is double-edged. Marginal groups can exist more autonomously in the city than elsewhere, yet their claim to 'take over the city' is always questioned, always challenged. For lesbians and gay men, urban life has almost seemed to be a condition of their social existence – the 'gay identity' appears to be a creation of the urban scene. There is no identity without visibility, and the city spectacle encourages self-definition in its most theatrical forms. The irony – or tragedy – is that the act of self-affirmation and of community affirmation is ever in danger of arousing the paranoia of the authoritarian powerbrokers of urban life. In turn, however, the cultures created by urban blacks and lesbians and gays depend for their vibrancy on precisely this bitter paradox.

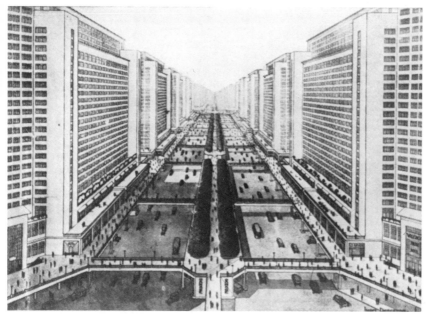

Le Corbusier's 'Radiant City' 'reproduced as a memory flicker' on the machines in the amusement arcade (see Ch. 2)
Courtesy Royal Institute of British Architecture

A SLIGHT MISTAKE,
CONSEQUENT ON THE FASHIONABLE RAGE FOR TARTANS.

Tipsy Recruit. "HULLO, CUMRAD! WHA' RESGH'MENT DO YOU B'LONG TO?"

A DISCUSSION.

Mrs. Brown (at the left of the Picture) THINKS IT A GREAT SHAME THAT A LADY CANNOT WALK BY HERSELF IN LONDON WITHOUT BEING FOLLOWED, ACCOSTED, AND OTHERWISE ANNOYED BY MEN. SUCH, AT LEAST, IS *HER* EXPERIENCE.
Mrs. Jones (with the feathers in her hat) IS OF THE SAME OPINION. *SHE* NEVER STIRS OUT ALONE—HER HUSBAND WOULD NEVER ALLOW SUCH A THING. BUT, EVEN THEN, MEN WILL STARE IN THE MOST OFFENSIVE MANNER.
Mrs. Robinson (in the middle) IS MUCH SURPRISED TO HEAR THIS. ALTHOUGH IN THE CONSTANT HABIT OF WALKING BY HERSELF, SHE HAS NEVER YET MET WITH ANY ANNOYANCE OF THE KIND MRS. B. AND MRS. J. HAVE DESCRIBED.

These cartoons from *Punch* in 1870 illustrate the dangers – imagined or real – for 'ladies' when exposed to the rough and tumble of the city street. The drunken Scotsman mistakes the young woman for a fellow soldier; alternatively the cartoonist implies that women have only their own vanity to blame if men annoy them in the public thoroughfare (see Ch. 3)
Courtesy *Punch*

Statues of women cast as representations of abstract entities, in this case the continents of the world (these two symbolise South America and Asia). Today they are displayed outside the Musée D'Orsay, Paris (see Ch. 4)
Photograph by the author

Colette in drag (see Ch. 4)
Courtesy Roger Viollet

Life on the streets: 'A Street Row in East London', drawn by Phil May in 1898 (see Ch. 3 and 7) Courtesy *Illustrated London News*

. . . or in the Garden City: 'The Garden Citizens of the Future', a 1909 Letchworth painting by Horace Taylor (see Ch. 7) Courtesy First Garden City Heritage Museum

Smartly dressed Black women in Harlem in the 1920s (see Ch. 5) Courtesy New York City Library

Doomed love in postwar Vienna: Alida Valli and Joseph Cotton in Carol Reed's
The Third Man (see Ch. 6)
Courtesy Weintraub Entertainments

A Gorbals pavement conversation in the late 1960s (see Ch. 9)
Courtesy W. Morton Gillespie

'Dwellings of the Poor in Bethnal Green' – Women queuing for water at a standpipe in the London slums in 1863 (see Ch. 3) From *Illustrated Times*

Woman fetching water in Rio de Janeiro in the 1970s (see Ch. 8) Courtesy Mark Edwards

The Postmodern City: Princes Square
shopping arcade, Glasgow, 1989
(see Ch. 9)
Photograph by the author

The Postmodern City: The 'Cascades',
Docklands, seen through the cranes of
'the biggest building site in Europe'
(see Ch. 9)
Photograph by the author

The Postmodern City: woman living in a
cardboard box on London's South Bank
Courtesy Mark Edwards

8

World Cities

The train swept in . . . From the third class coaches there emerged first the experienced Nairobi wives, hefty women with calf-length skirts and aggressively set sleeves, passing tin and wooden suitcases through windows, bunches of green bananas, squawky hens and passive children. Next . . . came the men . . . After them the rearguard, the mothers-in-law and the young brides, not very pushing . . .

At last Paulina came into sight, clutching a triangular bundle . . . She was wearing a faded blue cotton dress and a white headscarf. Her rubber shoes were scuffed and brown . . . He could see that . . . the journey had frightened her . . .

The front of the station was full of taxis and cars meeting trains. People thronged together. Ahead of them lay a street of tall buildings and rushing traffic. She supposed it was normal for big cities to be like this, but . . . she wanted to leap away from the kerb each time a car came close and felt, being new and strange, that she must be the one to give way whenever she came face to face with someone hurrying in the opposite direction.

Marjorie Oludhe Macgoye, *Coming to Birth* (1964)

When in the nineteenth and early twentieth centuries writers and planners viewed urban growth with anxiety, feeling that these vast conurbations had run out of control, the city they discussed was the western city. Theoretical writings usually either defined the city in such a way as to exclude all but western cities, or simply did not take non-western cities into account. The assumptions of the town-planning movement, which grew out of this anxiety, were subsequently applied to the fast-growing cities of the 'third world', to their great detriment.*

Since the Second World War, new forms of colonialism and capitalism have contributed to the creation of huge population centres in the non-western world. Between 1950 and 1970 the population of São Paulo grew from just under two and a half million to eight and a half million; that of Delhi from 1,737,000 to 3,100,000; while that of Lagos grew from 267,000 in 1952 to between two and a half and three million by 1980.[1] Thus the experience of urbanisation in nineteenth-century Europe and America is being repeated in Latin America, South-East Asia and Africa.

* The term 'third world' is used as a familiar, although unsatisfactory, shorthand.

At least two-thirds of this growth has been due to the migration of rural peasants to the city. Sometimes migrants travel from one country to another. Workers from Mozambique and Malawi find work in South Africa, for example. As in the early years of the Industrial Revolution in Europe, rural migrants are often attracted to the cities by the promise of work. Numbers in the present-day world city are also swelled by those who have been pushed off the land by changes in farming patterns and land development, as was also to some extent the case in pre-Victorian Britain. Patterns vary from one country and one continent to another; in tropical Africa, the majority of town dwellers retain strong links with their rural family of origin and often continue to farm in the countryside.

It has been usual to take the view that the cities of the third world are becoming, at least superficially, more like western cities, but that in some more fundamental way urbanisation in the third world is actually different from that both of the west and of the Soviet Union and eastern Europe. Such a view is itself ethnocentric and oversimplified. For one thing it ignores the differences among various third-world countries and their cities. In Africa and South Asia, for example, the level of urbanisation is much lower than in Latin America – although Africans are now migrating to the cities at a faster rate than are the populations of Latin America. It is also ahistorical to lump all third-world cities together, given that most Latin American cities were founded in the sixteenth century and are therefore much older than the majority of African, or indeed North American cities, while many cities of the Middle East are older still.[2]

Another difference is that in many Latin American and Middle Eastern countries power in the cities lies with long-established local elite families, part of a rigid class structure. By contrast, the African urban elite have maintained close links with rural-based extended families, many members of which remain very poor. In African cities there is usually no one dominant language, and this too makes for a difference from Latin America, where Portuguese or Spanish is universal.[3]

In Latin America urbanisation has, as in the west, gone in tandem with industrialisation. In Africa 'urbanisation without industrialisation' has been more usual – although of course there is some industrialisation as well.

At issue in the whole debate about urbanisation in the third world is an underlying presumption that urbanisation must always follow the same path – that taken historically by western cities in the industrial period. This may not be so for Africa; a form of urbanisation based on manufacturing industry may be a pattern that will no longer apply by the time full industrialisation reaches Africa – if it does.[4]

Despite the changing form of colonialism, the west has not lost interest in former dependencies and new 'spheres of influence'. On the contrary, research on a huge scale has been undertaken into the problems of the new world mega-cities. Sometimes this research is financed by the countries concerned, but often by United Nations, American, or other global interests. As a result, there is today a mass of information about non-western cities, but this knowledge is itself used as an instrument of power and domination. Researchers and planners have extended their former concern for the moral, physical and eugenic well-being of the inhabitants of their own cities, and have often treated third-world population centres as caricatures of the 'parent' cities of the west – as reproducing their worst problems in grotesquely exaggerated form. 'Detached observers' have attempted to investigate and describe the life of the 'teeming' cities, not in order to enter into the experience of urban life – as the *flâneur* of nineteenth-century Paris or twentieth-century São Paulo had done – but in order to change and reform. Plans for third-world cities have been stamped, like those of the nineteenth century, with the utopianism of those who aim to do away with poverty and crime while preserving capitalist interests.

Yet the history of urbanism and planning in Europe and the United States has continued largely to overlook the way in which the economies of countries that were being colonised in the nineteenth and twentieth centuries contributed to the urbanisation of the west. The histories of Bournville and Port Sunlight do not refer to the source of the cocoa that supported Cadbury's profits or the coconut oil that went into the making of Lever's soaps.

As part of the same process of colonialism, the British (and other colonising nations) sent more than cheap cotton or other manufactured goods to their colonies. They also exported the emergent town planning of the early twentieth century. 'We want not only England but all parts of the Empire to be covered with Garden Cities', wrote one of Ebenezer Howard's disciples.[5] In 1912, Captain Swinton, Chairman of the London County Council and a member of the New Delhi Planning Committee, enthused: 'I hope that in the new Delhi we shall be able to show how those ideas which Mr [Ebenezer] Howard put forward . . . can be brought in to assist this first Capital created in our time. The fact is that no new city or town should be permissible in these days to which the word "Garden" cannot be rightly applied.'[6]

In the 1950s, *Town and Country Planning*, the vehicle of the Garden City movement, was still praising the benign influence that British town planning had had in the 1930s on the countries of the British Empire. The 1932 Town and Country Planning Act had been used first in Trinidad, later in Uganda, Fiji, Aden, Sarawak, Mauritius and in Sierra Leone and East Africa: 'thus, the 1932 Act has left its mark in all corners of the world . . . Modern developments in British planning procedure are followed closely by colonial planning officers who are always ready to profit by the experience of the mother country.'[7] The earliest colonial settlements were often explicitly military towns. The later developments, built in order to promote the garden-city obsessions of physical health, sanitation and social orderliness, constituted a form of 'cultural colonialism'.[8]

The influence of British colonialism was not confined to developing countries; it equally determined the shape of cities in Canada and Australia. Australia, which is economically part of the 'west', is an interesting example of a highly urbanised society (85 per cent of its population was living in cities in 1971), which urbanised faster than either the United States or Canada. Its suburbs and urban transport systems anticipated similar developments in Europe and the United States; in the late nineteenth century Melbourne and Sydney rivalled London as centres of culture and commerce – Augustus Sala referred to 'marvellous Melbourne', and Melbourne was also compared to Chicago and to Paris.[9] Yet the Australian heritage has been largely defined in terms of the outback and the 'bush ethos', – just as Americans continued to be obsessed with the Frontier. The intensity and savagery of the Australian landscape, such a stark contrast to a caricatured suburban banality, has been perceived as a source of truth and inspiration. 'Depressed urban workers were led to believe that the bush was a place of healing away from the diseased life of the city. Furthermore the bush was regarded as masculine in gender, a place to escape from the ladylike refinements of the city and women's challenge to [male] supremacy.'[10] In the loneliness of the outback, the solitary male could pit himself against raw nature, although in practice, of course, he was usually supported by the unstinting and unrecognised labour of women, a situation subtly explored by Henry Handel Richardson in her great novel of Australian pioneering, *The Fortunes of Richard Mahony*. Recent attempts to atone for the great wrongs done to the Aboriginal peoples, however well intentioned, have served to reinforce the contrast between inauthentic city and the spiritual qualities of the Bush.

In India, the British imposed their own form of urban planning on a civilisation that already boasted many cities, although they paid little attention to the traditional forms of Indian urban life. New Delhi, built by the English architect Edwin Lutyens, was an administrative and bureaucratic centre, not a modern industrial city. In this it was typical of the way in which urbanisation in dependent imperial territories, such as India then was, took place without the industrialisation which had been key to urbanism in the West.

In Africa the old urban centres such as Kano in Northern Nigeria, Ibadan in Southern Nigeria and Benin were likewise disregarded. West Africa was the site of long-established pre-industrial indigenous cities, especially amongst the Yoruba. The Yoruba civilisation was based on an agricultural economy, but the farmers lived in the cities. The farms were set in belts of agricultural land that surrounded the towns to a distance of about fifteen miles. Within the cities craft specialisation and guilds on the one hand and market trading on the other were important activities. The markets were large, involving entrepreneurs and a money economy based on cowrie shells. The traditional extended family, or lineage system, remained important in the cities, partly because of the value of the land. Women played a subordinate role in the lineage family system, but occupied a central place in the market system, retailing being largely in their hands.[11]

In fact the lineage family remained important in urban life all over west Africa. A variety of urban housing forms developed to house these extended families. In the towns settled by the Mende tribe, the household typically consisted of a group of houses built round a compound, with separate one-room apartments for the male head of the family, for young wives and their children, for a head wife and for the male head of household's mother and for younger men and other dependants. The Ga, living in older districts of Accra, in the Gold Coast, had a residential unit consisting of two adjoining establishments, one occupied by men and the other by their wives. By the 1950s, though, educated Ga, working in clerical occupations in Accra, had adopted a much smaller nuclear family type of unit.[12]

New cities along more colonial lines also grew up in twentieth-century west Africa. These were not 'the place of the white man' in the way that the copperbelt towns of southern Africa, or Cape Town, or Johannesburg were. The colonial administration adapted in some degree to them. Control over housing and housing conditions was less direct, and the cities offered many different forms of employment, the whole way of life was diversified, and the inhabitants were more independent. The commercial nature of these cities, based on the export of cash crops, favoured the expansion of an educated indigenous professional and business middle class.[13]

These cities brought changes to the lives of women. They represented choice. The lives of women in the traditional lineage family outside the city, living in a compound which a head of family shared with his wives and mother and where a wife would come under the authority of these women and the wives of her husband's brothers, had been lives of submission to the family, who would be primarily interested in the economic advantages, in the shape of bridewealth, to be obtained from an impending marriage. Increasingly in the twentieth century girls could escape an unwelcome marriage by leaving for the city; and young couples could also break free to some extent of family restrictions by the same route.[14] This is not to imply that women always or even often wished for a different kind of life; simply to indicate the way in which the very existence of cities made it clear that other ways of life were possible.

In any case, life for the west African woman in the towns of mid-twentieth-century west Africa was not easy. Freedom from the restrictions of traditional ways of life brought insecurity as well as opportunities. Traditional marriage might be replaced by a statutory form of legal marriage, made possible by the introduction of western legal systems. Formal polygamy declined, but men were rarely monogamous. Nor did a husband have an individual obligation to support a deserted wife; that was still the responsibility of the lineage. Many men found it hard to earn enough money to support a family single-handed. Yoruba women were expected to wear as much new clothing and jewellery as possible on the many social occasions and ceremonial events in which they participated, and the employment of servants often also fell to the wife. Therefore, the majority of women in west African towns worked, and set great store by work. From their traditional sphere of marketing they expanded into nursing and other professional vocational training. They also set up voluntary associations, some for both sexes, which played a social and professional role, and some of which were women's associations. Through these associations they were enabled to raise capital to expand their trading opportunities. For this reason the associations presented to some extent an alternative to the family.[15]

In east Africa new urban forms were imposed upon a rural population. Lusaka, for example, in what is now Zambia, was planned and built as the capital of British Northern Rhodesia. Like New Delhi it was to be a governmental centre, and here – as in South Africa today – the colonial authorities attempted to restrict the participation of the African population in urban life. They were to be migrant labourers whose period of residence in an urban area was regarded as strictly temporary. It was assumed that African women would remain permanently in the rural areas.

The garden–city ideal inspired Lusaka, which was planned by Stanley D. Adshead, an enthusiastic disciple of Ebenezer Howard. The colonial version of the Letchworth/Welwyn ideal lacked, however, even the moderate reformism of those experiments. It is easy to dissent from the reformism, or laugh at the quaint utopian socialist lifestyle of the more eccentric Letchworth residents, but at least they were attempting to create a less hierarchical and non-oppressive community; the garden city in its English incarnation had aimed to foster neighbourhoods and communities. In Africa, by contrast, reading rooms, libraries and lecture halls were replaced by the races, the club and the golf course. In Lusaka and Delhi, an outmoded British way of life was artificially preserved. Middle-class bureaucrats and professionals were able to aspire to an aristocratic way of life with retinues of servants and an aura of ruling-class grandeur.[16]

In the building of colonial cities the environment created was a visible expression of the ideas upon which colonial rule was based. Lusaka, for example, was built as a city for Europeans. The Africans were to remain in the rural hinterland, with the exception of able-bodied men who would be needed to undertake manual work, and of men and women needed for domestic service.

Housing for these workers was minimal, since they were expected to make periodic migrations from the countryside, returning there when not needed. Sometimes workers built their own hutments. Sometimes employers provided very basic housing free. They did not mind doing this, because they were then able to pay labourers very low wages on the grounds that they had no housing costs.

In the original plans of the nineteenth- and early-twentieth-century utopias of the western world the intention had been to zone women safely into areas of domesticity and consumption. They were to be excluded altogether from the colonial city. Like the British working class, the indigenous population, particularly the female population, was totally written out of the colonial city utopia.

After the Second World War local authorities began to provide hostel accommodation, but as the African population expanded and changed, 'unauthorised' dwellings (squatters' areas or shanty towns) provided an important source of housing for Africans in Lusaka. By 1963 the idea that the African population consisted of a circulating labour force that frequently returned to a rural family was far from the reality; the census that year revealed that nearly as many African women as men were living in the city, and that over 50 per cent of its black inhabitants were under the age of twenty-one.[17]

In Latin America cities grew up in a number of different ways. There, the strong planning tradition of Spanish and Portuguese colonialism determined the form of the older cities. São Paulo, Brazil, for example, was founded in 1554 by the Jesuits as a bridgehead to the hinterland to further their 'domestication' of indigenous Indians. After independence in 1822 it became a provincial administrative and political centre. By the mid nineteenth century coffee-growing was substantial; this, and the related growth of a railroad network, transformed São Paulo by 1900 into a city of a quarter of a million inhabitants (as against 65,000 in 1890) and an important industrial centre.[18]

An infrastructure of sewage, roads, water supplies and lighting always lagged behind the needs of the raggedly growing city. By the 1930s, when Claude Lévi-Strauss was living there, the city was dealing with its housing problem by a variety of hand-to-mouth solutions, and 'in 1935 the citizens of São Paulo boasted that, on an average, one house per hour was built in their town . . . The town is developing so fast that it is impossible to obtain a map of it; a new edition would be required every week.' Everything was chaotic, and 'vast roadworks' were being built adjacent to old crafts quarters like Syrian bazaars. A new public avenue cut through a once exclusive neighbourhood, 'where painted wooden villas were falling to pieces in gardens full of eucalyptus and mango trees'; then came a working-class neighbourhood, 'along which lay a red light district, consisting of hovels with raised entresols, from the windows of which the prostitutes hailed their clients. Finally, on the outskirts of the town, the lower-middle-class residential areas . . . were making headway.'[19]

Today, many city dwellers live in shanty towns, and these have become the most telling and guilt-inducing image of 'third-world poverty', inviting the voyeuristic horror of the westerner. In the 1960s about one quarter of the population of cities such as Manila and Djakarta, one third of the population of Mexico City and half that of Lima lived in shanty towns. In the late 1970s it was estimated that by 1990 three-quarters of Lima's poor would be living in such conditions.[20]

The literature on shanty towns usually emphasises their squalor and poverty. Dwellings are constructed of wattle, cardboard or corrugated iron, and placed in close proximity, with narrow lanes running between them which also serve as open drains. Seven or eight members of a household sleep together in one room, and animals often share the human living space. Whether located in Venezuela or Calcutta, Cairo or Djakarta, the descriptions of the '*barrios*' are extraordinarily reminiscent of the Victorians' lurid depictions of nineteenth-century slums. Like the London or Paris poor of that time, women of the *barrios* queue for water, which is supplied – often intermittently – from standpipes. There are no proper sewage systems in the 'typical' shanty town, which in general lacks all basic amenities.

It is often assumed that the people living in such conditions must somehow themselves be inadequate, just as the Victorian reformers assumed for the most part that the poor were locked into the slums because they were lacking in moral fibre. For example, an American academic, M.H. Ross, described the Nairobi shanty towns as follows:

> Downtown Nairobi is beautiful, with its tall buildings, modern architecture and flowering trees . . . Four miles [away] . . . live some 10,000 to 20,000 urban squatters . . . The houses, crammed together in an apparently haphazard fashion dictated by the uneven terrain of the valley's walls, are built of mud and wattle and have roofs made of cardboard, flattened-out tin cans, or even sheet metal. A visitor entering the area is struck by the lack of social services; the roads are makeshift, garbage is piled high in open areas, and children play in the dust.[21]

He dismissed the inhabitants of Mathare as 'generally urban misfits and rural outcasts . . . [who] lack the skills necessary to find jobs in the modern economy' – yet went on to reveal that the community organised nursery schools, a co-op and social events, and that 'the most striking aspect of Mathare is that it is highly organised and politically integrated . . . There is a clearly identifiable group of community leaders.'

In the 1950s and 1960s governments in many countries responded to spontaneous settlements with harassment and evictions. Since the 1970s a different strategy has been more often used: a 'site and services' policy. This recognises the impossibility of providing better housing, and also that the squatters will not, indeed cannot, return to their former rural homes. The trend has therefore been to legalise the occupation of the shanty towns. Where possible sewage, electricity and water may be provided. The residents are encouraged to build their own homes (which they were already doing). National government and international agencies recognised that this self-help alternative could be a low-cost housing policy, and since 1974 self-help has been officially endorsed by the World Bank.[22]

Some researchers and planners have given these policies enthusiastic support. Critics, on the other hand, have argued that they simply let governments off the hook and act as a justification for low wages and frightful living conditions.[23]

Running through many of these debates, which for the most part originate in western institutions, has been the continuing theme of the planners' contempt for the poor. Individual studies of African or other non-western cities have testified to their ebullience, diversity and variety. There is friendliness, and social contacts are established with ease. Most of those who come to the towns do not come as strangers, but already have members of the family established there.

This family will cushion the shock of the transition to urban life, and provide much-needed help and support in the initial months. The new arrival relies precisely on ties of kinship to see her or him through the bewildering early days of life in the town.

Yet many who have written of third-world city life have emphasised poverty, the breakdown of family life, prostitution, crime and psychological maladjustment, and have blamed the impersonal nature of city life with its alienation and anomie. The work of Oscar Lewis, who described an alleged 'culture of poverty', was extremely influential in the 1950s and 1960s in the development of this view,[24] which, consciously or not, built on the assumptions of Georg Simmel and Louis Wirth, who had emphasised the impersonal factors in urban life.

More recently, there has been a greater recognition of the persistence of family obligations in the city. In the cities of the third world as in nineteenth-century New York or Chicago, or for that matter in the new industrial towns of nineteenth-century Lancashire, family connections play an important role in the process by which immigrants and rural workers are transformed into urban dwellers.

Yet the negative view of the effects of city life on the individual and the family has persisted. In addition, writers, planners and officials have then imposed the weight of the theories and assumptions of postwar western planning with its emphasis on zoning, segregation and surveillance. The result has been that in third-world cities, as in the cities of postwar Britain and the United States, redevelopment, zoning, skyscraper business districts and dormitory suburbs are to be the answers to the 'chaos' and 'moral breakdown' of the unplanned industrial city. The same exaggerated faith in the ability of neutral, scientific planning to solve the urban crisis has led to a reproduction of the same mistakes as in western cities, but with far more extreme results.

Western assumptions about the normality and universality of the nuclear family have been extended to the shanty towns and urban populations of the third world. The view that the slums of Latin America fostered unmarried motherhood, delinquency, prostitution and a psychology of apathy and living for the moment has ceded to that of writers who were more likely to emphasise the 'normality' and stability in western terms of family life and social existence in the shanty towns. 'Normality', however, has meant the stereotype of family life in which the husband works and the woman remains at home, engaged in full-time domestic work and child rearing. This is not the actual experience even of the majority of western families. It has been used to marginalise women in the paid workforce, and has also perpetuated inequalities generally between men and women inside and outside the family.[25]

It is even more inappropriate as a model of the family in non-western urban settlements. Its basic assumptions do not take into account the situation and crucial importance of women in and to these housing settlements. National and international investment in self-help housing projects has failed to answer the needs of women and, on the contrary, has excluded them. Governmental and financial policies tend to be based on the assumption that the nuclear family with a male breadwinner is the usual and indeed natural family form, whereas in fact different household forms coexist. Recent figures have suggested that one in three of the world's households are now headed by women. In urban areas, however, approximately 50 per cent of households are headed by women, and in the refugee camps of Central America the figure is closer to 90 per cent.[26]

Women-headed households are placed in a kind of double jeopardy. Their very existence is denied, minimised or not taken account of. Then, in addition, it is often assumed that only male-headed households are sufficiently stable to merit inclusion in housing schemes. In one project in São Paulo, funded by the Brazilian Housing Bank Profilurb programme, women who headed households were excluded by the criteria of eligibility. Yet some observers have argued that families headed by women may be more stable, show more responsibility in paying back loans, in paying rent and in improving properties.[27]

Governments have also failed to recognise that women play an especially important role in 'community management'. Because women are more directly concerned than men with the welfare of the household, and with 'community' issues such as water supply and safety, they are normally more aware than men of the needs of a housing project, and more committed to its succes.[28]

A neglect of the needs of women has often militated against the success of self-help housing projects. For example, a failure to recognise that women as well as men engage in paid employment leads to a male bias when 'squatters' are relocated, often miles from the centre of the city. This bias arises either when rehousing is near factories or other sites of male employment, or simply because it is assumed that men can travel long distances to work. Planners pay little heed to the fact that women both need work, and need to be near their work if, as they invariably have to, they are successfully to combine it with domestic duties. For example, many women take in laundry or have jobs as maids, and for this they need to live near to their employers. Even if it is acknowledged that the relocation has created transport difficulties, these may be interpreted as difficulties for men. In Belo Horizonte, Brazil, for example, public transport was laid on at peak hours, so that men could travel to work, but was withdrawn during the day when women needed to use the service, either to take children to school, to go shopping, or get to their own part-time jobs.[29]

Another way in which women are ignored and excluded is that they are not consulted on issues such as the design of houses. For example, the object of the Tanzanian 'Better Housing Campaign' was to persuade people to build more durable houses, built of imported materials, to replace traditional ones built with local materials. One unintended effect of the higher costs of building with imported materials was that it impeded the tradition of building separate accommodation for male and female members of families. As a result, women were redefined as dependants, and their traditional autonomy was undermined. In two housing projects in Tunis, houses were designed with a much smaller courtyard than in traditional design. Because Muslim women, spending most of their time in the home, needed this internal space, its absence caused depression and even suicide.[30]

In spite of all the obstacles and prejudice, women have managed to involve themselves in many local housing projects. They have organised locally against the fearful hardships of the majority of the *barrios*. In one settlement in Guayaquil, capital of Ecuador, initial conditions were terrible, as the settlement consisted of swampland. Settlers bought plots on which they then had to build their own houses. To begin with, the settlement had no services, not even water. It was approached by perilous catwalks above the swamps. These were so dangerous that two children drowned, while two women died as a result of wading through the swamp, and a man was electrocuted while trying to fix a light connection.

Women, given that they less frequently went out to work than did their male partners, were particularly isolated. Many had only just left their parents' home, others had given up paid work, and for those who tried to carry on with their laundry work the shortage of water was a disaster. They became more economically dependent than hitherto on their husbands or partners. So, while to settle on the swamp had economic advantages – they no longer had to pay rent and therefore had more money for education and consumer goods – the disadvantages of the area bore particularly upon women. Soon, however, they established mutual-aid networks, and this led to the formation of organised committees to agitate for change. To take a leading role in these did involve a challenge to traditional views of how woman should behave (submissively, with the emphasis on her role as mother and homemaker); on the other hand, the traditional role itself validated membership of groups seeking to improve domestic living conditions.[31]

In Nicaragua, the Sandinista Revolution in 1979 resulted in a political commitment to tackle problems such as these, but changes were brought about only with great difficulty. In one project in Managua, men objected to women sharing in the actual work of house construction, but, after considerable discord, some women did manage to learn the basic building skills. The women in the project were more radical than the men in that they wanted the finished houses allocated according to need, while the men wanted them to be allocated according to the amount of work put in (advantageous to them, since on the whole the men had fewer alternative calls on their time). During a dispute over the allocation of one particular house, the issues of *machismo* (also referred to as *somocismo*, i.e. behaviour worthy of the Somoza regime, overthrown by the Sandinistas) was raised. This was possible because the revolution had initiated a reassessment of the roles of men and women, and was committed in principle to the equality of women.[32] Increasingly throughout the 1980s, however, the Nicaraguan experience was distorted by the incursions of the Contras and American destabilisation, so that towards the end of the decade, the mounting economic crisis was testing the survival strategies of urban women to the limit.[33]

Throughout Latin America, the position of single mothers is ambiguous. Confined to low-paid work, they, with their children, are among the poorest in the community, and still tend to be stigmatised, blamed for their plight, although many have been irresponsibly deserted by husband or lover. Some, however, have made the choice to bring up the children on their own, preferring the hardships of this way of life to the domineering behaviour of their menfolk, many of whom refuse to allow their women freedom of movement, abuse them physically, and spend the family income on heavy drinking. An Ecuador study showed that participation in the organisation of the *barrio* had also enabled some of the cohabiting women involved to achieve economic independence so that they were in a much more powerful position in relation to their husbands/ partners.[34]

In countries such as Brazil, where feminism influenced radical middle-class women in the 1970s, the general turbulence of the political situation made possible, for a time at least, alliances between the feminists and women's groups from the working class and the poorest sections of society, including women in the shanty towns who were fighting for the provision of basic needs. In this way, the impact of feminist ideas on an educated middle class affected a much broader group of women, although in different ways. Female domestic servants, for example, became a militant and well-organised force – a far cry from the usual picture of maids as unorganised, and, indeed, impossible to organise.[35] For these women, life in the *barrios* and settlements was not a life of apathy and despair. Most of those living there neither came from nor wished to return to a rural life.

Life in the city provides the preconditions for continuing struggle, since in the city the poor, although 'excluded from the comforts of the city, are exposed to its modernity'.[36] The existence of the benefits of urban life – even though they are excluded from them – justifies their demands for *inclusion*. The gulf between what is and what might be may appear to widen; on the other hand, the city both raises aspirations and gives more chance of their realisation.[37]

Although cities in the non-western world differ both from one another and from the cities of Europe and North America, it has become customary to refer to the 'third-world city' or the 'world city' as a separate and recognisable entity. A global capitalism must surely be creating a global city: this seems to be the assumption upon which such a generalisation is based, although it is also recognised that global capital may act to differentiate one city, and one economy, from another. A fear remains that the world, and its cities, are becoming homogenised: difference is ironed out and everything is the same. At the same time, within every city a growing distance between rich and poor makes for another kind of unreality, and a gulf in experience that cannot be bridged. We move, then, from world city to postmodern city.

9

Beyond Good and Evil

San Narciso lay farther south, near LA. Like many named places in California it was less an identifiable city than a group of concepts – census tracts, special purpose bond-issue districts, shopping nuclei, all overlaid with access roads to its own freeway . . . Nothing was happening. She looked down a slope . . . onto a vast sprawl of houses which had grown up all together, like a well-tended crop, from the dull brown earth; and she thought of the time she'd opened a transistor radio to replace a battery and seen her first printed circuit. The ordered swirl of houses and streets, from this high angle, sprang at her now with the same unexpected, astonishing clarity as the circuit card had . . . there were to both outward patterns a hieroglyphic sense of concealed meaning, of an intent to communicate . . .

Smog hung all round the horizon, the sun on the bright beige countryside was painful; she and the Chevy seemed parked at the centre of an odd, religious instant.

Thomas Pynchon, *The Crying of Lot 49* (1965)

By the 1980s the grand attempts to build classless utopias in real life had resulted, with horrible irony, in inner-city ghettoes, residential wastelands and polluted peripheries where urban debris leaked into a fast-disappearing countryside. Social segregation by race, class and income was as pervasive as ever, and as fast as old slums were demolished new forms of urban decay appeared. This was not entirely the fault of town planners, still less was it the fault of architects. The designer of cities were, however, blamed for mounting social problems, and disillusionment with modernist architecture was one factor leading to the idea of the postmodern city.

The word postmodern has been used to describe such a wide range of cultural experiences that it is in danger of coming to mean little more than a vague sense of the flavour of our times. For some writers it has positive, for others negative meanings; it can be used to suggest diversity and cultural variety, but also to describe sameness and emotional flatness. In two ways the term is relevant to a discussion of the contemporary city: it is used to describe a sensibility or state of mind; and it is a key concept in contemporary debates about architecture and urban space.

The postmodern urban sensibility is typically described in negative terms, as a form of disorientation, meaninglessness and fragmenta- tion. Postmodernism is more than an aesthetic experience; postmodernism perceives *all* experience in aesthetic terms. In post-modernism the city becomes a labyrinth or a dream. Its chaos and senselessness mirror a loss of meaning in the world. At the same time, there may be an excess of meaning: the city becomes a split screen flickering with competing beliefs, cultures, and 'stories'.

This play of unnerving contrasts and extremes is the essence of the 'postmodern' experience. In the postmodern world we all become hysterics as we travel the city of skyscraper and abyss, alert with feelings of horror and excitement, but free from guilt or sadness. Or the eerie sameness of a thousand urban peripheries may flatten all feeling; the world has become one endless suburb and we watch with hallucinating blankness as it timelessly unrolls. Everything is the same, and nothing is quite real; the schizoid world anaesthetises us. Such, at least, is a common interpretation of the contemporary urban landscape, found, for example, in Fredric Jameson's extremely influential article on postmodernism, from which much current dete has arisen.[1] Some writers, John Thackara for example, have argued that we should be very cautious in accepting this version of subjective experience, which implies that we are '*victims* of modernity', and that the 'project of modernity' is finished.[2] The post-modern view of the contemporary world as caught in an imploding catastrophe is nonetheless widely popular.

The debate on postmodernism perpetuates the long-standing suspicion of the city expressed by so many writers and reformers, yet differs from them in obtaining a perverse pleasure from the horrors of the postmodern kitsch-scape. Postmodern aesthetics makes a virtue out of 'ugliness', often appearing to celebrate the very debris that threatens to suffocate all meaning. So, we celebrate Las Vegas and the architecture of the fast food outlet, find an eerie pleasure in the junkyard, the shopping mall and the cardboard city. Their onslaught on the received meaning of city life, its order, regularity and grace, are precisely what makes them radical and exciting; they 'make strange' the perhaps too familiar, outmoded structures of 'classic' city life. Horror, fear and ugliness are aestheticised, and thus become easier to live with, at least for the new urban aesthete, the voyeur – although presumably not for the poor and the homeless. Postmodernism thus expresses an urban sensibility, although a perverse one.

California provides one version of the ultimate postmodern experience. As popularly described, it combines kitsch architecture – and kitsch nature for that matter – a whole 'inauthentic' lifestyle, in fact, with a population of transients. LA is the 'nowhere city' (the title of a novel by Alison Lurie) in which lives are inconsequential, fugitive and timeless in the sense of lacking both past and future.

Since Nathanael West's bitter, 1930s satires on Hollywood, *Miss Lonely Hearts* and *The Day of the Locust*, the metaphor of the celluloid city has been consistently used to refer to the unreality of Californian life. Sometimes a kind of weird humour or unfettered eccentricity saves the characters of the typical LA novel from becoming tragic or sinister, as in Gavin Lambert's *The Slide Area* or the recent *Los Angeles without a Map* by Richard Rayner; but in Brett Easton's *Less than Zero* or Thomas Pynchon's *The Crying of Lot 49* the blank affectlessness of Californian life does become sinister, because human behaviour appears unintelligible. *Less than Zero* cleverly exploits the deadpan language of the wealthy Californian youth it portrays, but it relies on an assumed moral position from which the hero seems to criticise the hideous behaviour of his peers. Within the terms of the book there is no basis for this moral stand, however: its message is that the rich Los Angelenos have created a generation of young women and men entirely without moral perspective, and the hero is one of them, so the source of his moral judgments, such as they are, is unclear.

These recent novels may be contrasted with the cynicism of Raymond Chandler's classic LA thrillers of the 1940s, which did not preclude a clear sense of good and evil consistent with the position of the hero as the upright man in a crooked world. This was reflected in the 'film noir' versions of the 1940s, such as *The Big Sleep*. By contrast, the 1973 version of Chandler's *The Long Goodbye* was set in a California so spaced out that 'commonsense' definitions of good and bad were derailed, and the sharp-edged private eye became merely a puzzled, crumpled, passive observer.

Moral extremes lose their meaning. In New York, the lesbian heroine of *After Dolores* notices the way in which the derelicts who hang out in Tomkins Park 'moved slowly like . . . movie screens as the projector breaks down. It was like the last moment of a dream.' Scenes on the street verge on the horrific, yet this seems to destroy the observer's capacity to feel. The unnamed heroine notices a bag lady on the street, crying on account of her homelessness, but adds, 'I was crying too. It was so hot. But the whole time it was like she was on a television set and I wasn't crying for her because there are people just like her everywhere you look.'[3] The direst misery has become another spectacle.

The young middle-class heroines of stylish New York novels suffer at the hands of their indifferent or sadistic lovers, engage in some high-class prostitution or take jobs as strippers (although, really, they're artists), yet they never seem vulnerable, only masochistic. Even when driven by economic necessity, degradation seems more like a chosen style than a necessity. Catherine Texier, for example, finds a heartrending yet aesthetically satisfying sense of romance in a doomed city:

> The night is black and wet, the lights on the Hudson and along the New Jersey shore shattered in red and green and silver splinters blurred by the rain, the tip of Manhattan vanishing in the fog. Once in a while the hoot of a ship throbs darkly across the river . . .
>
> I see Manhattan like an ocean liner adrift in the middle of the Atlantic, never reaching its port. The moorings have been cast off. There's no turning back to dry land. We're all thrown together on this phantom ship, hallucinating, without connection to the other world. It's a trip from which we'll never come back.[4]

This postmodern city recalls the medieval 'ship of fools', in which the mad were herded on to a ship that endlessly sailed the rivers and seas of Europe.

Manhattan becomes a state of mind: a state of insanity. It reveals postmodernism as a late-romantic sensibility, in which loss of control is pleasurable as well as frightening. Sensation is valued more highly than sense. In the New York novels of Catherine Texier, Mary Gaitskill and Tama Janowitz, the heroines do not go with dangerous men just for the thrill; there is no alternative – sex *is* danger. The classic moral dilemmas of fiction – so often the moral dilemma of the heroine – have vanished, displaced by a 'decadence' in which sensation and aesthetics hold sway. Postmodern philosophers have suggested that a postmodern ethics should be based on what is aesthetically pleasing, but here we have the reverse: the aestheticisation of what is unpleasing; and it is unclear what kind of morality can be based on that.

Women take a central place in this disordered city, in which the idea of disorder can no longer be expressed, since there is no prior order from which to deviate. Gone is the hero who metaphorically carved his name on the city; now men are petulant, temperamental and uncertain; they have become the 'Other' to a female subjectivity, which endures but would never claim to shape the city.

In the Hollywood 'film noir', urban space became a powerful metaphor for the angst and paranoia of the 1940s. Then, the male figure was at hand to restore patriarchal control and punish the woman who had tried to usurp power: such was the plot of classics such as *Double Indemnity*, *Out of the Past* and *Mildred Pierce*. Today, the city with no boundary, which goes on for ever, has become a metaphor for confusion as a condition of existence. In the absence of any clear moral outlook, contemporary postmodern films perhaps surprisingly tend to fall back on very traditional attitudes. Jay McInerney's New York novel *Bright Lights, Big City* became a film in which the old contrast between evil city and redemptive country-side was wheeled on as the solution to his drug and emotional problems. In *Blade Runner*, one of the most acclaimed 'postmodern' films, the hero eventually escapes from a futuristic (yet almost medieval) Los Angeles peopled mostly by a Chinese sub-proletariat (racist shades of the 'yellow peril') and gains the refuge of an empty rural landscape with his robot lover.

One aspect of postmodern confusion and endlessness is the promise of consumer culture, with its strange euphoria. The con-temporary urban woman is both consumer and consumed. In her automobile she may seem the predator of the freeways – she may even become the female private eye.[5] Yet she remains an object of consumption at the same time as she becomes an actor. The ambivalence of her role was forcefully illustrated by the real-life tragedy of Suzy Lamplugh, who worked as an estate agent in London. At her place of work she was seated in a prominent position in the office window, so that her good looks would attract custom, yet she was expected to go out unaccompanied with male clients. When she disappeared, it was assumed that one of these clients had murdered her: the mystery has never been solved. Her car, her experience, her streetwise knowledge, did not save her. In a curious way, her alleged sexual past was even used against her in the media story that was created.[6] Women like Suzy Lamplugh embody the ambivalence of the postmodern city.

Postmodern ambivalence is played out in cities whose contours have changed, and here a second postmodern debate becomes relevant. Since the 1960s cities have been giving place to vast new 'urban regions'. The north-eastern seaboard of the United States is one such region, stretching from Boston to Washington. In these regions town and country intermingle. In what were once the outer suburbs, whole new city rings and clusters have formed around the decayed industrial nineteenth-century cores, extending into the countryside to annihilate the very division between rural and urban. Any rural enclaves in such areas are no longer simply dotted with commuter villages or surviving remnants of truly rural life; they are developing industrial centres as well, for many industries are leaving the old cities. Networks of transport and communications are creating an urban region that resembles a centreless web, rather than the traditional industrial city form of a core surrounded by concen-tric rings largely zoned into areas of commerce, manufacturing and residential use; this is the 'outer city', the endless suburb or urban region – the 'non-place urban realm',[7] with shopping malls and out-of-town hypermarkets, rural factories, home-based work and revamped heritage-industry leisure complexes.

Another form of postmodern city is the third-world city with its shining skyscrapers and rotting slums. Cruel and vibrant, it is a city in which medieval transport and side streets coexist with the new feudalism of the multinational corporations, conspicuous wealth and conspicuous poverty outbidding each other in a spiral of excess.

A third kind of postmodern city involves the privatisation of public space in the old city centres, their conversion from commerce and industry to spectacle and museum status. Examples are the Boston Waterfront, Fisherman's Wharf in San Francisco and Liverpool's Docklands. It has even been suggested that the Italian city of Florence might be preserved as a museum, while a new city of Florence for those who live and work in it be built some miles away. Thus where cities have been preserved from the developers, they become too precious to live in.

Postmodernity may alternatively mean simple banality. Basingstoke, a London overspill city in Hampshire, once a pleasant market town, has become a satellite centre for office and computer industries. Two hundred thousand people live in its new, undistinguished housing complexes, but there is only one cinema and one city-centre grocery supermarket. The new shopping is out on the periphery. In the shopping centre, owned by the Prudential insurance company, it is hard to know even what town you are in, since there is nothing to differentiate it from all other new shopping centres with the same chain-store outlets, the same grey architecture. Out of shopping hours it is deserted and dangerous. Leisure is "'a wine box and a video'". Its chief characteristic is vacancy and the absence of civic culture, collective institutions, such as trades unions, or public life.[8] Basingstoke is not unusual; rather, it is typical of cities across Britain, the USA and Europe. It is sometimes argued that these postmodern cities are the portents of a turning point in history as momentous as the Industrial Revolution two hundred years ago, and that soon even these new urban centres will disappear. We are on the threshold of a new era in which telecommunications will replace face to face contact and the city as a fixed urban space will eventually become redundant.

In Japan, high-tech city plans – 'Technopolis', 'Teletopia' – have been promoted. They will use communications systems to link agricultural communities in new ways, and to create enhanced leisure and welfare facilities. Research parks, high-tech industrial zones, tourist resorts, cable television and computer networks will be used in regions earmarked for development. An Australian version, proposed by Japan's Ministry of Trade and Industry, the

Multifunctional Polis, has been under discussion since 1987. This would combine high-tech operations with luxury leisure provision, financed largely by the private sector. One commentator has suggested that such a city would embody an international culture: that of the technocratic elite; another that it would constitute a kind of utopia as envisaged by capitalist property developers; a third that such plans raise, but do not address issues of democracy, surveillance and conformity.[9]

Just as there is no single type of postmodern city, so there is no one postmodern architectural style. Rather, postmodern architecture is distinguished by its mixing of styles and borrowings from historical periods and regional traditions. The rhetoric of postmodern architecture has emphasised 'human proportions', yet postmodern architecture looks to the planning of civic space made popular by the City Beautiful movement and Albert Speer. Some postmodern architects have revived traditional urban forms, such as the piazza and the street, and, like so many before them, invoke Christopher Wren in support of their plans; others have adopted the language of Disneyland and Las Vegas, using playful kitsch motifs, and relishing the 'vulgar' over-decoration of billboard, casino and fast food outlet. What makes today's revivalism different from Raymond Unwin's Letchworth cottages or from the tasteful Queen Anne style of Bedford Park is the tongue-in-cheek use of pastiche and period 'feel'. It appears to take itself less seriously than the garden city.

Yet postmodern architecture is serious, and has become the spearhead of a well-publicised attack on modernism and town planning. It has come forward as the David to rout the Goliaths of the inner city, and as a populist voice against the municipal bureaucrats. Its best-known supporter is, of course, Prince Charles. In sneering at the 'glass stumps' or 'carbuncles' that, for him, sum up modernist design, Prince Charles speaks both to genuine anxieties and to hardcore philistinism; either way, his opinions have touched a popular chord. In 1989 a MORI opinion poll showed that 87 per cent of the public approved of his support for traditional architecture and attacks on modernism; 81 per cent approved of his favourite neo-Georgian style; and only 25 per cent favoured modern architecture.[10]

An aura and rhetoric of humane popularity has bathed postmodernism and its exponents and buildings in a self-righteous glow. In Britain, it is associated with the community architecture movement. Community architects emphasise consultation, working closely with local groups to create buildings that satisfy local needs, and have, among other things, worked with the residents of council estates to improve amenities and safety. One group of woman architects, commissioned to build a centre for Asian women in the East End of London, made use of forms traditional to and suitable for that community.[11]

Leon Krier, an architect and adviser to the Prince, whose work has included efforts to rehabilitate Albert Speer, has attacked zoning and other forms of planning with social-engineering objectives as intrusive and mistaken, preferring an aesthetic concept of the city as a conglomeration of urban quarters and 'cities within the city'.[12] Traditional forms, such as piazzas and radial streets, similar to those planned by Wren for London after the Great Fire of 1666, should replace the over-unified principles of zoning. Diversity and tradition are the keys. Krier's pious hope is that architectural diversity will mirror a diversity of communities and individual needs in a less authoritarian city. Has this become the reality of the postmodern city? Why, if that is the case, is there still an 'urban crisis'?

Perhaps we can begin to answer this question by comparing the postmodern urban realm to Broadacre City, the utopia imagined by the influential American architect Frank Lloyd Wright. Wright was an intemperate anti-urbanist, but he also believed that the distinction between town and country was obsolete. Famous for the beautiful houses he designed all over the United States, his unfulfilled vision was to create a society in which the great cities, with their smoke, poverty and disease, were replaced by homesteads, each surrounded by at least an acre of land, and connected to others and to centres of work, leisure and commerce by a road network: in this utopia every family would have a car. His plan differed from Ebenezer Howard's garden city, since Howard had desired the survival of cities, although he had wished to limit their size. The two plans were alike, on the other hand, in that both envisaged the decentralisation of land ownership, believing that this would equalise wealth between classes.

For Wright, Broadacre City was desirable because it would preserve and strengthen the family, and even re-create an earlier (patriarchal, of course) family form. Once more, as in the pre-industrial period, every family would farm its own plot. Each homestead would also be a craft unit. There would be no urban shopping centres or department stores; instead, all members of society would come together at the roadside market, to sell their own produce as well as to buy what they needed. Schooling, entertainment and government would all be decentralised, and the state would to a large extent wither away.[13]

Although there are superficial resemblances between the contemporary urban region and Broadacre City, politically and economically the two are very different. There has been remarkably little diffusion of wealth in the western world, despite an expanding middle class of well-off salaried and professional workers. Politically, the urban region is neither decentralised, nor is it the outcome of a coherent plan. It is both chaotic and tightly controlled by the movement and development of capital. Today this is a global movement; the fate of London or Boston is related to the fate of São Paulo, Lima or Delhi.

Local municipal planners may have colluded in the property-speculation enterprises of global capital, but it is the movement of capital and the changing world economy that have ultimately determined the development of cities all over the world. The shutdown of factories and especially the loss of skilled, relatively well paid, unionised jobs in industrial centres such as the north of England and Scotland and the 'rust belt' of the United States (in cities such as Detroit and Pittsburgh) is one result of the movements of international capital. Multinational corporations (MNCs) have increasingly been able to export parts of the manufacturing process to 'third-world' countries, attractive because they offer cheap, 'disciplined' (that is to say non-unionised) labour.

At the same time, the corporate headquarters of the MNCs have remained in a few 'core command cities'. New York City heads the list with fifty-seven, London comes second with thirty-four, Tokyo third and Paris fourth. One result is the building of new prestige office blocks in such cities. These in turn attract a huge service sector, ranging from the highly paid specialist skills of lawyers and accountants through the provision of gourmet restaurants and designer boutiques to the employment of messengers, prostitutes and domestic cleaners. The high value of land in the city centre means that the working-class populations are shovelled out (as happened in the Marais district of Paris), to be replaced by glamorous and profitable property developments.[14]

City economies have responded to the restructuring of capital by pursuing a range of policies in the hope of capitalising on the changes that have occurred. The development of the financial sector in New York brought the city back from the brink of the bankruptcy that had threatened in the 1970s. In some centres the development of manufacturing or of the new, particularly the 'high-tech', industries has ensured financial viability. A third option has been the heritage and culture road; a fourth, as in Bristol or Los Angeles, the development of an armaments industry, one of the few still supported by government funding.[15]

London's Docklands development has been one of the best documented and most criticised results of the Big Bang in the City of London and of the City's continuing success as a financial centre.

The Isle of Dogs, an isthmus in the Thames, was a long-established, close-knit and rather isolated white working-class community. It was devastated in the early 1970s by the loss of employment consequent upon the closure of the docks. At that time a campaign for the regeneration of the whole docklands area tried to secure acceptance by the government of a plan that would have provided well paid, skilled jobs, homes and facilities for local people. Instead, in the 1980s, an 'enterprise zone' was created, which meant that planning restrictions were to a large extent set aside. The 'Island' was seen as the natural extension of the City of London finance sector, half a mile further west. Despite the bitter resistance of long-term working-class residents (most of them council tenants), the plan took shape. Instead of local government, Docklands was to be organised by a specially created, non-elected body, the London Docklands Development Corporation (LDDC), modelled on the postwar New Town Corporations. Offices, prestige private housing, including the postmodern high-rise called the Cascades, a marina, restaurants, wine bars and an entertainment arena rose on the 'biggest building site in Europe'. Yet the area heralded as the future of the inner cities and the Thatcherite enterprise culture city *par excellence* lacked basic roads, public transport and shopping facilities. By 1989 the depression in the London housing market had quelled the euphoria, and the local council was using the Cascades to house families, some of whom were in receipt of rent rebates (means-tested subsidies).

Meanwhile, two other districts adjacent to the City of London, Spitalfields and the Liverpool Street area, were being drawn into the plans for the expansion of the City of London. Successive immigrant communities had lived in Spitalfields since the Huguenots had arrived there in the seventeenth century, to be followed by the Jews in the nineteenth and early twentieth centuries, and in the last twenty years by the Bangladeshis. Once again, the proposed architecture for the 'new' Spitalfields claims to draw on the inspiration of Sir Christopher Wren, but takes little account of the Bangladeshi industries, restaurants and cultural institutions that have taken root. The development is centred on the site of Truman's brewery, established in the seventeenth century, but now scheduled for demolition and replacement with a mammoth office block. Some local businessmen welcome the plans, but others fear that rents will be pushed up and the local community pushed out, as the garment industry of 'Banglatown' is crushed and the local groceries and cafés are replaced by restaurants and cocktail bars designed for businessmen rather than for local workers.[16]

Even more dramatic is the example of Los Angeles, which contains within its huge extent almost every contradictory tendency of contemporary urban capitalism. Although Reyner Banham felt that its development was the unique outcome of geography and history, Los Angeles is more usually seen as a prototype.

In Los Angeles the richest and the poorest almost in the world live cheek by jowl, yet rigidly segregated. The *barrios* and ghettoes of latinos and blacks are surrounded by outlying suburbs along the coastline ('surfurbias' as Reyner Banham called them) with private beaches and psychedelic pollution sunsets. The black area of Watts is like a Hollywood set of the Deep South in the 1930s: old men and women sit on the stoops of single-storey shacks along roads that stretch dustily into nothingness – no shops, no businesses. Enclaves of bohemianism are tolerated at Venice Beach and West Hollywood, but the whole region is alive with armament factories, nuclear arsenals and military establishments, and in these installations some of the most highly paid white men in the world work in engineering and for the military.[17] The area is also stuffed with garment sweatshops, homeworkers, the homeless and unemployed.

While jobs at the highest and lowest level have multiplied, the organised blue-collar workforce has been decimated, with the loss of fifty thousand jobs between 1979 and 1982. This has had especially disastrous results for the black community. Women, too, were hit by the loss of skilled manual work. For example, after General Electric closed down its Flatiron plant at San Bernardino, the only alternative for its workers was to become a checkout clerk at local supermarkets – work that was much lower paid; predictably, women form a large part of the army of low-paid, often part-time, often undocumented and migrant workers.[18]

Up to a quarter of a million in Los Angeles are homeless, living in garages and sheds; approximately 125,000 subsist in motels and hotel rooms. Some of the homeless spend the night in cinemas, which charge less after midnight. This is quite apart from those on Skid Row. There, in the cold winter of 1986–7, people actually froze to death. The mayor's response was to have the police destroy the cardboard camps and tents that the homeless had erected. It was made clear that sleeping unprotected in the street was not in itself illegal: 'The camping aspect is what we are trying to get at, the jumble of furniture on the street, the open fires.'[19] Here, in fact, is the third world in the first world with a vengeance.

There is also Hollywood – the world's biggest dream factory, porno factory, nightmare factory. Here, the image of the perfect woman has been mass-produced since the 1920s: 'It is as if the whole race of gods had come to California . . . I see classic faces [worthy of the ancient Greeks]. The girls are all bleached and painted with sunburn enamel . . . desperate blondes in black satin, osprey and furs', wrote Cecil Beaton in 1930.[20] Hollywood has continued to turn them out ever since.

It is equally appropriate that the first Disneyland was built here, at Anaheim. Disneyland is the perfect utopia/dystopia, where fantasy seems to reign, a kind of infantile paradise cleansed of all adult emotions or concerns. It remains, nonetheless, a distorted reflection of LA itself, in that its enclosed spaces are invisibly controlled: the appearance of openness and choice is an illusion, since the visitor is subtly directed at every turn.

Fragmented yet structured perfectly to the logic of capital, LA, the West Coast 'capital of capital', seems to be all cities in one, containing within its boundaries not only sunbelt prosperity but also 'the far-reaching industrial decline and bankrupt urban neighbour-hoods of rust-belted Detroit or Cleveland. There is a Boston in Los Angeles, a Lower Manhattan and a South Bronx, a São Paulo and a Singapore.'[21]

Glasgow, in Scotland, illustrates, on a smaller and more easily grasped scale, the fate of the urban environment as we approach the year 2000: the industrial city become postmodern enterprise zone. Glasgow was already an urban centre in the early middle ages. In the eighteenth century it became an important entrepôt for tobacco, and it was at this time that the Glasgow tobacco lords built the section of the city now known as Merchant City. Glasgow's period of greatest expansion and wealth was in the nineteenth century. Between 1801 and the First World War its population grew from 77,000 to one million, but slump hit Clydeside shipbuilding in the 1920s. By 1930 there was 30 per cent unemployment in the city. At this time, Glasgow was famous for its militancy; 'red Clydeside' became a legend, and this reputation lasted right up until the Clydeside shipyard occupation of 1971. After the Second World War Scottish industry recovered, but by the 1960s it was once more going into steep decline.[22]

Overcrowding and housing problems had plagued nineteenth-century Glasgow, although municipal building started earlier in Glasgow than in comparable English cities.[23] Most famous of all the tenement slum areas was the Gorbals, a byword for overcrowding, poverty and crime. The 'first' Gorbals – one of the most notorious slum districts in Europe – was demolished in the 1860s, to be replaced by streets of stoutly built, grim, three- or four-storey tenements. Most of the dwellings in the tenements consisted of one room plus a kitchen, although some had only a single room. In the kitchen was the characteristic recess which held the parental bed. There was usually one lavatory to each cluster of three tenements, normally on a landing. Ralph Glasser, a child of the Gorbals Jewish community in the 1920s and 1930s, described its squalor, the crumbling buildings, the stench of urine and above all the rats round the ash pits:

> No one could afford to throw away food leavings that had any good left in them . . . but a final residue . . . was thrown on the ash pits, whence it was scavenged by rats and stray cats. At dead of night, sometimes even in daytime, one heard their furious scrabblings there, resulting in a scatter of rubbish all over the close,' so that one picked one's way among little heaps . . . far gone in putrefaction.[24]

The Gorbals, famous for violence – razor gangs waged war with one another – as well as for poverty, was also renowned for its close-knit culture, which lasted well into the 1950s. In his autobiography Jimmy Boyle, who served prison sentences as a result of his razor-gang activities, described the intimacy of the life, the 'warm blend of character' so 'comforting to the locals':

> There was a tremendous community spirit about the Gorbals people, and this extended to all things fortunate and unfortunate that occurred in our lives . . . [yet] although the architectural structure of the old buildings may have encouraged a sort of closeness, I think the dominant factor for this unity was that everyone was in the same boat, and didn't have two pennies to rub together.

A whole school of postwar 'Glasgow novels' emphasised the violence, especially sexual violence, the drink and the razor gangs.[25] Hard men, and women who were either victimised or exceptionally tough, peopled this legendary slum:

> The women of the district would either lean out of their windows, or, if the weather was good, take chairs down to the streets to sit and gossip about anything and anyone . . . The best nights of the whole week . . . were Friday and Saturday at pub closing time. It was a sort of occasion as all the women would be looking out of their windows for the pubs coming out. This was when all the fights took place.[26]

By 1957 Glasgow Corporation had approved the redevelopment plan for the Gorbals. The whole area was demolished, and most of its 26,000 inhabitants were relocated to bleak new estates on the outskirts of the city. Industry was moved out of the Gorbals altogether, the 444 shops reduced to fifty-seven and the forty-six pubs to nine.

A new housing estate was to be built on the site. The design of the high-rise flats and low-rise (four-storey) blocks was an 'award-winning' one, and Basil Spence, the architect of Coventry Cathedral, was to have designed 'hanging gardens' for them. The towers and slabs were to have risen from a grassy park uncontaminated by anything resembling the crowded business of city streets.

Before many of the prefabricated blocks had been built, it was becoming clear that they were a disaster; they were plagued with damp, and the electric heating which might have dried them out was far too expensive for most of the tenants.[27] Today, what used to be the Gorbals is still more like a bomb-site than a central city district, the few towers rising in an unplanned and meaningless way.

However squalid the old Gorbals had been, there was a terrible cost in the urban renewal that destroyed memories as well as streets. Ralph Glasser, returning to the Gorbals, felt as if his whole childhood had been erased. Nothing was left but 'a bit of broken masonry, a jagged piece of railway arch, a gable with only the sky behind it'. He could not find a single landmark from his childhood, not even the house in which his mother had died, and, 'all points of reference gone, I threaded my way among great piles of fallen stone, builders' debris, isolated lumps of blackened masonry'.

As he surveyed the social blitzkrieg, he asked the question so often asked by those who have resisted the demolition squads: 'Why had they erased the old Gorbals? Class guilt about its sordid slums, its poverty? A fear of folk memories, in the new days of discontent, if its identity was encouraged to survive?'[28]

Many of the former residents, transferred to outlying estates, clamoured to return. Housing allocation policies in Glasgow, as elsewhere, and the gradual postwar 'residualisation' of public housing, had created estates on which whole populations were stigmatised.

By residualisation is meant the process whereby public housing in Britain, which was once housing for the bulk of the white working class, became housing for the unemployed, minorities, single parents (mostly women) and others on benefit. In the American inner city, too, the housing-project population has become a population whose income comes largely from the state. Not surprisingly, petty thieving and drug dealing flourish where a whole local population lives below the poverty line.

Women are especially trapped in these estates, prevented by lack of money and public transport from travelling to the shops, to make social calls or to hospitals. On one outlying Glasgow estate, an ante-natal clinic was set up to make visits easier and to prevent the high rate of complications at birth, and deaths of infants. A survey of the results of this initiative found, however, that although this was the explicit purpose of the clinic, it did not have the technology that would have been appropriate for this end. The main purpose of the clinic appeared to be 'social monitoring'. Mothers who were unable to attend appointments were regarded as 'defaulters', making excuses for no good reason. The women's sobriety, the legitimacy of their children, their literacy and their ability to manage were constantly questioned by both doctors and other professional workers at the clinic. Judgments about medical problems rapidly extended to comments on lifestyle, and women were condemned for the 'extravagance' of colour television and other 'luxuries'. Although not all the professional staff at the clinic demonstrated these attitudes, they did appear to be common.[29]

In the early 1970s local authorities all over Britain, aware of the massive problems on many new estates, began to reject the insensitive mass demolitions of the 1950s and 1960s and turned instead to rehabilitation.[30] Glasgow was finally recognised as probably Britain's finest surviving Victorian city. Tragically, the Gorbals tenements had been for the most part structurally sound, and could have been rehabilitated. The shift to renovation in Glasgow led to the gentrification and upgrading of many of the remaining tenement-type blocks of flats.

In the 1980s rehabilitation extended to the renovation of central Glasgow as a showcase for culture and consumerism. 'Merchant City' was redeveloped as a sophisticated area of wine bars, restaurants, and warehouses converted into expensive 'loft-living' apartments. Some of the largest shopping malls in Britain created the now familiar environment of chain-stores located along galleries surrounding courts furnished with palm trees and tinkling fountains.

The most successful of the new marketing ventures was Princes Square, a small, four-storey mall built round a glazed-in courtyard, and designed in a style reminiscent of art nouveau with a hint of Charles Rennie Mackintosh, Glasgow's most famous designer/artist. Rippling staircases of parquet and wrought iron, open escalators and a glass lift offered exciting views into the well of the building. Live music and performances in the central court entertained shoppers, who could sit on the shallow steps surrounding the court, or while away an afternoon in one of the many cafés while sipping an expensive cappuccino. They could browse in designer boutiques instead of the usual multiple chain-stores, while a Foucault's pendulum swung from the ceiling in the well beside the escalator.[31]

Despite the 1980s rhetoric of the free market, the renovation of central Glasgow did not conform to free-market principles at all. Initially it was financed largely by public funds. A proposal that hypermarkets might be built in the deprived and shop-less outlying estates was thwarted because of fears that they would compete with the centre, which had been designated as the area to be devoted to consumer retail development.[32] A 'dual city' emerged: a prosperous middle-class core, and grimly deprived marginal estates; stylish renovation for the centre, and a (declining) welfare culture for the new urban wastelands on the periphery. The middle-class university district of Hillhead had the highest percentage of graduates in the country; the outlying estates the lowest.

By the late 1980s Glasgow was building its reputation as a 'city of culture'. The arts were bringing £200 million a year to the city and had created 14,000 jobs. Glasgow also had its own stock exchange, employing 2500 people. Meanwhile unemployment was running at 60 per cent in the outlying estates, and homelessness and debt had reached epic proportions.[33]

We can now revisit 'postmodernism of the mind' and the Prince Charles debate about architecture, and see that the urban crisis is neither simply a matter of architectural style, nor is it best understood as a crisis of consciousness. It is the economic restructuring of cities that has brought about a change in the way in which their inhabitants experience urban life.

Postmodernism, often criticised as a reactionary or frivolous approach to a general sense of crisis, does acknowledge the way in which familiar landscapes of existence are dissolving, and speaks to our sense of ambivalence and uncertainty in the face of large-scale change. Its preoccupation with style and subjectivity, and its tendency to aestheticise experiences instead of responding morally or emotionally, act to mask the role of global capital.

In three major spheres changes are occurring which have implications for the future of cities. These three areas are: our relationship to nature; the evolution of the family; and the wider economic and political sphere. In today's great cities, with their overblown private financing and under-resourced public sector, the desolation created by insensitive private development and paternalistic public projects contrasts with the glitter of shops, restaurants and arts projects hanging in the battered urban fabric like baubles on a worn-out Christmas tree. Our cities are as full of horrifying contrasts as those of the nineteenth century.

But although our problems may appear similar, we no longer trust the solutions of the late nineteenth and early twentieth centuries. Then, utopians, planners and architects believed that the only solution was to scrap the existing unplanned, irrational cities and build new, planned ones. Today, by contrast, planning, planners and architects are blamed for having *caused* the current state of our cities by their overweening interference.

The fashionable 'postmodern' solution is to reject plans in favour of piecemeal design initiatives. Now that the municipal authority is billed as a Stalinist juggernaut, the private developer may re-emerge in the guise of an Enlightenment benefactor. Property developers have consistently tried to argue that their schemes for massive redevelopment are in the interests of local communities or the public at large; the fact remains that their projects are largely outside democratic control.[34]

The postmodern solution may seem an elegant one to those who have followed Jane Jacobs in targeting paternalistic public-development projects as the source of the urban crisis. As we saw, she mounted a spirited attack against the horrors of urban renewal and clean-sweep planning, and eloquently celebrated the vitality of dense, bustling inner-city street life. She believed that large cities were 'just too big and too complex to be comprehended in detail from any vantage point'. For this reason, individuals should be left alone, and cities would spontaneously create themselves. 'It is the thousands of individuals who create, by making their own choices and operating without guidance from the planners, the exciting fabric of the cosmopolitan city.'[35]

In her wake, Richard Sennett argued for an anarchic city in which zoning, policing and many city services were either eliminated or at least entirely locally controlled. The resulting conflict and tension would force all citizens to take an active part in the running of their city.

Such a view assumes a plural society in which different interest groups have more or less equal power: 'the community is so diverse that its institutions cannot be pushed in any one direction'.[36] This appears at best naive. Jane Jacobs said nothing about the role of capital development. Sennett excluded the power of property and finance capital from his considerations. Such arguments appear surprisingly compatible with the views of New Right economists such as Milton Friedman and Friedrich Hayek, both of whom have argued that capitalist economies must be left entirely to their own devices, since command planning can never anticipate accurately the millions of private individual wishes that make possible the smooth running of the private market.

What has been forgotten in the optimistic scenarios of Jacobs and Sennett (which, to be fair, date from a more optimistic time, the 1960s) is the way in which postmodern solutions rely on market-led initiatives. Less and less are they built on the enterprise of the 'little people' in the old working-class and ethnic districts that she and

Marshall Bermann described so lovingly; more and more are they simply sophisticated top-down property developments. The example of Docklands proves that postmodern urban solutions fail to provide either housing or amenities for 'ordinary people'. The growth in all major western cities of homelessness to an extent not experienced for nearly a century alone demonstrates the glaring insufficiences of the postmodern scenario.

Critical of the disasters of utopian planning, we are in danger of forgetting that the unplanned city still *is* planned, equally undemocratically, by big business and the multinational corporation. Women, ethnic minorities and the working class in general have been caught between a paternalistic form of planning in which surveillance and regulation played a key role, and a profit-driven capital development that has been unbelievably destructive of urban space, and thus of supportive communities, killing whole cultures as the loved and familiar buildings and streets were bulldozed away.

Municipal authorities do not control their own territory, but are forced to subordinate their plans to the imperatives of the developers. Unless a given municipal planning body creates the transport facilities, public buildings and planning permissions for the private developer, it will have difficulty in realising its own schemes. As the economist François Lamarche has expressed it, 'it is as if the role of the city was to clear and plough its own land in order for others to sow and harvest the best fruit'.[37] The urban crisis is not, then, symptomatic of a loss of meaning in the world, but, on the contrary, has identifiable causes and effects which can be explained in economic and political terms.

There is a second source of anxiety, related to the changes in city fabric and social structure: changes in the composition of the family and the experience of family life. Family size has declined. One in four urban households in Britain is now a single-person household, while in Manhattan this is the commonest size of household. One in five children in the western inner city is growing up in a single-parent family. The old, the majority of whom are women, and ethnic minorities remain in the inner city, and are vulnerable to its crime, poverty and lack of transport.

The postmodern view of urban life is less prescriptive than the utopian or modernist solution, and has not set the preservation of the family as an overt goal. The debate on architecture has, nonetheless, implied a conservative vision of family and community life. It has also, ironically, started from the same assumption as its opponents: that architecture does change behaviour. If the nineteenth-century philanthropists believed that to change buildings and spatial planning would be to reform and regularise human beings, then so do the promoters of today's fashionable solutions. The terms of the debate have implied an unspoken but powerful belief not only in traditional architecture, but also in the traditional (that is, the patriarchal) family. The 'neo-vernacular' style favoured in both public and private housing schemes in recent years carries with it a nostalgia not only for traditional architecture, but for 'traditional' ways of life and romanticised visions of a 'natural' working-class family in which the role of women was domestic subordination and confinement to the home. Nostalgia in the mind has produced an equation in which brick buildings and closed-in courtyards equals happy families and traditional (i.e. white) communities.

This architecture also implies a rejection of the public values of municipal buildings in favour of the reinforcement of privacy. The reinforcement of privacy has become an explicit policy, especially since being advanced by Alice Coleman, an adviser to Mrs Thatcher. In *Utopia on Trial*, published in 1984, Mrs Coleman drew on the ideas of the American writer Oscar Newman, who as far back as 1966 had argued that the best way to reduce violence and crime on large housing estates was to reduce the amount of public or 'unowned' – communal – space.[38] He argued that individual residents were more prepared and better able to police space surrounding their dwelling if it belonged to them, and developed a concept of 'territory' that was taken up by Alice Coleman. This relies on a profoundly reactionary belief that human beings, like certain animal species, have an inbuilt 'territorial instinct' and will only defend their own territory. The reverse side of this belief is that there can be no public or social responsibilities or obligations.

The ideology of 'defensible space' legitimates a paranoid attitude to 'strangers' and 'aliens' and easily fits into racist paradigms of who 'intruders' are. Pitched roofs, red tiles and ornamental brickwork symbolise an unbalanced explanation of the ills of public housing – unbalanced because deep-seated causes such as poverty, unemployment, alienation and isolation are left out of the picture, pushed aside by racial and gender stereotypes and fantasies of a lost past.[39]

The third area of change is the loss of the balance between city and countryside. As cities spread over the whole globe we may be approaching the 'eclipse of nature' – losing entirely our relationship with nature. The 'urban realm' replaces the natural world. The invasive city, bleeding further and further into its surroundings, appears as a threat to our very survival – civilisation's toxic waste-dump poisoning the water-table. The loss of the contrast between the urban and the rural appears to drain the city as well as the countryside of meaning, for the city has always been defined in terms of its contrast with nature and the countryside. With the loss of that contrast everything becomes simply an endless sprawl of contingent matter.

Yet as nature retreats, many city dwellers also retreat into what remains of rural life, even though in so doing they hasten its demise. In Britain and France, Cotswold or Provençal villages become commuter havens. Manufacturing begins to return to villages and secluded rural towns, and thus the city begins to disintegrate alongside the natural realm.

These developments have uncertain implications for women. On the one hand, the loss of the traditional contrast between 'nature' and 'culture' with its parallel contrast between male and female may weaken traditional cultural barriers to the participation of women in all spheres of urban life. A culture with weak or disintegrating barriers and slack compartmentalisation may make it easier for women to slip into new terrain. On the other hand, the rural retreat and the re-industrialisation of the countryside open the way to the 'small is beautiful', ecologically sensitive decentralisation scenario. Alison Ravetz, a trenchant critic of postwar planning, has tried to reassure us that this will not mean 'a return to stultifying rural parochialism'. On the contrary, she regards the possible dispersed communities of the twenty-first century as an exciting prospect, linked as they will be by global information and communications systems. Yet she does not justify her preference for the small rather than the large community, or explain why it would operate in the interests of women.[40]

To create the society she envisages, it would be necessary to engage in precisely the clean-sweep planning of which she so greatly disapproves. In the foreseeable future it would almost certainly mean even greater reliance on the automobile. The pattern of small, interlinked communities in a technologically advanced world may attract many, given that it has become the lifestyle of the affluent in the 'urban regions'. Yet as it currently exists it depends on the great cities for its very being. Washington, DC, New York and Boston are indispensable to the existence of the north-eastern seaboard region of the United States, just as London is the very *raison d'être* of the whole of south-east England.

To destroy the cities and return to us all to small communities would be to capitulate to the puritanical and controlling elements that critics of town planning, including Alison Ravetz herself, have identified as its hidden agenda. There is no evidence that the small community would necessarily be a society freed from surveillance. Indeed, it is much more likely to be more strictly controlled, and would offer none of the opportunities for escape, anonymity, secret pleasures or even public crowds that the great city offers. For women especially, a return to the small community might mean the return of the paid work to the home in the expectation that this would do away with the need for the public provision of childcare, and, historically, homeworking has been the reverse of liberating for women. More women – and men, too – *are* undertaking paid work at home; the small business, communications and computers all hasten this trend, but its implications for women are uncertain and in many ways alarming.

In any case, although a rural commuter lifestyle is fashionable, not everyone even today wants to live in a stockbroker belt mansion behind a wall of rhododendrons – or, if you are in outer LA, behind an electrified fence patrolled by security guards and notices which state that 'trespassers will be shot'. Despite the flight from the central city, there is also a continuing back-to-the-city movement.

As Margo Huxley said at the Socialist Scholars Conference in Sydney, Australia, in the autumn of 1990, the contemporary city is an integral part of the crisis of capitalist accumulation, and it is also the case that 'revolutionary' governments have usually sought to shape cities as the symbol of their regimes (Hitler being a case in point). However, this does not mean, she argued, that we should turn our backs on the city. Cities are our treasure houses of cultural capital and wisdom, and to destroy them would be to will a state of collective amnesia. What *is* needed is non-commodified space, space that is democratically controlled.

The Green parties urge decentralisation and a return to the small community for a number of reasons. On ideological grounds they appear to believe that the only morally justifiable social order is one based on traditional forms of self-reliance. It may seem regrettable that the Greens, who speak to such serious and important concerns, have carried forward the anti-urbanism of many nineteenth-century utopians. On the other hand, there is genuine cause for concern in the extravagant use of energy encouraged by urban living and the amount of pollution it currently causes. As public transport systems have decayed, pollution from automobile traffic has become an ever more serious threat both to the health of individuals and to the survival of the planet itself. More immediately, cities such as London were being brought close to permanent standstill by traffic congestion by the early 1990s.

There are nonetheless possible solutions to these problems which do not involve wholesale decentralisation. LA itself, in unplanned California, has been forced to take a lead in the control of car use. The LA Plan, published in 1989, is concerned primarily with air pollution. In order to reduce this the plan not only proposes wholesale conversion to clean fuels, but would also penalise companies that did not introduce flexitime, commuter car-pools and financial incentives for their employees to travel by public transit systems yet to be built. There have already been experiments with freeway fast lanes reserved for buses and cars containing more than two persons.[41]

To reverse the present reliance on the car would also make for safer streets. The corridor street, as Jane Jacobs argued, was once a relatively safe place for women and children, informally monitored by those living and working in it. In addition, most streets were safer at night, since pedestrians used them until a late hour. Now, after workers have returned home, streets are deserted throughout the evening, and thus encourage muggings and attacks on women. Better public transport coupled with an extensive system of 'dial a ride' taxis and buses could be provided in cities if the will was there. In Italian cities such as Bologna and Florence public-transport systems were created in the 1970s which, coupled with strict regulations against cars and parking in the historic centres, did improve the environment. In the last decade of the twentieth century there is growing public demand for restrictions on the motor car and for the improvement of public transport in cities such as London, where public transport has been allowed to decline to the point at which not only the environment but also commerce and business are threatened.

Richard Sennett was right to grasp the nettle of disorder, and to recognise that the excitement of city life cannot be preserved if all conflict is eliminated. He was right to emphasise the positive aspects of conflict, and to understand that life in the great city offers the potential for greater freedom and diversity than life in small communities. This is particularly important for women.

Nevertheless, planning is necessary if cities are to survive. What needs to change is the ultimate purpose of planning. Hitherto, town planning has too often been driven by the motor of capitalist profit and fuelled by the desire to police whole communities. Planners considered it desirable to provide a civilised standard of housing for the masses, but this was less as a right than because they imagined that better housing would lead to a docile and domesticated populace. They wished to eliminate not just dirt and disease, but slovenly housewives and rioting workers. The colonial imperative was close to the surface even in the imperial heartlands: the city was essentially for the white, male bourgeoisie; all others were there on sufferance. The purpose of the plan was to create a city of order and surveillance rather than one of pleasure and opportunity.

Stated thus, such a proposition may seem crude and simplistic. Even in the nineteenth century, however, there was an awareness of the surveillance aspects of town improvement. The large tenement blocks built, largely in London, by Peabody and other private philanthropic organisations were even criticised by other reformers. General Booth condemned them as being 'only a slight advance upon the Union Bastille' (i.e. the workhouse), while the Fabian Society spoke of 'so-called model dwellings with all their repulsive features'. Furthermore, the Royal Commission on Housing of 1885 heard much evidence of the unpopularity of model dwellings. Tenants disliked the regulations, and, in particular, reported one witness to the Commission, the tenements were experienced as 'a sort of prison: they look upon themselves as being watched'.[42]

Planning has tended to express the deep ambivalence towards city life that has characterised modern western culture. This ambivalence (the city is seductive, but for that very reason dangerous) has led to mutually incompatible solutions, and the worst of all worlds in many city centres and peripheries: drab and alienating environments, the domination of the office block, the destruction of urban neighbourhoods. Market forces, wishing to capitalise on the pleasures and consumerism of the city, have as often as not killed the goose that laid the golden egg.

Ambivalence expresses fear and desire fused into one. What is feared is also desired: the Sphinx in the city. In the Greek legend, the Minotaur at the centre of the Cretan labyrinth was half man, half bull. In the cities of modernity and postmodernity, it is the Sphinx, half woman, half animal, that has represented what is feared and desired at the heart of the maze. She may take the shape of the Victorian prostitute, of the red whore of the barricades, of the evil genius of *Metropolis*, or of the slatternly fishwife of the slums.

Women have fared especially badly in western visions of the metropolis because they have seemed to represent disorder. There is fear of the city as a realm of uncontrolled and chaotic sexual licence, and the rigid control of women in cities has been felt necessary to avert this danger. Urban civilisation has come, in fact, to mean an authoritarian control of the wayward spontaneity of all human desires and aspirations. Women without men in the city symbolise the menace of disorder in all spheres once rigid patriarchal control is weakened. That is why women – perhaps unexpectedly – have represented the mob, the 'alien', the revolutionary.

It is therefore rather ironic that women have often appeared less daunted by city life than men. For example, most of the male modernist literary figures of the early twentieth century drew (as we saw earlier) a threatening picture of the modern metropolis (an exception being James Joyce), but modernist women writers such as Virginia Woolf and Dorothy Richardson responded with joy and affirmation. In *Mrs Dalloway*, Virginia Woolf exulted in the vitality of a summer's morning in London, in the 'swing, tramp and tread; in the bellow and uproar . . . in the triumph and the jingle and the strange high singing of some aeroplane overhead'.[43] Acknowledging the unstable and uncertain nature of personal identity, she does not find this alarming, as did Kafka and Musil. She often wrote of her love of London in her letters and diaries.[44]

Dorothy Richardson, who pioneered the 'stream of consciousness' in her long novel sequence *Pilgrimage*, predating both Virginia Woolf and James Joyce, also portrayed London life as a source of liberation. Her heroine, Miriam Henderson, is an unattached, lower-middle-class woman with no means of support other than her meagre secretarial wage, who is trying to make her way in a largely male literary world. She is therefore a far more marginal intellectual than Musil's wealthy Ulrich or even Kafka's clerical worker, K. Yet London life as she experiences it contrasts strongly with the threatening ambience of Vienna and Prague seen through male eyes. Mrs Dalloway and Miriam Henderson are not estranged. For them urban life offers not only adventure, but reassurance. The city is an enveloping presence in their work, and they seem to find its vast amorphousness maternal or even womblike. Instead of disintegrating, they are held by it. Why is it that these feminine experiences are denied?

The urban crisis is a crisis of inequality, and of authoritarianism. Problems of overcrowding and population growth would always be difficult to solve, but they have been made much worse by the unequal competition for urban space and the ways in which the few have commandeered almost all the resources. I am not trying to reproduce the cliché of 'bright lights, big city' versus suburban respectability and drabness, to rely on a superficial stereotype of urban chic. It is essential to acknowledge that city centres have become increasingly places of paradox: playgrounds for the rich, but dustbins for the very poor. Nor do I have a solution for the complex problems facing city dwellers and city governments. I am arguing that we will never solve the problems of cities unless we *like* the urban-ness of urban life. Cities aren't villages; they aren't machines; they aren't works of art; and they aren't telecommunications stations. They are spaces for face to face contact of amazing variety and richness. They are spectacle – and what is wrong with that?

The failure of many well intentioned planners was to allow the horrors of city life to blind them to its virtues. Those who believe that spiritual values can develop only in an atmosphere of calm and orderliness will always dislike and fear the city. For others it will represent the possibility of the highest levels of spirituality in its excesses and extremes: the city as the ultimate sublime. Such a city must, however, be a city for all, not just for a few.

★   ★   ★

My own corner of the inner city offers other qualities, typical of city life, yet less often remembered or remarked upon. The startling contrasts are there: I look out at my 'postmodern' garden, a Victorian grotto bounded by a high wall which hides the surprise of the main railway line. Trains trumpet past with nineteenth-century energy. In the adjacent streets the houses with burglar alarms and ruched blinds, pastel frontages and flowery wallpapers stand cheek by jowl with the run-down flats and the wasteland of disused yards where cats and winos congregate at night.

Further east, one of the richest squares in the borough lies close to a notorious estate, famed for its drug problems, its refuse and its leaking Corbusian flat roofs. Down towards King's Cross and the railway termini we are promised a Channel Tunnel terminal, and the biggest shopping mall in Europe inside Gilbert Scott's Victorian Gothic hotel building. What will happen to the poverty-stricken working class, both white and Bangladeshi, in the estates behind the station, currently plagued by prostitution and racial attacks, when they have to make way for the developers? They will be shovelled out to even less desirable locations, while their flats and shops are upmarketed or pulled down to be replaced by hotels, offices and a privately owned park. What will happen then to our quiet streets, with their little shops, local eccentrics and leafy squares?

We who live here wear this corner of the city like a comfortable old coat, an extension of our personalities, threadbare yet retaining a beauty of its own. This is the intimacy of cities, made more precious and more secret by our knowledge that it is one of many cells or corners in a great city that is not so much a labyrinth as a web or a shawl. We wrap ourselves in the city as we journey through it. Muffled, we march, 'like Juno in a cloud',[45] drawing it around us like a cloak of many colours: a disguise, a refuge, an adventure, a home.

References and Notes

1 Into the Labyrinth

1 Benjamin (1979), p. 296.
2 ibid., p. 312.
3 See Pike (1981), passim, to which I am indebted for the ideas developed in this section. See also Sizemore (1984).
4 Frisby (1985), p. 139, quoting Kracauer, Siegfried (1932) 'Strasse ohne Erinnerung', *Frankfurter Zeitung*, 16 December.
5 Benjamin, op. cit., p.309.
6 Lévi-Strauss (1976), pp.120–21.
7 Tocqueville (1966), p.256, footnote.
8 Huyssen (1986), pp.52–3, quoting Le Bon, Gustave (1981) *The Crowd*, Harmondsworth: Penguin, pp. 39, 52.
9 See, particularly, Little, Peake and Richardson, eds. (1988).
10 Proust (1981), vol. 3, p.665.

2 From Kitsch City to the City Sublime

1 Brunhoff (1987).
2 Marin (1977), especially pp. 54, 58, 61–4.
3 Lerner, Gerda (1986a). See also Lerner (1986b).
4 Alberti (1969).
5 Osgood (1951), pp.145–6.
6 Piggott (1967), p.15 and passim.
7 Eliade (1955), pp.7–12.
8 Mumford (1961), p. 25. See also Waterhouse (1990).
9 Kahn (1987).
10 Tod and Wheeler (1978).
11 Choay, (1980) passim, to whom I am indebted for the ideas discussed in this section.
12 Tod and Wheeler, op. cit.
13 Summerson (1962). See also Stelter (1984).
14 Burke, Edmund (1987), pp.39, 81. See also Taylor (1973), in Dyos and Wolff, eds. (1973), vol. 2.
15 Honour (1987), passim.
16 Dickens (1970), pp.120–21.
17 Hugo (1976), pp. 338–9.
18 Williams (1982), pp.186, 188, quoting Mauclair, Camille, 'Le nouveau Paris du peuple' and 'Le style de la rue moderne'.

19 Frisby (1985), p.139, quoting Kracauer, Siegfried (1928) 'Analyse einer Stadtplans', in *Das Ornament der Masse*; and p.138, quoting Kracauer, Siegfried (1932) 'Berlin in Deutschland', *Frankfurter Zeitung*, 14 August.
20 Burke, Edmund, op. cit., pp.116, 124.
21 See Schor, Naomi (1987).

3 *Cesspool City: London*

1 See Lampard (1973) and Lees (1985), p. 5. In 1801, 20 per cent of the population lived in cities, and one in twelve of the population was a Londoner. By 1851 38 per cent of Britons lived in cities; by 1875 more than half the population had become urban, and by 1901 75 per cent. The population of Paris grew from half a million in 1801 to nearly three million in 1910; that of New York from 60,000 to 4,700,000; Berlin from 172,000 to two million; and Chicago, which did not exist in 1801, also had two million–odd inhabitants by 1910.
2 Godwin (1854), p.1. See also Wordsworth (1982), p.264; and Mayhew (1983), p.43.
3 Thompson and Yeo, eds. (1984).
4 Sala (1859), p.220.
5 Lampard, op. cit., quoting Cooke Taylor, William (1840) *Natural History of Society in the Barbarous and Civilised State*.
6 Baines (1843), p.9, quoting Lord Shaftesbury.
7 ibid., p.54.
8 Vaughan (1843), p.103.
9 Darley (1989), p.172.
10 Davidoff (1973), p. 50.
11 Brontë (1979), p.109.
12 ibid., p.121.
13 Lambert (1963). For an account of women connected to the Pre-Raphaelite movement, see Marsh (1985) *The Pre-Raphaelite Sisterhood*.
14 Darley, op. cit., pp.135–6, 318–19.
15 Davidoff and Hall (1987), p.415.
16 Dodd (1843), p.5.
17 Yeo, Eileen (1984) 'Mayhew as a Social Investigator', in Thompson and Yeo, eds., op. cit.
18 Wohl (1973), p. 651.
19 Engels (1973), p.182.
20 Chadwick (1965), p.190.
21 See Gauldie (1974).
22 See Finn (1965).
23 Chadwick, op. cit., p.193.
24 Godwin, op. cit., p.70.
25 Chadwick, op. cit., p. 205.
26 Simon, Sir John (1854), p. 38.
27 ibid., p. 39.
28 ibid., p.42.

29 ibid.
30 Godwin, op. cit., p.21.
31 See Wohl (1983).
32 Cruikshank, Percy (1854), pp.29–30, 33.
33 See Walkowitz (1980).
34 Ryan (1840), p.146.
35 ibid., p.149.
36 Walkowitz, op. cit., p.34, quoting Bevan, William (1843) *Prostitution in the Borough of Liverpool*, Liverpool; and Tait, William (1840) *Magdalenism: An Inquiry into the Extent, Causes and Consequences of Prostitution*, Edinburgh.
37 Patterson (1955), p.163, quoting a letter from Charles Dickens to Angela Burdett Coutts.
38 Johnson, ed. (1955), pp.152, 154.
39 Acton (1968), p.72.
40 ibid., p.60.
41 ibid., p.24.
42 ibid., p.49.
43 Benevolo (1967).
44 See Hareven (1982).
45 Hayden (1981).
46 Gaskell (1987), p.135. See also Creese (1966), p.1.
47 Creese, op. cit., p.40.
48 ibid., pp.55–6.
49 Buckingham (1849), p.xxii.
50 ibid., p.193.
51 Lehan (1986), pp.100–102.
52 Richardson (1876).
53 Edwards (1981), p.9, citing Summerson (1962).
54 Davidoff, op. cit., p.31; and Olsen (1986), p.185.
55 Dyos (1982), p. 88.

4 *The City of the Floating World: Paris*

1 Baldick (1984), p.83.
2 Citron (1961), Chapter 17.
3 Chevalier (1973), pp.20–21, quoting Bertillon, Louis Adolphe, Introduction to a Census of Paris, 1881.
4 See Hertz (1983), discussing Hugo, Victor (1955) *Choses vues, oeuvres complètes*, tome 31.
5 Warner (1985), Chapter 2, 'The Street (Paris)'.
6 Leroy-Beaulieu (1873), p.93. See also Zola (1970).
7 ibid., p.108.
8 Parent-Duchâtelet (1836).
9 ibid., pp.91–2.
10 See Clarke (1984).
11 Sue (n.d.), p.9.
12 Knepler, ed. (1972), p.38.

13 Richardson, Joanna (1969), p.76.
14 ibid., p.41, quoting Stern, Daniel (Madam d'Agoult) *Mes Souvenirs, 1806–1833*, pp. 355–7.
15 Dijkstra (1984), p.21.
16 Moers (1978), p.9, quoting Sand, George, *Histoire de ma vie*, Part 4.
17 Baldick, op. cit., p.53.
18 Trollope (1985), p.165.
19 See Pinkney (1958), passim.
20 Choay (1969).
21 Clarke, op. cit., p.29, citing Lazare, Louis, quoted in Lavedan (1952).
22 Kracauer (1937), p.202.
23 Frégier (1840), pp.104–10.
24 Marx (1978), pp.311–25.
25 Benjamin (1973), p.57, quoting Baudelaire, Charles, 'Crépuscule du Soir', in *Les fleurs du mal*, trans. David Paul.
26 Zola, op. cit., pp. 396–7.
27 See Wolff (1985) and Pollock, 'Modernity and the Spaces of Femininity', in Pollock (1985).
28 Richardson, Joanna (1971), p.149.
29 Baldick, op. cit., p.68.
30 Kracauer, op. cit., Part 2, Chapter 6, 'Operetta World', especially p.206.
31 Zola (1972), pp.44–5.
32 Richardson, Joanna (1967), pp.295–303, quoting Goncourt, Jules and Edmond, *Journals*, 10 March 1862.
33 Zola (1984), p.120.
34 See Williams (1982); Miller (1981); and Bowlby (1985).
35 See James, Henry (1968), p.102; and Frisby (1985), Chapter 3, Section 3, pp. 126–34, in which Frisby discusses Kracauer, Siegfried (1922–5) *Der Detektiv-Roman*, especially p.127.
36 Citron, op. cit., Chapter 21.
37 Rudorff (1972), Chapter 2, 'The Pleasure Capital'.
38 ibid., pp.381–2.
39 Benjamin, op. cit., pp.90, 95.
40 Colette (1971), p.61; see also Blankley (1984).
41 Vincendeau (1982); see also Chevalier (1980), Part 6, 'De la crise à la guerre'.
42 Vincendeau, op. cit., p.126, footnote.
43 See Greco, Juliette (1982) and Webster and Powell (1984).
44 Beauvoir (1984), pp.11–12.

5 *Cities of the American Dream*

1 Glaab and Brown (1976), p.23.
2 Wright, Gwendolyn (1981), p.48.
3 Glaab and Brown (1976), p.126.
4 Dreiser (1981), pp.16, 23.
5 ibid., p.323.
6 Burnham and Bennett (1970).

7 ibid., for example, pp.33, 79.
8 Bellamy (1982), p.55.
9 Tichi (1982), p.25.
10 See Hayden (1981).
11 ibid., p.151, and Chapter 8, passim.
12 Addams (1910), p.136.
13 See Hayden, op. cit., and Wright, op. cit., Chapter 11.
14 Addams, op. cit., p.227; see also Hyman (1985).
15 Williams (1982), pp.303 et seq.
16 Addams (1909), p.5.
17 See Osofsky (1971), p.56; Hayden, op. cit., Chapter 9; and Wright, op. cit., p.138, and Chapter 8, passim.
18 Chernin (1985), p.100.
19 Parry (1933), pp.75–80; and Bremer (1984).
20 Parry, op. cit., p.199.
21 ibid., p.176.
22 Dos Passos (1986), pp.190–91.
23 Park (1929) Introduction to Zorbaugh (1929), pp.viii–ix.
24 Zorbaugh, op. cit., pp.91–2.
25 Parry, op. cit., p.270; and see Hayden, op. cit., Chapter 9.
26 Starr (1973); and Starr (1985), Chapter 4.
27 Parry, op. cit., p.107; see also Trimberger (1984).
28 Osofsky, op. cit., pp.4, 15.
29 ibid., p.56.
30 ibid., p.151.
31 Hughes (1941), p.173.
32 Malcolm X (1965), p.210.
33 Osofsky, op. cit.
34 Anderson (1982).
35 Marshall (1982), p.3.
36 Guy (1984), p.15.
37 Petry (1986), p.7.
38 Jackson (1984).
39 See Ballard (1989).
40 Hardwick (1980), pp.34–5.
41 ibid., p.32.
42 Lévi-Strauss, 'New York in 1941', in Lévi-Strauss (1987), pp.258–9.
43 ibid., p.261.

6 *Architecture and Consciousness in Central Europe*

1 Schorske (1961), p.47.
2 ibid., p.xxvi.
3 Musil (1979), vol. 1, p.3.
4 ibid., p.182.
5 ibid., p.132.
6 See Smith (1980), Chapter 2.

7 See Weininger (1906) and Schorske, op. cit., Chapter 5, 'Gustav Klimt: Painting and the Crisis of the Liberal Ego'.
8 Janik and Toulmin (1973), pp.47–8; and see Zweig (1943) and Schnitzler (1968).
9 Timms (1986), especially Chapter 4.
10 Kafka (1953) *The Trial*, p.43.
11 ibid., p.156.
12 Kafka (1983), p.130; see also Wilson, 'Love', in Wilson (1988).
13 See Huyssen, 'The Vamp and the Machine: Fritz Lang's *Metropolis'*, in Huyssen (1986).
14 Spender (1951), p.120.
15 I am indebted to Tony Halliday and to Anthony Burke for these insights. See Burke, Anthony (1990).
16 Döblin (1978), p.29; see also Scholvin (1985).
17 See Naylor (1985).
18 Loos (1900) 'Ladies Fashion', in Loos (1982), p.99; see also Wollen (1987) and Loos (1964).
19 Sant' Elia and Marinetti (1964), pp.36–7.
20 Schorske, op. cit., p.97, quoting Wagner, Otto (1911) *Die Groszstadt: Eine Studie über dieses Vienna*, pp.3, 73–4.
21 Meyer (1965), pp.91–2.
22 Gropius (1935), p. 56.
23 See Willett (1978), p.124.
24 Banham (1971), p.65.
25 Hayden, op. cit., Chapter 11.
26 Anscombe (1984), and Whitford (1984), p.144.
27 Walker (1990), pp.6–8 passim.
28 Le Corbusier (1933), p.11.
29 Frisby, op. cit., p.168.
30 Le Corbusier, op. cit., p.117.
31 ibid., p.46; and see pp.112–15 for his views on women and child-rearing.
32 Speer (1976), p.129.
33 Giese (1979), p.45.
34 Kopp (1970).
35 Bater (1980), pp.22–4.
36 See Hayden (1983), pp.67–9.
37 See Larsson (1984), p.203.
38 See Hitler (1969), Chapter 2; and Timms (1985).
39 Speer, op. cit., pp.120, 122.
40 ibid., p.198, and see p.199 for Speer's description of the projected plans for Berlin.
41 See Jellonek (1987).

7 *The Lost Metropolis*

1 Henslowe (1984), p.4.
2 Edwards, (1981), p.61, quoting Carr, Jonathan, in *Building News*, 22 December 1876.

3 Geddes and Thomson (1890), p.271.
4 Mairet (1957), pp.177–8, quoting Patrick Geddes, letter to his daughter Norah, written in 1917.
5 Howard (1946), p.48.
6 See Fishman (1977), passim.
7 McFarlane (1984), p.34.
8 Fishman, op. cit.; and Swenarton (1981), p.12.
9 Osborn (1953), p.406.
10 Henderson (1953), p.457.
11 Linnell (1953); see also Mabel Barry, Parker, and numerous other contributions in *Town and Country Planning*, vol. 21, no. 113, Golden Jubilee issue.
12 Corbett Fisher (1957), pp.310–11.
13 Another influential utopian writer was Tony Garnier, whose *Cité industrielle* contained many of the features, such as zoning, to be found in the garden city. Garnier worked on his plan from before 1900 to 1917, when it was published. It is uncertain whether or not he was influenced by Patrick Geddes. See Wiebenson (1969).
14 McFarlane, op. cit., p.32; see also Ravetz (1989).
15 See White (1986).
16 Durant (1939), passim.
17 Burnett (1986), p.188, quoting Masterman, C.F.G. (1909) *The Condition of England*, p.58.
18 See Samuel (1983); see also Rothblatt, Garr and Sprague (1979), p.13, quoting Grace Goodwin in *Good Housekeeping*, 1909.
19 Geddes (1915), p.129.
20 Edwards, op. cit., p.130, quoting Thomas Sharp.
21 Rothblatt, Garr and Sprague, op. cit., p.13.
22 Schaffer (1982).
23 Sharp (1940), p.23; see also Adshead (1941); Williams Ellis (1941); and Ravetz (1980), who discusses these town planners at length.
24 Coe and Reading (1981).
25 Abercrombie (1945), p.14.
26 I am grateful to Elizabeth Beskine for discussing her experience with me.
27 See Young and Willmott (1957) and Townsend (1958).
28 Robertson (1945), pp.83–4.
29 See Wilson (1980).
30 Lawrence (1987).
31 Mumford (1945), p.5.
32 Newsom (1948), p.103.
33 Attfield (1989).
34 See Partington (1990).
35 See Ravetz, op. cit., passim.
36 Nairn (1955), p.365.
37 Spectorsky (1955).
38 Lefebvre (1968), p.73.
39 The block of flats designed by Le Corbusier and built in Marseille after

the Second World War had many amenities, and is still popular with residents, some of whom have inherited their flats from their parents or other relatives.

40 See Harvey (1989), p.70.
41 See Zukin (1982).
42 Berman (1982), pp.292–3; see also Caro (1974).
43 See Evenson (1981) and Kain (1981).
44 Abrams (1967), Chapter 1.
45 Wallace (1982), quoting Moynihan, Daniel (1965) *The Negro Family*, which is reprinted in Rainwater and Yancy (1967).
46 Roberts (1975), p.25.
47 Rosenthal (1975), p.46.
48 Carter (1977), pp.11–12.
49 Hobsbawm (1987).
50 *Signs* (1980); see also Birch, ed. (1985).
51 See Thane (1978) and Chapter 4, note 7, above.
52 Castells (1983), especially Part 3, Chapter 14, 'Cultural Identity, Sexual Liberation and Urban Structure: the Gay Community in San Francisco'.

8 World Cities

1 Moser (1987a), pp.4–5.
2 O'Connor (1983), p.315.
3 ibid.
4 ibid., p.316.
5 King (1980).
6 ibid., quoting Swinton, G. (1912) 'Planning an Imperial Capital', *Garden Cities and Town Planning*, 2 (4).
7 ibid., quoting Stevens, P.H.M. (1955) 'Planning Legislation in the Colonies', *Town and Country Planning*, March.
8 ibid.
9 Briggs, 'Melbourne, a Victorian Community Overseas', in Briggs (1968), p.278.
10 Butel, (1985), p.3; Sandercock (1976), p.7.
11 Bascom (1955), p.239.
12 Little (1959).
13 O'Connor, op. cit., Chapter 2.
14 Baker and Bird (1959).
15 ibid.
16 Collins (1980).
17 See O'Connor, op. cit.
18 Cunningham, Susan (1980).
19 Lévi-Strauss (1976), pp.120–23.
20 Lloyd (1970), p.20.
21 Lloyd, op. cit., p.17, quoting Ross, M.H. (1973) *Grass Roots in an African City: Political Behaviour in Nairobi*, Cambridge, Mass.: The MIT Press, pp.5–8.
22 Moser, op. cit., p.5.

23 ibid.
24 Lewis (1961).
25 Moser, op. cit.
26 Moser (1987b), p.14.
27 See Machado (1987).
28 Chant (1987).
29 Moser (1987b), p.21; and see Machado, op. cit.
30 Moser (1987a), p.19.
31 Moser (1987c), pp.169–78.
32 Vance (1987).
33 Collinson, ed. (1990).
34 Moser (1987c).
35 Sarti (1989), p.77.
36 ibid., p.75.
37 ibid.

9 Beyond Good and Evil

1 Jameson (1984); see also *Theory Culture and Society* (1988); *Zone* n.d.; Wilson (1988) and Thackara, ed. (1988).
2 Thackara (1988).
3 Schulman (1989), pp.100–101.
4 Texier (1987), p.130.
5 See, for example, Forrest, Katherine (1990) *Beverley Malibu*, London: Pandora; Wilson, Barbara (1988) *The Dog Collar Murders*, London: Virago; Paretsky, Sara (1990) *Toxic Shock*, Harmondsworth: Penguin; and O'Rourke, Rebecca (1988) *Jumping the Cracks*, London: Virago.
6 See Stephen (1989).
7 Sharpe and Wallock (1987), p.29, quoting Webber, 'The Urban Place and the Nonplace Urban Realm', in Webber, ed. (1964).
8 See Campbell (1989).
9 Sugimoto (1990a), (1990b); Morris-Suzuki (1990); Huxley (1990).
10 Jencks (1989).
11 See Cunningham, John (1988).
12 Harvey (1989), pp.67–8, quoting Krier, Leon (1987) *Architectural Design Profile*, no. 65; and see Banham et.al. (1969).
13 Fishman (1977).
14 Feagin and Smith (1987).
15 Harvey (1988); see also Hebdige (1988) and Mulgan (1989).
16 O'Neill (1990); see also Cruikshank (1989) and Samuel (1989).
17 Soja (1989); Davis (1985); Davis (1987); and Davis (1988).
18 Soja, op. cit. I have made extensive use of Edward Soja's and Mike Davis's articles in this section.
19 Davis (1987), p.79, quoting Jim Woods, Chairman of the Community Redevelopment Agency, in *Los Angeles Times*, 19 February 1987, section 4, p.1; and see Davis (1990).
20 Beaton (1982), p.14.
21 Soja, op. cit.

22 Keating (1988).
23 See Allan (1965).
24 Glasser (1987), p.75.
25 The most famous of the 'Glasgow novels' is McArthur, Alexander and Long, H. Kingsley (1935) *No Mean City*, London: Longmans Green. See Burgess (1986).
26 Boyle (1977), pp.8, 15.
27 Keating, op. cit.
28 Glasser, op. cit., p.45.
29 Reid (1983), p.172 passim.
30 Keating, op. cit., p.196.
31 Thanks to Harvie Ferguson for showing me round Glasgow and sharing his enthusiasm for the city with me.
32 Cosgrove and Campbell (1988).
33 ibid.
34 See Pearman (1989).
35 Jacobs (1961); see also Fishman (1980).
36 Sennett (1970).
37 Lamarche (1976), p.103.
38 Coleman (1984) and Newman (1973).
39 See Boys (1989). I have made extensive use of Jos Boys's arguments in this section.
40 Ravetz (1980), p.347.
41 See Reed (1989).
42 See Dyos (1982), p.87, quoting General Booth's *In Darkest England*; Ashworth (1954), p.150, quoting Fabian Society Pamphlet (1900) *The House Famine and How to Relieve It*; and Burnett (1986), p.178.
43 Woolf (1989), p.6.
44 Woolf (1979), pp.9, 31, 35; see also Squier (1984) and Hanscombe (1979).
45 Dryden, 'The Sixth Satire of Juvenal', in Dryden (1987), p.341.

Bibliography

Abercrombie, Patrick (1945) *The Greater London Plan 1944*, London: HMSO

Abrams, Charles (1967) *The City is the Frontier*, New York: Harper & Row

Acton, William (1968) *Prostitution*, ed. Peter Fryer, London: McGibbon & Kee (originally published 1857)

Addams, Jane (1909) *The Spirit of Youth in City Streets*, New York: Macmillan

——(1910) *Twenty Years at Hull House*, New York: Macmillan

Adshead, S.D. (1941) *A New England*, London: Frederick Muller

Alberti, Leon Battista (1969) *The Family in Renaissance Florence*, trans. Renée Neu Watkins, Columbia, South Carolina: University of South Carolina Press (originally written 1434)

Allan, C.M. (1965) 'The Genesis of British Urban Redevelopment with Special Reference to Glasgow', *Economic History Review*, 2nd series, vol. 18

Anderson, Jervis (1982) *Harlem, the Great Black Way, 1900–1950*, London: Orbis

Anscombe, Isabelle (1984) *A Woman's Touch: Women in Design from 1860 to the Present Day*, London: Virago

Ashworth, William (1954) *The Genesis of Modern British Town Planning*, London: Routledge & Kegan Paul

Attfield, Judith (1989) 'Inside Pram Town: A Case Study of Harlow House Interiors, 1951–1961', in Attfield and Kirkham, eds, (1989)

Attfield, Judith and Kirkham, Pat, eds (1989) *A View from the Interior*, London: The Women's Press

Baines, Edward (1843) *The Social, Educational and Religious State of the Manufacturing Districts*, London: Simpkin Marshall & Co. and T. Ward & Co.

Baker, Tanya and Bird, Mary (1959) 'Urbanisation and the Position of Women', *Sociological Review*, vol. 7, no. 1

Baldick, Robert (1984) *Pages from the Goncourt Journals*, Harmondsworth: Penguin

Ballard, J.G. (1989) 'In the Voyeur's Gaze', *Guardian*, 25 August

Banham, Reyner (1971) *Los Angeles: The Architecture of Four Ecologies*, Harmondsworth: Penguin

Banham, R., Barker, Paul, Hall, Peter and Price, Cedric (1969) 'Non Plan: an Experiment in Freedom', *New Society*, 20 March

Bascom, William (1955) 'Urbanisation Among the Yoruba', *American Journal of Sociology*, vol. 60, no. 5, March, special issue on world urbanisation

Bater, James H. (1980) *The Soviet City: Ideal and Reality*, London: Edward Arnold

Beaton, Cecil (1982) *Self Portrait with Friends: The Selected Diaries of Cecil Beaton 1926–1974*, Harmondsworth: Penguin

Beauvoir, Simone de (1984) *The Prime of Life*, Harmondsworth: Penguin (originally published 1960)

Bellamy, Edward (1982) *Looking Backward: 2000–1887*, Harmondsworth: Penguin (originally published 1888)

Benevolo, Leonardo (1967) *The Origins of Modern Town Planning*, trans. Judith Landry, London: Routledge & Kegan Paul

Benjamin, Walter (1973) *Charles Baudelaire: A Lyric Poet in the Era of High Capitalism*, London: New Left Books

—— (1979) *One Way Street*, London: New Left Books

Bensman, Joseph and Vidich, Arthur, eds (1975) *Metropolitan Communities: New Forms of Urban Sub-Communities*, New York: Franklin Watts

Berman, Marshall (1982) *All that is Solid Melts into Air*, London: Verso

Birch, Eugenie Ladner, ed. (1985) *The Unsheltered Woman: Women and Housing in the Eighties*, New York: New York Center for Urban Policy Research

Blankley, Elyse (1984) 'Return to Mytilène: Renée Vivien and the City of Women', in Squier, ed. (1984)

Bowlby, Rachel (1985) *Just Looking: Consumer Culture in Dreiser, Gissing and Zola*, London: Methuen

Boyle, Jimmy (1977) *A Sense of Freedom*, London: Pan Books

Boys, Jos (1989) 'From Alcatraz to the OK Corral: Images of Class and Gender', in Attfield and Kirkham, eds (1989)

Bremer, Sidney H. (1984) 'Willa Cather's Lost Chicago Sisters', in Squier, ed. (1984)

Briggs, Asa (1968) *Victorian Cities*, Harmondsworth: Penguin

Brontë, Charlotte (1979) *Villette*, Harmondsworth: Penguin (originally published 1853)

Brunhoff, Jean de (1987) *Babar the King*, London: Methuen (originally published 1936)

Buckingham, James Silk (1849) *National Evils and Practical Remedies and the Plan for a Model Town*, London

Burgess, Moira (1986) *The Glasgow Novel: A Survey and Bibliography*, Glasgow: Scottish Libraries Association and Glasgow District Library

Burke, Anthony (1990) *Georg Grosz and Otto Dix's Representations of Women in the Early Years of the Weimar Republic*, unpublished report, Courtauld Institute, University of London

Burke, Edmund (1987) *A Philosophical Enquiry into the Origin of our Ideas of the Sublime and the Beautiful*, Oxford: Basil Blackwell (originally published 1757)

Burnett, John (1986) *A Social History of Housing 1915–1985*, London: Methuen

Burnham, Daniel and Bennett, Edward (1970) *Plan of Chicago*, New York: Da Capo Press (originally published 1909)

Butel, Elizabeth (1985) *Margaret Preston: The Art of Constant Rearrangement*, Ringwood, Australia: Penguin

Campbell, Beatrix (1989) 'The Citizen as Consumer', *Guardian*, 6 September

Cannadine, David and Reeder, David, eds (1982) *Exploring the Urban Past: Essays in Urban History of H.J. Dyos*, Cambridge: Cambridge University Press

Caro, Robert (1974) *The Power Broker: Robert Moses and the Fall of New York*, New York: Alfred Knopf

Carter, Angela (1977) *The Passion of New Eve*, London: Virago

Castells, Manuel (1983) *The City and the Grassroots: A Cross Cultural Theory of Urban Social Movements*, London: Edward Arnold

Chadwick, Edwin (1965) *Report on the Sanitary Condition of the Labouring Population of Great Britain*, ed. M.W. Flinn, London (originally published 1842)

Chant, Sylvia (1987) 'Domestic Labour, Decision Making and Dwelling Construction: The Experience of Women in Querétaro, Mexico', in Moser and Peake, eds (1987)

Chernin, Kim (1985) *In My Mother's House: A Daughter's Story*, London: Virago

Cherry, Gordon, ed. (1980) *Shaping an Urban World*, London: Mansell

Chevalier, Louis (1973) *Labouring Classes and Dangerous Classes in Paris during the First Half of the Nineteenth Century*, trans. Frank Jellinek, London: Routledge & Kegan Paul

—— (1980) *Montmartre du Plaisir et du Crime*, Paris: Editions Robert Laffont

Choay, Françoise (1969) *The Modern City: Planning in the Nineteenth Century*, London: Studio Vista

—— (1980) *La règle et le modèle: sur la Théorie de L'architecture et de l'urbanisme*, Paris: Editions du Seuil

Citron, Pierre (1961) *La poésie de Paris dans la littérature française de Rousseau à Baudelaire*, Paris: Editions de Minuit

Clarke, T.J. (1984) *The Painting of Modern Life: Paris in the Art of Manet and his Followers*, London: Thames & Hudson

Coe, Peter and Reading, Malcolm (1981) *Lubetkin and Tecton: Architecture and Social Commitment*, London and Bristol: Arts Council of Great Britain and University of Bristol Department of Architecture

Coleman, Alice (1984) *Utopia on Trial*, London: Hilary Shipman

Colette (1971) *The Pure and the Impure*, trans. Herma Briffault, Harmondsworth: Penguin (originally published as *Ces Plaisirs*, 1932.)

Collins, John (1980) 'Lusaka: Urban Planning in a British Colony 1931–1964', in Cherry, ed. (1980)

Collinson, Helen, ed. (1990) *Women and Revolution in Nicaragua*, London: Zed Books

Conrads, Ulrich, ed. (1964) *Programmes and Manifestoes on Twentieth Century Architecture*, London: Lund Humphries

Corbett Fisher, Cicely (1957) in *Town and Country Planning*, vol. 25, no. 8, Hampstead Garden Suburb Golden Jubilee issue

Cosgrove, Stuart and Campbell, Denis (1988) 'Behind the Wee Smiles', *New Statesman and Society*, 16 December

Creese, Walter (1966) *The Search for Environment: The Garden City: Before and After*, New Haven: Yale University Press

Cruikshank, Daniel (1989) 'Towering Problems in Hawksmoor's Backyard', *Independent*, 6 December

Cruikshank, Percy (1854) *Sunday Scenes in London and the Suburbs*, London: published by the artist

Cunningham, John (1988) 'The House that Jill Built', *Guardian*, 6 January

Cunningham, Susan (1980) 'Brazilian Cities Old and New: Growth and Planning Experiences', in Cherry, ed. (1980)

Darley, Gillian (1989) *Octavia Hill: A Life*, London: Constable

Davidoff, Leonora (1973) *The Best Circles: Society Etiquette and the Season*, London: Croom Helm

—— and Hall, Catherine (1987) *Family Fortunes: Men and Women of the English Middle Classes 1780–1850*, London: Hutchinson

Davis, Mike (1985) 'The Postmodern City', *New Left Review*, no. 151, May/June

—— (1987) 'Chinatown Part Two?: The "Internationalisation" of Downtown Los Angeles', *New Left Review*, no. 164, July/August

—— (1988) 'Nightmares in Los Angeles', *New Left Review*, no. 170, July/August

—— (1990) *City of Quartz* London: Verso

Dickens, Charles (1970) *Dombey and Son*, Harmondsworth: Penguin (originally published 1848)

Dijkstra, Sandra (1984) 'The City as Catalyst for Flora Tristan's Vision of Social Change', in Squier, ed. (1984)

Döblin, Alfred (1978) *Berlin-Alexanderplatz*, Harmondsworth: Penguin (originally published 1929)

Dodd, George (1843) *Days at the Factories, or the Manufacturing Industries of Great Britain Described*, Series 1, London: Charles Knight & Co.

Dos Passos, John (1986) *USA*, Harmondsworth: Penguin (originally published 1938)

Dreiser, Theodor (1981) *Sister Carrie*, Harmondsworth: Penguin (originally published 1900)

Dryden, John (1987) *The Oxford Authors: John Dryden*, Oxford: Oxford University Press

Durant, Ruth (Ruth Glass) (1939) *Watling: A Survey of Social Life on a New Housing Estate*, London: P.S. King & Son

Dyos, H.J. (1982) 'Workmen's Fares in South London 1860–1914', in Cannadine and Reeder, eds (1982)

—— and Wolff, Michael, eds (1973) *The Victorian City*, vols. 1, 2, London: Routledge & Kegan Paul

Edwards, Arthur (1981) *The Design of Suburbia: A Critical Study in Environmental History*, London: Pembridge Press

Eliade, Mircea (1955) *The Myth of the Eternal Return*, trans. Willard Trask, London: Routledge & Kegan Paul

Engels, Friedrich (1973) *The Condition of the Working Class in England*, Moscow: Progress Publishers (originally published 1844)

Evenson, Norma (1981) 'The City as an Artefact: Building Control in Modern Paris', in Kain, ed. (1981)

Feagin, Joe R. and Smith, Michael Peter (1987) 'Cities and the New International Division of Labour: An Overview', in Smith and Feagin, eds (1987)

Fisher, Robert Moore, ed. (1967) *The Metropolis in Modern Life*, New York: Russell & Russell

Fishman, Robert (1977) *Urban Utopias in the Twentieth Century: Ebenezer Howard, Frank Lloyd Wright and Le Corbusier*, New York: Basic Books

—— (1980) 'The Anti Planners: The Contemporary Revolt against Planning and its Significance for Planning History', in Cherry, ed. (1980)

Flinn, M.W. (1965) 'Introduction' in Chadwick, E. (1965)

Frégier, H.–A. (1840) *Des classes dangereuses de la population dans les grandes villes*, Paris: H. Baillière

French, R.A. and Ian Hamilton, F.E. ed. (1979) *The Socialist City: Spatial Structure and Urban Policy*, New York: John Wiley

Frisby, David (1985) *Fragments of Modernity: Theories of Modernity in the Work of Simmel, Kracauer and Benjamin*, Oxford: Polity Press

Gaskell, S. Martin (1987) *Model Housing: From the Great Exhibition to the Festival of Britain*, London: Mansell

Gauldie, Enid (1974) *Cruel Habitations: A History of Working Class Housing, 1780–1918*, London: Allen & Unwin

Geddes, Patrick (1915) *Cities in Evolution: An Introduction to the Town Planning Movement and the Study of Civics*, London: Williams & Northgate

—— and Thomson, J. Arthur (1890) *The Evolution of Sex*, London: Walter Scott

Giese, Ernst (1979) 'Transformation of Islamic Cities in Soviet Middle Asia into Socialist Cities', in French and Ian Hamilton, eds (1979)

Glaab, Charles and Brown, A. Theodore (1976) *A History of Urban America*, New York: Macmillan

Glasgow Women's Study Group (1983) *Uncharted Lives: Extracts from Scottish Women's Experiences 1850–1982*, Glasgow: Pressgang

Glasser, Ralph (1987) *Growing up in the Gorbals*, London: Pan

Godwin, George (1854) *London Shadows: A Glance at the 'Homes' of the Thousands*, London: Routledge

Greco, Juliette (1982) *Jujube*, Paris: Editions Stock

Gropius, Walter (1935) *The New Architecture and the Bauhaus*, trans. P. Morton Shand, London: Faber and Faber

Guy, Rosa (1984) *A Measure of Time*, London: Virago

Hanscombe, Gillian (1979) Introduction to Richardson, Dorothy (1979)

Hardwick, Elizabeth (1980) *Sleepless Nights*, London: Virago

Hareven, Tamara (1982) *Family Time and Industrial Time: The Relationship between the Family and Work in a New England Industrial Community*, Cambridge, Mass.: Cambridge University Press

Harvey, David (1988) 'Voodoo Cities', *New Statesman and Society*, 30 September, special issue 'City Politti'

—— (1989) *The Condition of Postmodernity*, Oxford: Basil Blackwell

Hayden, Dolores (1981) *The Grand Domestic Revolution: A History of Feminist Designs for American Homes, Neighborhoods and Cities*, Cambridge, Mass.: The MIT Press

—— (1983) 'Capitalism, Socialism and the Built Environment', in Shalom, ed. (1983)

Hebdige, Dick (1988) 'A Tale of Two Cities', *New Statesman and Society*, 30 September, special issue 'City Politti'

Henderson, Ethel (1953) 'Letchworth Then and Now', *Town and Country Planning*, vol. 21, no. 113, 'Letchworth, Golden Jubilee Issue'

Henslowe, Philip (1984) *Ninety Years On: An Account of the Bournville Village Trust*, Birmingham: The Bournville Village Trust

Hertz, Neil (1983) 'Medusa's Head: Male Hysteria under Political Pressure', *Representations*, vol. 1, no. 4, Fall

Hitler, Adolf (1969) *Mein Kampf*, trans. Ralph Mannheim, London: Hutchinson (originally published 1925)

Hobsbawm, Eric (1987) 'Labour in the Great City', *New Left Review*, no. 166, November/December

Honour, Hugh (1987) *Neoclassicism*, Harmondsworth: Penguin

Howard, Ebenezer (1946) *Garden Cities of Tomorrow*, London: Faber & Faber (originally published 1898 as *Tomorrow: A Peaceful Path to Real Reform*)

Hughes, Langston (1941) *The Big Sea*, London: Hutchinson

Hugo, Victor (1976) *Les misérables*, trans. Norman Denny, Harmondsworth: Penguin (originally published 1862)

Huyssen, Andreas (1986) *After the Great Divide: Modernism, Mass Culture, Postmodernism*, London: Macmillan

Hyman, Colette A. (1985) 'Labor Organizing and Female Institution Building: The Chicago Women's Trade Union League, 1904–1924', in Milkman, ed. (1985)

Jackson, Kenneth (1984) 'The Capital of Capitalism: The New York Metropolitan Region 1890–1940', in Sutcliffe, ed. (1984)

Jacobs, Jane (1961) *The Death and Life of Great American Cities*, Harmondsworth: Penguin

James, Henry (1968) *The American Scene*, London: Rupert Hart Davis (originally published 1907)

Jameson, Fredric (1984) 'Postmodernism or the Cultural Logic of Late Capitalism', *New Left Review*, no. 146, July/August

Janik, Allan and Toulmin, Stephen (1973) *Wittgenstein's Vienna*, New York: Simon & Schuster

Huxley, Margo (1990) 'The Multifunction Polis: The Issues', *Arena*, 90, Autumn

Jellonek, Burkhard (1987) 'The Persecution of Homosexuals in the "Third Reich"' paper presented to the 'Homosexuality, Which Homosexuality?' International Scientific Conference on Gay and Lesbian Studies, Amsterdam, Free University, December 15–18

Jencks, Charles (1989) 'Public Opinion and Princely Intervention', *Independent*, 22 November

Johnson, Edgar, ed. (1955) *Letters from Charles Dickens to Angela Burdett Coutts 1841–1865*, London: Jonathan Cape

Kafka, Franz (1953) *The Trial*, trans. Willa and Edwin Muir, Harmondsworth: Penguin (originally published 1925)
—— (1983) *Letters to Milena*, Harmondsworth: Penguin
Kahn, Bonnie Menes (1987) *Cosmopolitan Culture*, New York: Antheneum
Kain, Roger (1981) 'Conservation and Planning in France: Policy and Practice in the Marais, Paris', in Kain, R., ed.
——, ed. (1981) *Planning for Conservation*, London: Mansell
Keating, Michael (1988) *The City that Refused to Die: Glasgow and the Politics of Urban Regeneration*, Aberdeen: Aberdeen University Press
King, A.D. (1980) 'Exporting Planning: the Colonial and Neo-colonial Experience', in Cherry, ed. (1980)
Knepler, Henry, ed. (1972) *Man About Paris: The Confessions of Arsène Houssaye*, London: Victor Gollancz
Kopp, Anatole (1970) *Town and Revolution: Soviet Architecture and City Planning 1917–1935*, trans. Thomas E. Burton, London: Thames & Hudson
Kracauer, Siegfried (1937) *Jacques Offenbach and the Paris of his Time*, London: Constable
Lamarche, François (1976) 'Property Development and the Economic Foundations of the Urban Question', in Pickvance, ed. (1976)
Lambert, Royston (1963) *Sir John Simon 1816–1904 and English Social Administration*, London: McGibbon & Kee
Lampard, Eric (1973) 'The Urbanising World', in Dyos and Wolff, eds (1973)
Larsson, Lars Olof (1984) 'Metropolis Architecture', in Sutcliffe ed. (1984)
Lavedan, P. (1952) *L'histoire de l'Urbanisme, époque contemporaine*, Paris: Henri Laurens
Lawrence, Hilda (1987) *Death of a Doll*, London: Pandora (originally published 1947)
Le Corbusier (1933) *The Radiant City*, London: Faber & Faber
Lees, Andrew (1985) *Cities Perceived: Urban Society in European and American Thought, 1820–1940*, Manchester: Manchester University Press
Lefebvre, Henri (1968) *Everyday Life in the Modern World*, trans. Sacha Rabinovitch, London: Allen Lane, The Penguin Press
Lehan, Richard (1986) 'Urban Signs and Urban Literature: Literary Form and Historical Process', *New Literary History*, vol. 18, no. 1, Autumn, 'Studies in Historical Change'
Lerner, Gerda (1986a) 'The Origin of Prostitution in Ancient Mesopotamia', *Signs*, vol. 11, no. 2
—— (1986b) *The Creation of Patriarchy*, New York: Oxford University Press
Leroy-Beaulieu, Paul (1873) *Le travail des femmes au XIXe siècle*, Paris: Charpentier
Lévi-Strauss, Claude (1976) *Tristes Tropiques*, Harmondsworth: Penguin
—— (1987) *The View From Afar*, trans Joachim Neugroschel and Phoebe Hoss, Harmondsworth: Penguin
Lewis, Oscar (1961) *The Children of Sanchez: The Autobiography of a Mexican Family*, New York: Random House

Linnell, Isabelle (1953) 'A Business Woman's Experience', *Town and Country Planning*, vol. 21, no. 113, Letchworth Golden Jubilee Issue

Little, Jo, Peake, Linda and Richardson, Pat, eds (1988) *Women in Cities: Gender and the Urban Environment*, London: Macmillan

Little, Kenneth (1959) 'Some Urban Patterns of Marriage and Domesticity in West Africa', *Sociological Review*, new series, vol. 7, no. 1, July, special issue on Urbanism in West Africa

Lloyd, Peter (1979) *Slums of Hope: Shanty Towns of the Third World*, Harmondsworth: Penguin

Loos, Adolf (1964) 'Ornament and Crime', in Conrads, ed. (1964)

—— (1982) *Spoken into the Void: Collected Essays 1897–1900*, trans. Jane Newman and John H. Smith, Cambridge, Mass.: The MIT Press

McFarlane, Barbara (1984) 'Homes Fit for Heroines: Housing in the Twenties', in Matrix (1984)

Machado, Leda (1987) 'The Problems for Women-headed Households in a Low Income Housing Programme in Brazil', in Moser and Peake, eds (1987)

Mairet, Philippe (1957) *Pioneer of Sociology: The Life and Letters of Patrick Geddes*, London: Lund Humphries

Malcolm X (1965) *The Autobiography of Malcolm X*, Harmondsworth: Penguin

Marin, Louis (1977) 'Disneyland: A Degenerate Utopia', *Glyph: Johns Hopkins Textual Studies*, vol. 1, number 1.

Marsh, Jan (1985) *The Pre-Raphaelite Sisterhood*, New York: St Martin's Press

Marshall, Paule (1982) *Brown Girl Brownstones*, London: Virago (originally published 1959)

Marx, Karl (1978) 'Review of *Les Conspirateurs* par A. Chenu, and *La Naissance de la république en Février 1848*, par Lucien de la Hodde', in Marx, Karl and Engels, Friedrich (1978) *Collected Works*, vol. 10 (originally published 1851)

Matrix (1984) *Making Space: Women and the Man Made Environment*, London: Pluto Press

Mayhew, Henry (1983) *London's Underworld*, London: Bracken Books

Meyer, Hannes (1965) 'The New World' (1926) in *Building Projects and Writings*, London: Alec Tiranti

Milkman, Ruth, ed. (1985) *Women, Work and Protest: A Century of U S Women's Labor History*, London: Routledge & Kegan Paul

Miller, Michael (1981) *The Bon Marché: Bourgeois Culture and the Department Store 1869–1920*, London: Allen & Unwin

Moers, Ellen (1978) *Literary Women*, London: The Women's Press

Morris-Suzuki, Tessa (1990) 'Futuristic Cities: Japanese Models for Australian Followers?' *Arena*, 91, Winter

Moser, Caroline (1987a) Introduction to Moser and Peake, eds (1987)

—— (1987b) 'Women, Human Settlements and Housing: A Conceptual Framework for Analysis and Policy Making', in Moser and Peake, eds (1987)

—— (1987c) 'Mobilisation is Women's Work: Struggles for Infrastructure in Guayaquil, Equador', in Moser and Peake, eds (1987)

—— and Peake, Linda, eds (1987) *Women: Human Settlements and Housing*, London: Tavistock

Mulgan, Geoff (1989) 'A Tale of New Cities', *Marxism Today*, March, special issue 'Cities: A Vision of the Future'

Mumford, Lewis (1945) 'On the Future of London', *Architectural Review*, vol. xcvii, no. 577, January

—— (1961) *The City in History*, Harmondsworth: Penguin

Musil, Robert (1979) *The Man without Qualities*, trans. Eithne Wilkins and Ernst Kaiser, London: Picador (originally published 1930)

Nairn, Ian (1955) 'Outrage', *Architectural Review*, vol. 117, no. 702, June

Naylor, Gillian (1985) *The Bauhaus Reassessed*, London: The Herbert Press

Newman, Oscar (1973) *Defensible Space*, London: Architectural Press

Newsom, John (1948) *The Education of Girls*, London: Faber & Faber

O'Connor, Anthony (1983) *The African City*, London: Hutchinson

Olsen, Donald (1986) *The City as a Work of Art: London, Paris, Vienna*, New Haven, Conn.: Yale University Press

O'Neill, Sean (1990) 'Battle Cries in Banglatown', *Guardian*, 5 June

Osborn, Frederic (1953) 'Letchworth's First Fifty Years', *Town and Country Planning*, vol. 21, no. 113, 'Letchworth Golden Jubilee Issue'

Osgood, Cornelius (1951) *The Koreans and their Culture*, New York: The Ronald Press Co.

Osofsky, Gilbert (1971) *Harlem, the Making of a Ghetto*, New York: Harper & Row

Parent-Duchâtelet, A.J.B. (1836) *De la prostitution dans la ville de Paris*, Paris: H. Baillière

Parry, Albert (1933) *Garrets and Pretenders: A History of Bohemianism in America*, New York: Covici Friede

Partington, Angela (1990) *Consumption Practices as the Production and Articulation of Differences: Rethinking Working Class Femininity and Consumer Culture in 1950s Britain*, unpublished PhD thesis, University of Birmingham, Department of Culture Studies

Patterson, Clara Burdett (1955) *Angela Burdett Coutts and the Victorians*, London: John Murray

Pearman, Hugh (1989) 'A Royal Vision with Distorted Perspectives', *Sunday Times*, 10 September

Petry, Ann (1986) *The Street*, London: Virago (originally published 1946)

Pickvance, Christopher, ed. (1976) *Urban Sociology: Critical Essays*, London: Tavistock

Piggott, Stuart (1967) 'The Role of the City in Ancient Civilisations', in Fisher, ed. (1967)

Pike, Burton (1981) *The Image of the City in Modern Literature*, Princeton, New Jersey: Princeton University Press

Pinkney, David H. (1958) *Napoleon III and the Rebuilding of Paris*, Princeton, New Jersey: Princeton University Press

Pollock, Griselda (1985) *Vision and Difference: Femininity, Feminism and Histories of Art*, London: Routledge & Kegan Paul

Proust, Marcel (1981) *Remembrance of Things Past*, London: Chatto & Windus (originally published 1925)

Rainwater, Lee and Yancy, William (1967) *The Moynihan Report and the Politics of Controversy*, Cambridge, Mass.: The MIT Press

Ravetz, Alison (1980) *Remaking Cities*, London: Croom Helm

—— (1989) 'A View from the Interior', in Attfield and Kirkham, eds (1989)

Reed, Christopher (1989) 'The Taxpayers Cough Up in Smog City', *Guardian*, 23 October

Reid, Margaret (1983) 'Helping those Mothers: Antenatal Care in a Scottish Peripheral Housing Estate', in Glasgow Women's Studies Group, ed. (1983)

Richardson, Benjamin Ward (1876) *Hygeia*, London

Richardson, Dorothy (1979) *Pilgrimage*, London: Virago

Richardson, Joanna (1967) *The Courtesans: The Demi Monde in Nineteenth Century France*, London: Weidenfeld & Nicolson

—— (1969) *The Bohemians: La Vie de Bohème in Paris 1830–1914*, London: Macmillan

—— (1971) *La Vie Parisienne 1852–1870*, London: Hamish Hamilton

Roberts, Steven (1975) 'Brownsville Sinks in Decay and Fear', in Bensman and Vidich, eds (1975)

Robertson, Howard (1945) 'Industrial Hostels: An Experimental Wartime Community', *Architectural Review*, vol xcvii, no 579, March

Rosenthal, Jack (1975) 'U S in Suburban Turmoil' in Bensman and Vidich, eds (1975)

Rothblatt, Donald, Garr, Daniel and Sprague, J. (1979) *The Suburban Environment and Women*, New York: Praeger

Rudorff, Raymond (1972) *Belle Epoque: Paris in the Nineties*, London: Hamish Hamilton

Ryan, Michael (1840) *Prostitution in London*, London: H. Baillière

Sala, George Augustus (1859) *Twice Around the Clock*, London: Houlston & Wright

Samuel, Raphael (1983) 'Suburbs under Siege', *New Socialist*, no. 11, May/June

—— (1989) 'A Plaque on all Your Houses', *Guardian*, 17 October

Sandercock, Leonie (1976) *Cities for Sale: Property Politics and Urban Planning in Australia*, London: Heinemann

Sant'Elia, Antonio and Marinetti, Filippo Tommaso (1964) 'Futurist Architecture', in Conrads, ed. (1964)

Sarti, Cynthia (1989) 'The Panorama of Feminism in Brazil', *New Left Review*, no. 173, January/February

Schaffer, Daniel (1982) *Garden Cities for America: The Radburn Experiment*, Philadelphia: Temple University Press

Schnitzler, Arthur (1968) *Jugend in Wien: Ein Autobiographie*, Vienna: Verlag Fritz Molden

Scholvin, Ulricke (1985) *Döblin's Metropolen: über reale und imaginäre Städte und die Travestie der Wünsche*, Weinheim and Basel: Beltz Verlag

Schor, Naomi (1987) *Reading in Detail: Aesthetics and the Feminine*, London: Methuen

Schorske, Carl E. (1961) *Fin-de-Siècle Vienna: Politics and Culture*, London: Weidenfeld & Nicolson

Schulman, Sarah (1989) *After Dolores*, London: Sheba Press
Sennett, Richard (1970) *The Uses of Disorder*, Harmondsworth: Penguin
Shalom, Stephen Rosskaum, ed. (1983) *Socialist Visions*, London: Pluto
    Press
Sharp, Thomas (1940) *Town Planning*, Harmondsworth: Penguin
Sharpe, William and Wallock, Leonard (1987) 'From "Great Town" to
    "Nonplace Urban Realm": Reading the Modern City', in Sharpe and
    Wallock, eds (1987)
——, ed. (1987) *Visions of the Modern City: Essays in History, Art and
    Literature*, Baltimore: Johns Hopkins University Press
Signs (1980) 'Special Issue on the City', vol. 5, no. 3
Simon, Sir John (1854) *Preface to Reports Relating to the Sanitary Condition of
    the City of London*, London: John Parker & Son
Sizemore, Christine (1984) 'Reading the City as Palimpsest: The Experien-
    tial Perception of the City in Doris Lessing's *The Four Gated City*', in
    Squier, ed. (1984)
Smith, Michael Peter (1980) *The City and Social Theory*, Oxford: Basil
    Blackwell
—— and Feagin, Joe, eds (1987) *The Capitalist City: Global Restructuring and
    Community Politics*, Oxford: Basil Blackwell
Snitow, Ann, Stansell, Christine and Thompson, Sharon, eds (1984) *Desire:
    the Politics of Sexuality*, London: Virago
Soja, Edward W. (1989) *Postmodern Geographies: The Reassertion of Space in
    Critical Social Theory*, London: Verso
Spectorsky, A.C. (1955) *The Exurbanites*, Philadelphia: J.B. Lippincott
Speer, Albert (1976) *Inside the Third Reich*, London: Cardinal Books
Spender, Stephen (1951) *World within World*, London: Hamish Hamilton
Squier, Susan Merrill (1984) 'Tradition and Revision: The Classic City
    Novel and Virginia Woolf's *Night and Day*', in Squier, ed. (1984)
—— ed. (1984) *Women Writers and the City: Essays in Feminist Literary
    Criticism*, Knoxville: University of Tennessee Press
Starr, Kevin (1973) *Americans and the Californian Dream 1850–1915*, New
    York: Oxford University Press
—— (1985) *Inventing the Dream: California through the Progressive Era*, New
    York: Oxford University Press
Stelter, Gilbert A. (1984) 'The Classical Ideal: Cultural and Urban Form in
    Eighteenth Century Britain and America', *Journal of Urban History*, vol.
    10, no. 4, August
Stephen, A. (1989) *The Suzy Lamplugh Story*, London: Faber and Faber
Sue, Eugène (n.d.) *The Mysteries of Paris*, New York: Daedalus/Hippocrene
    (originally published 1842–3)
Sugimoto, Yoshio (1990a) 'High-Tech Cities for Lonely Technocrats',
    Arena, 90, Autumn
—— (1990b) 'A Post-Modern Japan?' *Arena*, 91, Winter
Summerson, John (1962) *Georgian London*, Harmondsworth: Penguin
Sutcliffe, Anthony, ed. (1984) *Metropolis 1890–1940*, London: Mansell
Swenarton, Mark (1981) *Homes Fit for Heroes: the Politics and Architecture of
    Early State Housing in Britain*, London: Heinemann

Taylor, Nicholas (1973) 'The Awful Sublimity of the Victorian City', in Dyos and Wolff, eds (1973)

Texier, Katherine (1987) *Love Me Tender*, London: Paladin

Thackara, John (1988) 'The Pleasures of Unease', *Metropolis: New British Architecture and the City*, catalogue of an exhibition at the Institute of Contemporary Arts, London, curated and organised by Linda Brown and Deyan Sudjic

——, ed. (1988) *Design after Modernism*, London: Thames & Hudson

Thane, Pat (1978) 'Women and the Poor Law in Victorian and Edwardian England', *History Workshop Journal*, Issue 6, Autumn

Theory, Culture and Society (1988) *Postmodernism*, special issue, vol. 5, nos 2–3, June

Thompson, E.P. and Yeo, Eileen, eds (1984) *The Unknown Mayhew: Selections from the Morning Chronicle 1849–1850*, Harmondsworth: Penguin

Tichi, Cecilia (1982) 'Introduction', in Bellamy, Edward (1982)

Timms, Edward (1985) 'Musil's Vienna and Kafka's Prague: The Quest for a Spiritual City', in Timms and Kelley, eds (1985)

—— (1986) *Karl Kraus: Apocalyptic Satirist: Culture and Catastrophe in Hapsburg Vienna*, New Haven, Conn.: Yale University Press

—— and Kelley, David, eds (1985) *Unreal City: Urban Experience in Modern European Literature and Art*, New York: St Martin's Press

Tocqueville, Charles Alexis de (1966) *Democracy in America*, New York: Harper & Row (originally published 1835)

Tod, Ian and Wheeler, Michael (1978) *Utopia*, London: Orbis

Townsend, Peter (1958) *The Family Life of Old People*, Harmondsworth: Penguin

Trimberger, Ellen Kay (1984) 'Feminism, Men and Modern Love: Greenwich Village 1980–1925', in Snitow, Stansell and Thompson, eds (1984)

Trollope, Mrs Frances (1985) *Paris and the Parisians*, Gloucester: Alan Sutton (originally published 1836)

Vance, Irene (1987) 'More than Bricks and Mortar: Women's Participation in Self Help Housing in Managua, Nicaragua', in Moser and Peake, eds (1987)

Vaughan, Robert (1843) *The Age of Great Cities or Modern Society Viewed in its Relation to Intelligence, Morals and Religion*, London: Jackson & Walford

Venturi, Robert, Scott Brown, Denise and Izenour, Steven (1985) *Learning from Las Vegas: The Forgotten Symbolism of Architectural Form*, Cambridge, Mass.: The MIT Press (rev. edn)

Vincendeau, Ginette (1987) 'The Mise-en-Scène of Suffering: French *Chanteuses Réalistes*', *New Formations*, no. 3, Winter

Walker, Lynne (1990) 'Concrete Proof: Women, Architecture and Modernism', *FAN: Feminist Art News*, vol. 3, no. 4

Walkowitz, Judith (1980) *Prostitution and Victorian Society: Women, Class and the State*, Cambridge: Cambridge University Press

Wallace, Michele (1982) *Black Macho and the Myth of the Superwoman*, London: John Calder

Warner, Marina (1985) *Monuments and Maidens: The Allegory of the Female Form*, London: Weidenfeld & Nicolson

Waterhouse, Robert (1990) 'Obituary: Lewis Mumford: Civilisation in the City', *Guardian*, 29 January

Webber, Melvin M., ed. (1964) *Explorations in Urban Structure*, Philadelphia: University of Pennsylvania Press

Webster, Paul and Powell, Nicholas (1984) *Saint Germain-des-Prés*, London: Constable

Weininger, Otto (1906) *Sex and Character*, London: Heinemann

White, Jerry (1986) *The Worst Street in North London: Campbell Bunk: Islington between the Wars*, London: Routledge & Kegan Paul

Whitford, Frank (1984) *Bauhaus*, London: Thames and Hudson

Wiebenson, Dora (1969) *Tony Garnier: The Cité Industrielle*, London: Studio Vista

Willett, John (1978) *The New Sobriety: Art and Politics in the Weimar Period, 1917–1933*, London: Thames & Hudson

Williams, Rosalind (1982) *Dream Worlds: Consumption in Late Nineteenth Century France*, Berkeley: University of California Press

Williams Ellis, Clough (1941) *Plan for Living: The Architect's Part*, London: Faber & Faber

Wilson, Elizabeth (1980) *Only Halfway to Paradise: Women in Postwar Britain 1945–1968*, London: Tavistock

—— (1988) *Hallucinations*, London: Radius

Wohl, Anthony (1973) 'The Role of the Medical Officers in Preventive Medicine', in Dyos and Wolff, eds (1973)

—— (1983) *Endangered Lives: Public Health in Victorian Britain*, London: Methuen

Wolff, Janet (1985) 'The Invisible Flâneuse: Women and the Literature of Modernity', *Theory, Culture and Society*, special issue, vol. 2, no. 3, 'The Fate of Modernity'

Wollen, Peter (1987) 'Fashion/Orientalism/the Body', *New Formations*, no. 1, Spring

Woolf, Virginia (1979) *Diary*, vol. 1, Harmondsworth: Penguin

Wordsworth, William (1982) *The Prelude*, Harmondsworth: Penguin (originally written 1805)

Wright, Gwendolen (1981) *Building the Dream: A Social History of Housing in America*, New York: Pantheon

Young, Michael and Willmott, Peter (1957) *Family and Kinship in East London*, Harmondsworth: Penguin

Zola, Emile (1970) *L'Assommoir*, trans. Leonard Tancock, Harmondsworth: Penguin (originally published 1876)

—— (1972) *Nana*, trans. George Holden, Harmondsworth: Penguin (originally published 1880)

—— (1984) *Au bonheur des dames*, Paris: Bernard Grasset (originally published 1883)

Zone (n.d., circa 1987) 'City', issues 1–2

Zorbaugh, Harvey (1929) *The Gold Coast and the Slum*, Chicago: Chicago University Press

Zukin, Sharon (1982) *Loft Living: Culture and Capital in Urban Change*, Baltimore: Johns Hopkins University Press

Zweig, Stefan (1943) *The World of Yesterday*, London: Cassell & Co.

Index